THE AMERICAN COMMUNITY SURVEY AND SELECT SURVEY BRIEFS

GOVERNMENT PROCEDURES AND OPERATIONS

Additional books in this series can be found on Nova's website under the Series tab.

Additional E-books in this series can be found on Nova's website under the E-books tab.

AMERICAN POLITICAL, ECONOMIC, AND SECURITY ISSUES

Additional books in this series can be found on Nova's website under the Series tab.

Additional E-books in this series can be found on Nova's website under the E-books tab.

GOVERNMENT PROCEDURES AND OPERATIONS

THE AMERICAN COMMUNITY SURVEY AND SELECT SURVEY BRIEFS

Barry M. Russo
and
Alice D. Haffner
EDITORS

Nova Science Publishers, Inc.

New York

NOTICE TO THE READER

Library of Congress Cataloging-in-Publication Data
The American community survey and other survey briefs / editors,
Barry M. Russo and Alice D. Haffner.
  p. cm.
  Includes index.
  ISBN 978-1-61324-362-6 (hardcover)
  1. Social indicators--United States. 2. Social surveys--United States. 3. American community survey. I. Russo, Barry M. II. Haffner, Alice D.
  HN60.A44 2011
  300.72'073--dc22
                                                                        2011012576

Published by Nova Science Publishers, Inc.＋ New York

CONTENTS

PREFACE

In the mid-1990s, the U.S. Bureau of Census began developing and testing a new means of data collection called a "rolling sample" or "continuous measurement" survey that became the American Community Survey (ACS). Implemented nationwide in 2005 and 2006, the ACS collects data from a representative sample of about 250,000 housing units a month (totaling about three million a year). The Bureau issues one-year estimates for the most populous areas, those with at least 65,000 people; three-year estimates for areas with 20,000 to 65,000 people and five-year estimates for areas with fewer than 20,000 people. This book examines the development, implementation and issues for Congress of the American Community Survey, along with select survey briefs.

Chapter 1- The American Community Survey (ACS) is the U.S. Bureau of the Census's replacement for the decennial census long form, which, since 1940, had gathered detailed socioeconomic and housing data from a representative population sample in conjunction with the once-a-decade count of all U.S. residents. Unlike the long form, with its approximately 17% sample of U.S. housing units in 2000, the ACS is a "rolling sample" or "continuous measurement" survey of about 250,000 housing units a month (totaling about three million a year). The data are aggregated to produce one-year, three-year, and five-year estimates that are much more timely than the long-form estimates were. As were the long-form data, ACS data are used in program formulas that determine the annual allocation of certain federal funds, currently more than $400 billion, to states and localities.

Chapter 2- This report is one of a series produced to highlight results from the 2009 American Community Survey (ACS). It presents poverty estimates based on data from the 2008 and the 2009 ACS. The report compares national and state level poverty rates and summarizes the distribution of income-to-poverty ratios for each state and the District of Columbia.

Chapter 3- This report presents data on median household income at the national and state levels based on the 2008 and 2009 American Community Surveys (ACS). The data are presented first in tabular form and then displayed on maps. The ACS provides detailed estimates of demographic, social, economic, and housing characteristics for states, congressional districts, counties, places, and other localities every year. A description of the ACS is provided in the text box "What Is the American Community Survey?"

Chapter 4- This report presents data on men's and women's earnings at the national, state, and metropolitan levels based on the 2009 American Community Survey (ACS). "Earnings" are defined as the sum of wages, salary, and net self-employment income and do not include other income sources such as property income, government cash transfers, or other types of cash income. Estimates are restricted to full-time, year-round workers 16 years or older. To be considered a "year-round" worker, an individual must have worked 50 or more weeks in the past 12 months, including paid time off for vacation or sick leave. To be considered "full-time" an individual must have worked 35 or more hours per week in the weeks they worked in the past 12 months.

Chapter 5- Since the onset of the recession in December of 2007, work hours have trended downward because of increasing involuntary part-time work and a reduction in overtime hours. These trends vary by metropolitan statistical area (metro area) and by type of employment. This report will show where work-hour cuts have been most prevalent. It highlights changes in usual hours worked per week by sex, occupation, industry, and class of worker.

Chapter 6- This report presents data from the 2008 and 2009 American Community Surveys (ACS) on the percentage of commuters who used public transportation to get to work in U.S. metropolitan statistical areas (metro areas). The percentage of workers who usually travel to work using public transportation has remained at about 5 percent since the 1 990 Census.[2]

Chapter 7- This report presents data on property value at the national level and for metropolitan statistical areas (metro areas) based on the 2008 and 2009 American Community Surveys (ACS). The value of property is an important component in measuring neighborhood quality, housing aff ordability, and wealth. These data provide socioeconomic information not captured by household income and comparative information about metro housing markets.

Chapter 8- This report presents data from the 2009 American Community Survey (ACS) on rental market conditions, including share of occupied housing, housing costs, housing cost "burden," and vacancy rate at the national level and for metropolitan statistical areas (metro areas).

Chapter 9- This report presents data on food stamp/SNAP receipt for the past 12 months at the national and state levels based on the 2008 and 2009 American Community Surveys (ACS). The data in this report are for households, not individuals. If any person living at the sample address at the time of the interview received food stamps/SNAP, the household is included in the count. Respondents were asked to report any spells of food stamp/SNAP receipt for the past 12 months.

Chapter 10- The recent economic downturn has affected the labor force participation of men and women of all ages and education levels. Recent college graduates have had difficulty obtaining jobs, while older workers are returning to work or continuing to work in order to bolster their diminished retirement savings. Some younger workers may enroll in school or stay in school due to diminished job prospects, while others may end their job search out of frustration. The recession has also had an impact on workers in the prime working age group of 25 to 54, particularly for men and especially for those with less education. The largest job losses have been in male-dominated industries such as construction and manufacturing, whereas female-dominated industries such as healthcare have fared relatively better over the course of the recession. As a result of men bearing the brunt of the job losses, women are entering the labor force to supplement family income when their spouses have either lost their jobs or have had their work hours reduced. Consequently, workers of all ages and education levels will be competing for jobs within a smaller job market pool.

Chapter 11- Although the current recession has impacted the country in a variety of ways, a common scenario emerging from this economic climate is an increase in the number of women who are the sole worker within a married-couple family. In some cases, husbands have lost their jobs while their wives have not. In others, wives have reentered the labor force to help off set lost family income after their husbands' job loss. Between 2008 and 2009, the largest job losses were reported in male-dominated industries such as construction and manufacturing, whereas female-dominated industries such as healthcare have fared relatively better over the course of the recession.

Chapter 12- Health insurance coverage, whether private or public, improves children's access to health care services and the regularity with which children receive medical care. This improved access to care leads to better health for insured children compared to uninsured children.

Chapter 13- Many policies directed toward the population of people with disabilities have focused on expanding employment opportunities. Federal laws, like the Rehabilitation Act of 1 972 and the Americans with Disabilities Act of 1 990 (ADA), have attempted to improve workplace conditions by encouraging reasonable accommodation and reducing job discrimination. Over the two decades since the ADA was signed, countless numbers of people with disabilities have credited the legislation with improving their lives. Despite the progress made, barriers still remain that limit full participation in the labor force.

Chapter 14- This report presents data on public assistance receipt at the national and state levels based on the 2008 and 2009 American Community Surveys (ACS). Public assistance income, or welfare, provides cash payments to poor families and includes general assistance and Temporary Assistance to Needy Families (TANF), which replaced Aid to Families with Dependent Children (AFDC) in 1997. Public assistance income does not include Supplemental Security Income (SSI), noncash benefits such as food stamps, or separate payments received for hospital or other medical care (vendor payments). To qualify for public assistance benefits, the income and/or assets of an individual or family must fall below specified thresholds. However, unlike AFDC benefits, TANF benefits are time-limited, require most adult recipients to work, and give states increased flexibility in program design.

Chapter 15- This brief presents data on reported field of bachelor's degrees for the nation, the 50 states, the District of Columbia, and Puerto Rico based on the 2009 American Community Survey (ACS). It focuses on the distribution of degrees in science and engineering fields (S&E) compared to all other degree fields. The science and engineering category includes fields such as animal sciences, biology, psychology, engineering, and anthropology. Examples of nonscience and nonengineering fields include agriculture, business, communications, education, and social work.

Chapter 16- This report presents data on the foreign- born population at the national and state levels based on the 2009 American Community Survey (ACS). During the last four decades, the foreign-born population of the United States has continued to increase in size and as a percent of the total population: from 9.6 million or 4.7 percent in 1970, to 14.1 million or 6.2 percent in 1980, 19.8 million or 7.9 percent in 1990, and 31.1 million or 11.1 percent in 2000.[1] According to the 2009 ACS, there were 38.5 million foreign-born residents, representing 12.5 percent of the total population.[2] While the number of foreign born repre-sents a historical high, the proportion of the total population is lower than during the great migration of the late 1800s and early 1900s, when it fluctuated between 13 percent and 15 percent. But more notable than the growth of the foreign- born population is the change in the distribution of origin countries over time.

Chapter 17- This report presents data on nativity status and citizenship at the national and state levels based on the 2009 American Community Survey (ACS). During the last four decades, both the native and foreign- born populations have increased in size. While the native-born population has remained the majority during this period, the foreign-born population has come to represent a greater share of the total population, increasing from 9.6 million or 4.7 percent in 1970, to 31.1 million or 11.1 percent in 2000.[2] According to the 2009 ACS, 38.5 million of the 307 million residents in the United States were foreign- born, representing 12.5 percent of the total population.

Chapter 18- This report presents data on the year of entry of the foreign-born population at the national and state levels based on the 2009 American Community Survey (ACS). In 2009, an estimated 38.5 million foreign-born people lived in the United States, representing roughly 12.5 percent of the total population. The foreign-born population includes anyone who was not a U.S. citizen at birth.

Chapter 19- This report describes the population with Haitian ancestry living in the United States based on the 2009 American Community Survey (ACS). It also presents the distribution of people with Haitian ancestry across the United States.

Haitian is a relatively small, yet growing, ancestry group in the United States, increasing from 290,000 people with Haitian ancestry (0.1 percent of the total population) in 1990 to 548,000 (0.2 percent) in 2000. By 2009, an estimated 830,000 people with Haitian ancestry were living in the United States, or 0.3 percent of the total population.

Chapter 20- This report presents data on the proportion of people aged 5 and over who spoke a language other than English at home, based on the 2009 merican Community Survey (ACS). Data are presented at the national and state levels. Data in the state maps are reported for Hispanic origin and racial groups with a population of at least 65,000.

In: The American Community Survey ...   ISBN: 978-1-61324-362-6
Editors: B. M. Russo and A. D. Haffner   ©2011 Nova Science Publishers, Inc.

Chapter 1

THE AMERICAN COMMUNITY SURVEY: DEVELOPMENT, IMPLEMENTATION, AND ISSUES FOR CONGRESS

Jennifer D. Williams

SUMMARY

The American Community Survey (ACS) is the U.S. Bureau of the Census's replacement for the decennial census long form, which, since 1940, had gathered detailed socioeconomic and housing data from a representative population sample in conjunction with the once-a-decade count of all U.S. residents. Unlike the long form, with its approximately 17% sample of U.S. housing units in 2000, the ACS is a "rolling sample" or "continuous measurement" survey of about 250,000 housing units a month (totaling about three million a year). The data are aggregated to produce one-year, three-year, and five-year estimates that are much more timely than the long-form estimates were. As were the long-form data, ACS data are used in program formulas that determine the annual allocation of certain federal funds, currently more than $400 billion, to states and localities.

The ACS has several other features in common with the long form: the topics covered are largely the same; survey questionnaires are mailed to housing units, filled out, and returned by mail; responses are mandatory; and the Bureau follows up, by telephone or in-person visits, with households that do not return completed questionnaires. The ACS is conducted under the authority of Title 13, Sections 141 and 193, of the United States Code; so was the long form. Title 44, Section 3501, of the Code, the Paperwork Reduction Act of 1995, and its implementing regulations require federal agencies to obtain Office of Management and Budget approval before collecting information from the public. On the long form, the Bureau could gather only data that were mandatory for particular programs, required by federal law or regulations, or needed for the Bureau's operations. Likewise, the ACS can collect only necessary information.

The limited ACS sample size makes longer accumulations of data necessary to generate reliable estimates for less populous areas. Yearly averages have been available since 2006, but only for geographic areas with 65,000 or more people. The first three-year period estimates, for areas with 20,000 to 65,000 people, became available in 2008. They represent data collected in 2005, 2006, and 2007. The first-ever five-year averages, of data gathered from 2005 through 2009, were released on December 14, 2010, for areas with fewer than 20,000 people. A concern noted by some data users is that the present ACS sample size will result in less-detailed five-year data products for smaller geographic areas—census tracts and block groups—than were available every 10 years with the long form. A related issue is data quality, especially for small areas. Of the Obama Administration's $1 .267 billion appropriations request for the Bureau in FY20 11, $44 million, if approved, would go toward increasing the annual ACS sample size from about 2.3% to 2.5% of the population (3.5 million housing units), to improve the tract-level reliability of ACS estimates. Under an FY20 11 continuing appropriations act (H.J.Res. 101; P.L. 111-290), the Bureau is funded through December 18, 2010, at an annualized amount of $1 .223 billion.

An ongoing concern for some Members of Congress and their constituents is that responses to the ACS are required. The conferees on H.J.Res. 2, the Consolidated Appropriations Resolution, 2003 (P.L. 108-7; 117 Stat. 11), included $1 million for the Bureau to test a voluntary versus mandatory ACS. The test findings, reported in 2003 and 2004, showed a 20.7-percentage-point drop in the overall ACS response rate when answers were optional. The Bureau estimated that if the survey became voluntary, maintaining data reliability would necessitate increasing the annual sample size from about three million to 3.7 million housing units, at an additional cost of at least $59.2 million per year in FY2005 dollars. Two bills from the 111th Congress, H.R. 3131 and H.R. 5046, proposed making almost all ACS responses optional.

INTRODUCTION

In the mid-1990s, the U.S. Bureau of the Census began developing and testing a new means of data collection called a "rolling sample" or "continuous measurement" survey[1] that became the American Community Survey (ACS). Implemented nationwide in 2005 and 2006, the ACS collects data from a representative sample of about 250,000 housing units a month (totaling about three million a year). The data are aggregated over time to produce large enough samples for reliable[2] estimates, with longer cumulations of data necessary in less populous areas. The Bureau issues one-year estimates for the most populous areas, those with at least 65,000 people; three-year estimates for areas with 20,000 to 65,000 people; and five-year estimates for areas with fewer than 20,000 people.

Although conducted separately from the once-a-decade count of the whole U.S. population, the ACS is considered a part of the decennial census program[3] because it has replaced the census long form, which covered a representative sample of housing units every 10 years, from 1940 through 2000.[4] In the 2000 census, a set of basic questions on a short form went to most housing units; a sample of units—about 17% overall—received a long form containing the short-form questions and additional questions that collected detailed data on socioeconomic and housing characteristics. The data served myriad governmental, business, and research purposes, and were used in program formulas that determined the annual allocation of various federal funds to states and localities. ACS data, which serve the same purposes but are much more current than the long- form estimates were, are used to distribute more than $400 billion a year in funding. Thus, the timeliness and quality of ACS data are important for many reasons, but especially to promote the equitable allocation of scarce public resources.

Discussing in 2001 how the ACS evolved, the late Charles H. Alexander of the Census Bureau recalled that in the early 1 990s

[t]here was renewed Congressional interest in the intercensal characteristics data ... and a "continuous measurement" alternative to the census long form that was considered as part of the research for Census 2000, starting in 1992. [The] rolling sample design was eventually proposed for this purpose because it provided flexibility in making estimates, as well as the potential for efficient data collection ..."Continuous Measurement" was later renamed the "American Community Survey ...."

The proposed ACS was not adopted for Census 2000, but after limited testing during 1996- 1998, the ACS methodology was implemented in 36 counties for the years 1999-2001, so that ACS results could be compared to the 2000 census long form data. There was also a large-scale test in 2000, for a state-representative annual sample ... called the Census 2000 Supplementary Survey, of collecting long-form data separately from the census, using the ACS questionnaire.[5]

He explained that

[f]or the main ACS objective, to replace the census long form as a source of detailed descriptive statistics, we plan to use 5-year ACS cumulations, for a data product similar to traditional long form "summary files". This is the shortest time period for which the ACS sampling error is judged to be reasonably close to that of the census long form. All sizes and types of geographic areas would be included on these 5-year data files. ...

For individual areas, the most prominently published data will be one-year averages for areas greater than 65,000 population, and 3-year averages for areas greater than 20,000, in addition to the 5-year averages for all areas.[6]

REASONS FOR ADOPTING THE ACS

The Census Bureau had two main reasons for replacing the long form with the ACS. First was the intention to increase public acceptance of, and response to, the decennial enumeration by decoupling the count of the whole population from the sample-survey part of the census.[7] The Bureau strives, never entirely successfully, to achieve a complete count because it is a constitutional requirement for reapportioning the U.S. House of Representatives, and because the data serve many other important national, state, and local purposes.[8] According to a 2008 Government Accountability Office (GAO) report on the projected mail response rate[9] of 69% for the 2010 census, the Bureau calculated that eliminating the long form and moving to a shortform-only census would add one percentage point to the 2000 census initial mail return rate of 65%.[10] The second reason for adopting the ACS was to produce more timely information,[11] which was particularly needed in program formulas used to distribute certain federal funds to states and localities. Detailed socioeconomic and housing data not only were collected just once a decade on the long form, but also were up to three years old by the time the Bureau processed and released them. In 1976, Congress authorized,[12] but did not fund, a mid-decade census that would have provided more current data.[13] The ACS could be viewed as substituting for the never- implemented mid-decade census as well as the long form.

DEVELOPMENT AND LAUNCHING OF THE ACS

Before the ACS became fully operational, in 2005 and 2006, it underwent extensive development and testing, which began in the mid-1990s. The steps that led to full implementation are discussed briefly below.

Developing a Prototype

The Bureau's ACS designers decided, while developing a prototype of the survey, that it would have several features in common with the decennial census: survey questionnaires would be mailed to housing units, and completed questionnaires would be returned by mail; responses would be mandatory; and the Bureau would follow up, by telephone and, as necessary, in-person visits, with households that did not fill out and return their questionnaires.[14]

Unlike the census, however, the ACS would collect data continuously from independent monthly samples of the population and would aggregate the data over time to produce estimates[15] that would be controlled to intercensal population and housing estimates.[16] The designers "initially suggested" an ACS sample size of 500,000 housing units per month, but rejected it as prohibitively expensive and "determined that a monthly sample size of 250,000 would generate an acceptable level of reliability."[17]

Early Testing

Limited testing of ACS operations began in 1995 in Rockland County, New York; Brevard County, Florida; Multnomah County, Oregon; and Fulton County, Pennsylvania.[18]

In 1996, the Bureau extended testing to areas with varied geographic and demographic characteristics, including Harris County, Texas; Fort Bend County, Texas; Douglas County, Nebraska; Franklin County, Ohio; and Otero County, New Mexico. This testing led to further research into small-area estimation, estimation methods, nonresponse follow-up, weighting in ACS tests, item nonresponse, response rates, and the quality of data for rural areas.[19]

In 1998, operational testing expanded to Kershaw County, South Carolina; Richland County, South Carolina; and Broward County (which the Bureau substituted for Brevard County), Florida. Adding the two South Carolina counties enabled the Bureau to compare ACS test data with results from the 1998 dress rehearsal for the 2000 census, which included these counties.[20]

Testing was extended in 1999 to 36 counties in 26 states, "selected to represent different combinations of county population size, difficulty of enumeration, and 1990-1995 population growth," as well as "racial and ethnic diversity, migrant or seasonal populations, American Indian reservations, changing economic conditions, and predominant occupation or industry types."[21] In addition, during 1999 and 2001, the 36 counties were test sites for enumerating residents of group quarters, such as college residence halls, residential treatment centers, skilled nursing facilities, group homes, military barracks, correctional facilities, and workers' dormitories; and facilities for homeless people.[22] These tests, which concentrated on the methodology for visiting group quarters, selecting samples of residents, and conducting interviews,[23] "led to modification of sampling techniques and revisions to data collection methods."[24]

Although the primary objective of this testing phase "was to determine the viability of the methodologies utilized, it also generated usable data."[25] Data were released in 1999 on "demographic, social, economic, and housing topics."[26]

The Demonstration Phase

In 2000, the Bureau undertook a larger-scale test, or demonstration, originally called the "Census 2000 Supplementary Survey,"[27] to "assure Congress and other data users" that nationwide implementation of the ACS was feasible and that the rolling-sample survey could produce information comparable in quality and reliability to long-form data.[28]

The demonstration was conducted in 1,239 of the nation's 3,141 counties, the 36 ACS test counties, and 1,203 newly added counties. The number of housing units sampled annually increased from 165,000 in 1999 to 866,000 in 2000.

From 2001 through 2004, the Bureau issued 11 reports analyzing various aspects of the demonstration phase.[29] Overall, according to this analysis, the demonstration showed the ACS to be a success and supported proceeding with it, but with certain refinements. The demonstration's "planned tasks were completed on time and within budget, and the data collected met basic Census Bureau quality standards."[30] The ACS "was well-managed, was achieving the desired response rates, and had functional quality control procedures."[31] The ACS and census 2000 long- form estimates of economic characteristics were comparable. The same was true of social characteristics, except for the estimates of disability and ancestry. The analysis recommended further research concerning these discrepancies, and other research to reduce variance[32] in ACS estimates below the county level of geography.[33] Moreover, the analysis found that although the "ACS methodology was sound, its improvement needed to be an ongoing activity."[34]

At congressional direction,[35] part of the demonstration involved a test of voluntary versus mandatory compliance with the ACS. The test and its results, which have implications for ACS response rates, survey costs, and data reliability, are discussed later in this report.

Full Implementation

Full implementation of the housing unit component of the ACS occurred in January 2005, with the survey's expansion to all 3,141 U.S. counties,[36] covering approximately 250,000 housing units per month (totaling about 3 million a year). In January 2006, with an annual sample of approximately 20,000 group quarters, the Bureau fully implemented this part of the ACS.[37]

ACS DATA RELEASES ON THE WEB

In mid-2006, the Bureau began releasing, on its American FactFinder website,[38] annual ACS population and housing unit profiles for geographic areas—including congressional districts— with 65,000 or more people.[39] An estimate released in any given year is a period estimate, an average of data collected in every month during the previous year. Thus, for example, the data issued in 2006 represent information gathered throughout 2005, not at a particular point in 2005.

The first three-year period estimates, for areas with 20,000 to 65,000 people, became available in 2008. They represent data collected in 2005, 2006, and 2007.[40] The second three-year set, released in 2009, covers 2006 through 2008.[41] New three-year averages, for 2007 through 2009, are scheduled for release in January 2011.[42]

In areas with fewer than 20,000 people, generating an ACS sample large enough to provide estimates similar in accuracy to long-form estimates requires, as noted at the beginning of this report, data collection over a five-year period.[43] The first-ever five-year averages, of data gathered from 2005 through 2009, were released on December 14, 2010.[44] Five-year estimates are to be available "every year thereafter," in 2011 for the period 2006 through 2010, and so forth.[45]

The many tables of ACS data shown on American FactFinder include, beside each estimate, the margin of sampling error associated with it. As the Bureau has explained, "a margin of error is the difference between an estimate and its upper or lower confidence bounds. Confidence bounds can be created by adding the margin of error to the estimate (for an upper bound) and subtracting the margin of error from the estimate (for a lower bound)."[46] All published margins of error for the ACS are based on a 90% confidence level. That is, the data user can be 90% certain that the true value of an ACS estimate lies between its upper and lower confidence bounds.[47] The Bureau gave the following illustration using a one-year estimate from 2007. The estimate for the percentage of children under age 18 below the poverty level in Mississippi "is 29.3% and the margin of error is +/- 1.2." The data user can be 90% "certain that the true value is between 28.1% and 30.5%. This is calculated by first subtracting the margin of error (1.2%) from the estimate (29.3%), giving the lower bound for the estimate (28.1%)." Then, to calculate the upper bound, the data user adds "the margin of error (1.2%) to the estimate (29.3%), to get 30.5%."[48]

THE DETERMINATION OF QUESTIONNAIRE CONTENTS

Those who access ACS data tables on American FactFinder will see that the survey covers a broad array of topics, which are summarized in the appendix to this report. The brief explanation or description after each topic was adapted from the ACS questionnaire. Although—as the **Appendix** indicates—the questionnaire is quite detailed, the items on it, like the predecessor long-form items, underwent a precise selection process. A 2006 policy statement by the Bureau[49] pointed out that Title 44, Section 3501, of the *United States Code*, the Paperwork Reduction Act of 1995 (PRA), and its implementing regulations[50] require federal agencies to obtain Office of Management and Budget (OMB) approval before collecting information from the public.

On the long form, the Bureau could ask only for data that were

- mandatory: "a current federal law ... explicitly called for the use of decennial census data for a particular federal program";
- required: "it was unequivocally clear that a federal law (or implementing regulation) required the use of specific data and the decennial census was the historical or only source of data"; or
- programmatic: "the data were necessary for Census Bureau operational needs ...."[51]

"In accordance with the PRA," the policy statement continued, "the OMB, in consultation with the Census Bureau, is responsible for approving new content for the ACS."[52] Factors to be considered include

frequency of data collection; the level of geography needed ... ; and whether any other source of data would meet the requestor's need in lieu of ... the ACS. The Census Bureau recognizes and appreciates the interests of federal partners and stakeholders in the collection of data on the ACS. The fact that respondents' participation ... is mandatory requires that the OMB will only approve, and the Census Bureau will only ask, necessary questions. On a periodic basis, the Census Bureau will reassess the questions contained on the ACS to ensure that this survey remains the appropriate vehicle for collection of these data. The OMB's responsibility under the PRA requires that practical utility of the data be demonstrated and that the respondent burden be kept to a minimum. As such, the Census Bureau will refer all agency requests for new content to the OMB.[53]

The Bureau's website[54] reproduces each item from the ACS questionnaire and describes in general terms how the resulting data are used, including, as mentioned at the beginning of this report, in program formulas that determine the distribution of more than $400 billion a year in certain federal funds to states and localities.[55] Below are several examples of these program uses, paraphrased from the Bureau's descriptions.

- Various federal agencies use information about disability status to develop programs and distribute funds, such as grants based on the number of elderly people with physical and mental disabilities and funds for mass transit systems to provide facilities for the handicapped.
- Income data are part of the federal allocation formulas for many programs. Among other purposes, these data are used to allocate funds for home energy aid; provide funds for housing assistance; identify localities eligible for grants to promote economic recovery and conduct job-training programs; provide local agencies with funds for food, health care, and legal services for the low-income elderly; allocate funds for food, health care, and classes in meal planning to low- income women with children; and distribute funds to counties and school districts to improve the education of children from low-income households.
- Data on veteran status are used to distribute funds to states and localities for veterans' employment and job training programs.
- Data on language are the basis for allocating grants to school districts to benefit children with limited English proficiency.
- Data about plumbing facilities are used as one variable in assessing the quality of housing stock; an additional use is to allocate federal housing subsidies.

ISSUES CONCERNING THE ACS

Tension is inherent between the amount, quality, timeliness, and geographic coverage of data that the ACS provides, and the public cost—in both dollars and respondent burden—of gathering the information. Larger samples can provide better data and better coverage across different levels of geography, but they are more expensive and involve more respondents. Gathering a large amount of data monthly and aggregating it over one-, three-, and five-year intervals yields detailed, relatively current information, but also at considerable cost.

Sample Size

In a March 2009 Federal Register notice, the Bureau announced and sought public comments on its plans for releasing 2005 through 2009 ACS data products.[56] According to the notice, the release "will achieve a goal of the ACS to provide small area data similar to the data published after Census 2000, based on the long-form sample,"[57] but some who commented had a different assessment. As one observed,[58] with a "fixed sample size of three million households annually, the ACS 5-year sample is considerably smaller than the 1-in-6 household sample of Census 2000. ... The original ACS sample design was for three percent of households each year, a level that would have produced 5-year data for small geographic areas near the reliability and disclosure avoidance[59] levels of Census 2000." Because the Bureau "did not receive a budget for a sample similar to that of the long form ... , the 5-year data products cannot be as detailed for smaller geographic areas as they were in 2000." The correspondent called for the Bureau to acknowledge "openly" that, "given the smaller sample size, some ACS 5-year products cannot meet some user needs for detailed census tract[60] and block group[61] data."

The issue of sample size, especially as it affects small-area data, is not new. It was discussed, for example, in a 2007 publication by the National Academy of Sciences' Committee on National Statistics[62] and a 2004 GAO report.[63] Moreover, the fixed sample size of the ACS means that as the U.S. population grows, with a corresponding increase in housing units, the proportion of units surveyed decreases. This decrease could affect the quality of ACS data for all purposes, particularly for the equitable distribution to states and localities of more than $400 billion yearly in federal funds. In 2003, the Bureau reported that the fully implemented ACS would sample about 3 million of approximately 120 million housing units annually,[64] or about 2.5% of all units. By 2009, when the number of housing units was estimated at almost 130 million,[65] 3 million units represented about 2.3% of the total.

Of the Obama Administration's $1.267 billion appropriations request for the Bureau in FY2011, $44 million would go toward increasing the annual ACS sample size to 2.5% of the population, (3.5 million housing units), "to improve the reliability of the ACS estimates at the tract level." The funds also would "allow the Census Bureau to enhance field and telephone center data collection, conduct a 100 percent nonresponse follow-up operation in Remote Alaska and small American Indian, Alaska Native, and Native Hawaiian Homeland areas, and provide additional resources for the full review of the 3-year and 5-year data."[66] The level of ACS funding for FY2011 has yet to be determined. The Senate Committee on Appropriations recommended $1.245 billion for the Bureau, $22.3 million below the FY2011 request. The House Appropriations Committee did not report an FY2011 Commerce, Justice, Science, and Related Agencies appropriations bill. Under a continuing resolution,[67] the Bureau is funded through December 18, 2010, at an annualized amount of $1.223 billion.[68]

Public Perception

The ACS has encountered some public resistance, as did its long-form predecessor. One indication of the reaction to a mailed questionnaire from the Bureau is whether the recipients fill it out and mail it back before nonresponse follow-up begins. Long-form responses by mail tended to decrease over time, and the same has occurred with the ACS since 2000. A 2004 report by the National Academy of Sciences' Committee on National Statistics, Panel to Review the 2000 Census,[69] cited a two-percentage-point difference between short-form and long-form mail return rates[70] in 1980 (82% versus 80%), which widened to five percentage points in 1990 (76% versus 71%) and nine percentage points in 2000 (80% versus 71%).[71] The 71% mail return rate for the long form in 1990 and 2000 represented a nine-percentage-point decrease from the 1980 rate of 80%. A 2009 evaluation[72] by the Bureau found that ACS mail response rates[73] dropped 5.8 percentage points over eight years (from 40.6% in 2000 to 34.8% in 2008).[74] These rates, however, excluded questionnaires returned more than 25 days after being mailed out. When all the questionnaires were included, response rates were higher and the decrease over eight years was less (3.1 percentage points, from 59.7% in 2000 to 56.6% in 2008).[75]

Press reports,[76] a poll,[77] and a House subcommittee oversight hearing on the 2000 census reflected a degree of dissatisfaction with the 2000 census long form. In opening remarks at the hearing, the subcommittee chairman stated:

> Clearly the biggest controversy surrounding the census has been the perceived intrusiveness and the invasion of privacy of the long form.
> ...
> While the long form has always been less popular than the short form, the attitudes toward the 2000 long form seem to be particularly intense despite the fact that it ... only differs by one new question from 1990. During the 1998 dress rehearsals, the long form response

rate was between 10 and 15 percentage points lower than the short form. ....

From the first day that the forms were being received at millions of homes around the Nation, Members of Congress were receiving phone calls from constituents who were very upset about the long form. ...

Every major newspaper in the Nation has written about the long form and the privacy issue. Electronic media from talk radio to television have weighed in. ...

The reason why there is a long form controversy is because millions of Americans aren't comfortable answering the questions .... The News Hour on PBS had an entire segment on the privacy issue and the long form almost 2 weeks ago.[78] On 60 Minutes, one of the most popular news shows on television with almost 13 million viewers weekly, commentator Andy Rooney voiced to the Nation two Sundays ago his criticism of the long form.[79] He concluded ... by saying, "I am not going to fill out the long form."[80]

Whereas the long form could attract criticism once a decade, however, the monthly survey can generate some degree of negative attention more frequently.[81] Among the comments reported by the media are that the ACS asks for too much detail, and that certain questions—such as those about income, disability, and home plumbing facilities—invade respondents' privacy.[82] Reluctant respondents may ask whether, and why, they must answer these and other questions.[83]

As noted previously, the ACS can ask only "necessary questions,"[84] and responses are mandatory. The decennial census is conducted under the authority of Title 13, Sections 141 and 193, of the United States Code. Section 141 authorizes a census of population every 10 years for House reapportionment and within-state redistricting. This section also authorizes the Department of Commerce[85] Secretary "to obtain such other census information as necessary." Section 193 provides that "[i]n advance of, in conjunction with, or after the taking of each census ..., the Secretary may make surveys and collect such preliminary and supplementary statistics related to the main topic of the census as are necessary to the initiation, taking, or completion thereof." The Census Bureau considered long-form responses to be mandatory and has conducted the ACS as mandatory "since its inception" in the mid-1990s.[86] Title 13, Section 221, provides for a fine of not more than $100 for refusal or neglect to answer questions; pursuant to Title 18, Sections 3559 and 3571, the

Sentencing Reform Act of 1984, the possible fine has been adjusted to not more than $5,000.

In addition, current and former Bureau employees are required to maintain the confidentiality of census data about individuals. Under Title 13, Section 214, the wrongful disclosure of information is punishable by a fine of not more than $5,000, or not more than five years' imprisonment, or both. Pursuant to Title 18, Sections 3559 and 3571, the possible fine has been adjusted to not more than $250,000.

TESTING A MANDATORY VERSUS VOLUNTARY ACS

By late 2002, public complaints about the long form and congressional concern about the ACS had prompted some in Congress to inquire about the advisability of making responses to the latter survey voluntary.[87] Shortly thereafter, the conferees on H.J.Res. 2, the FY2003 Consolidated Appropriations Resolution,[88] included $1 million for the Bureau "to test the response rates of both a voluntary and a mandatory" ACS because "sufficient information is not available to [weigh] the benefits" of each approach.[89] The conferees directed the Commerce Secretary to report to the Appropriations Committees as soon as the test results were available.

Two reports about the test and its findings appear on the Bureau's website.[90] The first one, issued in December 2003, "was prepared on an expedited basis to meet Congressional needs."[91] A year later, the second report presented additional test results, "including greater detail for some of the measures included in the initial report."[92] The discussion below focuses on the 2003 report.

As the ACS is, the test of a voluntary ACS (hereafter called the "ACS test") was a mail-out, mail- back operation in which interviewers followed up with nonresponding households by telephone and, when necessary, personal visits.[93]

The ACS test studied four experimental treatments of mailed questionnaires, two instructing recipients that responses were mandatory and two treating responses as voluntary. The 2003 report highlighted two main treatments, one mandatory and the other voluntary: the benchmark "2002 Current Mandatory approach" was "identical to the mail treatment used in prior years and provided a control to previous years";[94] the "Standard Voluntary treatment" used "a standard survey approach" to explain that responses were not required.[95]

The Bureau's sample design for the test divided the universe of approximately 140,000 housing units[96] into two strata, high-response areas (HRAs) and low-response areas (LRAs), which were designated on the basis of "tract-level long form mail return rates from Census 2000."[97] Data from the 2001 ACS indicated that people in the LRAs were younger, more likely to be Hispanic, more likely to be non-White, less likely to be college educated, and more likely to be renters than in the HRAs. The LRA stratum had more households with lower incomes, more that included "other relatives"[98] or "nonrelatives," and more where languages "other than English" were spoken at home.[99]

The ACS test was conducted in March and April 2003. The tables in the report issued later that year compared the results from the Standard Voluntary treatment of test questionnaires (hereafter, the "2003 voluntary survey") with those from the mandatory ACS for March and April 2002 (hereafter, the "2002 mandatory ACS"), as discussed below.[100] The Bureau applied the HRA-LRA stratification to the 2002 mandatory ACS results.[101]

Key test results pertained to the mail cooperation rate.[102] It was 20.7 percentage points lower overall for the 2003 voluntary survey than for the 2002 mandatory ACS (3 8.8% compared with 59.5%, a 34.8% decrease). In the HRAs, the decrease was 22.2 percentage points (42.4% versus 64.6%, a 34.4% drop). In the LRAs, the percentage-point decrease was less, 15.9 points, but the already low 2002 mail cooperation rate of 43.6% dropped to 27.7% in 2003 (a 3 6.5% decrease).[103]

Lower mail cooperation in the 2003 voluntary survey meant a heavier workload of nonresponse follow-up by telephone. Moreover, cooperation with telephone interviewers was lower when it was optional (66.5% overall in 2003 versus 80.7% in 2002, a 14.2 percentage-point or 17.6 % decrease). Although the 2003 rates of telephone cooperation were almost identical in the HRAs and LRAs, cooperation decreased more from 2002 to 2003 in the HRAs (by 15.6 percentage points or 19%, from 82.1% to 66.5%) than in the LRAs (by 10.2 percentage points or 13.4%, from 76.4% to 66.2%).[104]

Personal visits for nonresponse follow-up closed "some, but not all,"[105] of the gap in mail and telephone cooperation between 2002 and 2003. As with telephone nonresponse follow-up, the workload of personal visits increased in 2003; responses decreased when they were optional; and the percentage-point decline in cooperation was greater in the HRAs than in the LRAs, suggesting that the voluntary approach had a greater negative effect on compliance in areas that usually tend to be cooperative. Overall response to personal visits was 89% in 2003, down from 95.6% a year earlier (a 6.6 percentage-point or

6.9% decline). In the HRAs, the 2003 response rate was 88.2% versus 95.7% in 2002 (a 7.5 percentage-point or 7.8% drop). The comparable figures for the LRAs were 90.7% versus 95.6% (a 4.9 percentage-point or 5.1% decrease).[106]

The Bureau observed that when ACS responses were voluntary instead of required, respondents tended to shift "from participating by mail to participating by telephone or personal visit followup."[107] Because personal interviews are about 10 times more expensive than data collection by mail or telephone,[108] survey costs rise as mail and telephone cooperation fall. Further, since the Bureau selects a subsample of ACS nonrespondents—not all nonrespondents—for personal visits, reliability of the data is a concern. A decrease in the percentage of responses by mail and telephone means "fewer total interviews and thus, a reduction in reliability."[109] If the survey became voluntary, the Bureau concluded, maintaining the same data reliability as under the 2002 mandatory ACS would necessitate increasing the annual sample size from about 3 million to an estimated 3.7 million housing units,[110] at an additional cost of at least $59.2 million per year in FY2005 dollars.[111] The latter estimate reflected "direct data collection costs only"; it did not include the expense of hiring and training more ACS staff, and purchasing additional equipment.[112]

PROPOSALS IN THE 111TH CONGRESS FOR A VOLUNTARY ACS

Two bills introduced in the 111th Congress sought to make almost all ACS responses optional. They received no action beyond committee and subcommittee referrals.

- H.R. 3131, to Make Participation in the American Community Survey Voluntary, Except with Respect to Certain Basic Questions, was introduced on July 8, 2009, by Representative Poe. The bill would have prohibited applying any criminal penalty to people who refused or willfully neglected to answer ACS inquiries, except those about the respondent's name and contact information, the date of the response, and the number of residents at the respondent's address.
- H.R. 5046, the Census Clarification and Privacy Act, introduced on April 15, 2010, by Representative Akin. This measure called for a statement, on the front of the decennial census and ACS

questionnaires, that the respondent was constitutionally required only to provide the number of people living at the residence, and that all other answers were optional. The bill also would have made penalties applicable only for refusing or willfully neglecting to answer this question on any census or survey conducted under Title 13, Sections 141 or 193, *United States Code*, or for falsely answering any question on any census or survey conducted under these sections.

POSSIBLE ACS OPTIONS FOR CONGRESS

Noted below are several possible options that Congress could have regarding the ACS, now that the survey is fully implemented and the long form of previous decennial censuses no longer exists.

Congress could support the status quo, providing oversight and funding of the ACS into the future. Oversight issues might include ACS methodology and any advisable improvements in it. Three other related issues are how large the ACS sample should be to ensure reliability of the data, particularly for small areas; what funding levels would be necessary to achieve and maintain such a sample size; and what funding levels would be feasible, given the likelihood of continuing federal budgetary constraints.

Some Members of the 112th Congress could propose making ACS responses voluntary, as two Members did during the 111th Congress. Another congressional approach—because the test results discussed above indicate that a voluntary survey might well lower response rates and raise costs—might involve inquiring into the extent and sources of public dissatisfaction with the ACS and exploring remedies short of voluntary responses. Possible questions to consider are how to explain more effectively why ACS data are necessary and how best to engage the public in nonresponse follow-up. Congress could assess with the Bureau whether an advertising campaign, perhaps modeled on that for the 2010 decennial census,[113] might heighten awareness of the ACS and its value to states and localities. A related consideration is whether the Bureau might enhance the appeal of the ACS by posting on its website estimates of the funds provided each year to specific states and localities on the basis of program formulas that use ACS data. In addition, Congress could direct the Bureau to offer respondents the convenience of answering the ACS questionnaire by Internet instead of on paper, if the Bureau determines that this option would not jeopardize the confidentiality of personal data.

Congress could examine alternatives to the ACS. If the past is an accurate predictor, returning to an approximately 17% sample of U.S. housing units via the long form would depress decennial census response rates somewhat and complicate the count; this reprise also would generate less timely data than does the ACS. Congress could set as a priority research into whether administrative records might substitute for the ACS. Possible points to consider would be the operational feasibility of this approach, its expense, the quality and completeness of administrative records, privacy concerns, and acceptability to the public.

The ACS is arguably an efficient means of gathering data for many purposes. Congress could direct that the Bureau and other federal statistical agencies expedite research into whether the ACS could replace certain other surveys. This research might involve identifying duplicative data collections, if any; estimating what savings, in both money and respondent burden, might occur from having the ACS substitute for these collections; and assessing any disadvantages of replacing them.

APPENDIX. ACS TOPICS

The topics covered by the ACS are summarized below. Following each topic is a brief explanation or description of it, adapted from the ACS questionnaire.[114]

Demographic Characteristics

- Age: each person's age and date of birth
- Sex: male or female
- Hispanic or Latino origin: whether a person considers himself or herself to be of Hispanic or Latino ethnicity; and if so, whether the person is Mexican, Puerto Rican, Cuban, Argentinean, Colombian, Salvadoran, etc.
- Race: a person's self-classification as White; Black or African American; American Indian or Alaska Native, with the tribal name specified; Asian or Pacific Islander, with the specific group, such as Chinese or Samoan, named; belonging to more than one of these groups; or belonging to some other race, with the name specified

- Relationship: the relationship of each person listed on the ACS form to the person filling out the form; examples are husband or wife, roomer or border, and foster child

Social Characteristics

- Ancestry: a self-classification based on the country from which each person, or the person's parents or ancestors, came; examples of ancestries include Jamaican, Korean, and Ukrainian
- Citizenship status: whether a person is a U.S. citizen, either by birth or by naturalization
- Disability status: whether a person has various physical or mental impairments, such as serious difficulty hearing, seeing, walking, dressing, bathing, concentrating, or remembering
- Educational attainment: the highest degree or level of schooling that a person has completed
- Fertility: whether a person gave birth to any children in the past 12 months
- Field of degree: major field of study for a bachelor's degree
- Grandparents as caregivers: whether a person has any grandchildren under age 18 living with him or her; if so, whether the person is responsible for their needs, and how long the person has had this responsibility
- Language: whether a person speaks a language other than English at home; if so, what the other language is and how well the person speaks English
- Marital status and marital history: whether a person currently is married, divorced, widowed, etc.; whether the person was married, divorced, or widowed within the past 12 months; how many times the person has been married; and the year when he or she last married
- Place of birth: either the U.S. state or the place outside the 50 states
- School enrollment: whether a person attended public or private school or college in the last three months; if so, the grade or level
- Residence one year ago and migration: whether a person has moved from one residence to another in the past year; if so, what his or her previous address was

- Veterans: whether and when a person served on active duty in the U.S. military, whether the person has a service-connected disability rating; if so, what it is
- Year of entry: the year when a person born outside the United States came to live in this country

Economic Characteristics

- Class of worker: whether a person employed during the past 12 months worked for a private for-profit company, a private nonprofit organization, or federal, state, or local government; was self-employed; or was an unpaid worker for a family business or farm
- Employment status: whether a person worked for pay during the past week or was on layoff from a job, whether the person was actively looking for work in the past four weeks, and when the person last worked
- Health insurance coverage: whether a person currently is covered by any heath insurance plan, such as through a current or former employer, Medicaid, or Medicare
- Income: income in the past 12 months from various sources, including wages and salary, interest and dividends, and Social Security
- Industry: the type of activity where a person was employed during the past 12 months, such as manufacturing, retail trade, or construction
- Journey to work: where a person worked in the past week; what mode of transportation the person used to commute to work; whether the person commuted with other people in an automobile, a truck, or a van; and how much time the commute took
- Occupation: the kind of work a person did during the past 12 months, such as nursing, personnel management, or accounting
- Poverty: determined from income data
- Work status: the number of weeks a person worked during the past year, and the number of hours he or she usually worked each week

Housing Characteristics

- House heating fuel: the fuel that is used most for heating the house, apartment, or mobile home

- Kitchen facilities: whether the housing unit has a sink with a faucet, a stove or range, and a refrigerator
- Owner statistics: the owner's mortgage payments; condominium fees; real estate taxes; payments for utilities; and payments for fire, hazard, or flood insurance
- Plumbing facilities: whether the housing unit has hot and cold running water, a flush toilet, and a bathtub or shower
- Renter statistics: the renter's payments for rent and utilities
- Rooms and bedrooms: number of rooms in the housing unit, excluding bathrooms
- Supplemental Nutrition Assistance Program (SNAP, formerly the Food Stamp program): whether, in the past 12 months, anyone in the household received benefits from the program
- Telephone service available: whether the housing unit has telephone, including cell-phone, service
- Tenure: whether the housing unit is rented or owned, with or without a mortgage, by someone in the household
- Units in structure: whether the housing structure is a mobile home, a single-family detached house, a building with two apartments, etc.
- Value of home: the estimated dollar value of the home, the number of acres on which it is located, and whether the property includes a business or medical office
- Vehicles available: the number of motor vehicles kept at the home for household members' use
- Year householder moved into unit: the year the person in whose name the housing unit is rented or owned moved into the unit
- Year structure built: the year the housing structure was built

End Notes

[1] The idea for a rolling sample survey originated with statistician Leslie Kish. When interviewed toward the end of his life, Kish described the concept this way: "I want to call it rolling sample or rolling census because instead of taking the sample or census all at once, as you go through successive periods, you roll the samples gradually over the whole population. The name gives the idea." Martin Frankel and Benjamin King, "A Conversation with Leslie Kish," *Statistical Science*, vol. 11, no. 1 (February 1996), p. 79. For further discussion, see Leslie Kish, "Population Counts from Cumulated Samples," pp. 5-50 in U.S. Congress, House Committee on Post Office and Civil Service, Subcommittee on Census and Population, *Using Cumulated Rolling Samples to Integrate Census and Survey Operations*

of the Census Bureau: An Analysis, Review, and Response, committee print, 97th Cong., 1st sess., June 26, 1981, CP 97-2 (Washington: GPO, 1981).

The Census Bureau has explained the rolling-sample concept as follows: "A rolling sample design jointly selects *k* nonoverlapping probability samples, each of which constitutes 1/*F* of the entire population. One sample is interviewed each time period until all of the sample has been interviewed after *k* periods." U.S. Bureau of the Census, *American Community Survey, Design and Methodology* (Washington: GPO, 2009), glossary, p. 13.

[2] "An indicator is reliable if it consistently assigns the same numbers to some phenomenon." Kenneth J. Meier and Jeffrey L. Brudney, *Applied Statistics for Public Administration* (Belmont, CA: Wadsworth, Inc., 1987), p. 98.

[3] U.S. Bureau of the Census, "Policy on New Content for the American Community Survey," p. 1, http://www.census.gov/acs/www/Downloads/operations

[4] U.S. Bureau of the Census, *American Community Survey, Design and Methodology* (Washington: GPO, 2009), p. iii.

[5] Charles H. Alexander, "Still Rolling: Leslie Kish's 'Rolling Samples' and the American Community Survey," *Survey Methodology*, vol. 28, no. 1 (June 2002), p. 36; the article earlier was a paper presented at the Proceedings of Statistics Canada Symposium 2001, Achieving Data Quality in a Statistical Agency: A Methodological Perspective.

[6] Ibid., p. 38.

[7] See, for example, testimony of then-Census Bureau Director Kenneth Prewitt in U.S. Congress, House Committee on Government Reform, Subcommittee on the Census, *The American Community Survey—A Replacement for the Census Long Form?*, hearing, 106th Cong., 2nd sess., July 20, 2000, no. 106-246 (Washington: GPO, 2001), p. 29: "The ACS will revolutionize the way we take the decennial census and for the better. With good reason, the Congress has been concerned that the long form is a drag on the decennial census, that it introduces a complication in carrying out the basic constitutional purpose of the census. The best solution is to radically simplify the census by eliminating the long form."

[8] Article I, Section 2, clause 3 of the Constitution, as modified by Section 2 of the Fourteenth Amendment, mandates a count of the "whole number of persons in each State" every 10 years for House reapportionment. Decennial census data are used, too, for within-state redistricting and, like ACS data, as a component of certain program formulas that determine the annual allocation of more than $400 billion in federal funds to states and localities. For background information about the decennial census and a discussion of the 2010 census, see CRS Report R40551, *The 2010 Decennial Census: Background and Issues*, by Jennifer D. Williams.

[9] The "mail response rate" is "the percentage of census forms completed and returned for all housing units that were on the Bureau's address file eligible to receive a census questionnaire delivered by mail or by a census enumerator. The denominator used in calculating the response rate includes vacant housing units" and other addresses where questionnaires were determined to be "undeliverable" or that were "deleted through other census operations." U.S. Government Accountability Office, *2010 Census: Census Bureau Needs Procedures for Estimating the Response Rate and Selecting for Testing Methods to Increase Response Rate*, GAO-08-1012, September 2008, p. 6. Another measure of response is the "mail return rate," the percentage of questionnaires completed and returned from "occupied housing units with deliverable addresses." Ibid., footnote 6, p. 6.

[10] When the Bureau compared 2000 census short-form and long-form mail response rates, it found a nine-percentagepoint higher rate for the short form. Constance F. Citro, Daniel L. Cork, and Janet L. Norwood, eds., *The 2000 Census: Counting Under Adversity* (Washington: National Academies Press, 2004), p. 100. Because the long form went to only about 17% of housing units in 2000, however, its "overall effect on the response rate estimate was small ...." U.S. Government Accountability Office, *2010 Census: Census Bureau Needs Procedures for Estimating the Response Rate and Selecting for Testing Methods to Increase Response Rate*, GAO-08-1012, September 2008, pp. 12-13.

The Bureau's projected mail response rate of 69% for the 2010 census was based on more than limiting the census to a short form, for a one-percentage-point increase over the initial 65% response rate in 2000. The projection also assumed a seven-percentage-point increase in 2010 from mailing replacement questionnaires to selected nonresponding households and a four-percentage-point decrease because of generally declining public participation in surveys. Ibid., p. 12.

The National Academy of Sciences' Committee on National Statistics, Panel to Review the 2000 Census, reported a mail response rate of 67%, two percentage points higher than the earlier-reported 65% rate. Constance F. Citro, Daniel L. Cork, and Janet L. Norwood, eds., *The 2000 Census: Counting Under Adversity* (Washington: National Academies Press, 2004), p. 100.

[11] U.S. Bureau of the Census, *American Community Survey, Design and Methodology* (Washington: GPO, 2009), p. 2-1.

[12] An act to Amend Title 13, *United States Code*, to Provide for a Mid-Decade Census of Population, and for Other Purposes, P.L. 94-521; 90 Stat. 2459; 13 U.S.C. §141(d).

[13] U.S. Bureau of the Census, *American Community Survey, Design and Methodology* (Washington: GPO, 2009), p. 2-1.

[14] Ibid. The Bureau attempts to reach all nonrespondents by telephone, but conducts personal visits with a subsample of the original ACS sample who have not answered the survey.

[15] Ibid., p. 2-2.

[16] As the Bureau has explained, a "controlled estimate of a characteristic is forced to conform to the official estimate from the ... Bureau's Population Estimates Program (PEP)," which is separate from the ACS. "The total housing unit and the total population estimates are controlled at the county (or groups of counties) level. In addition, estimates of some combinations of age, sex, race, and Hispanic origin are controlled .... This process is implemented to improve person and housing unit coverage and to reduce the variability of the ACS estimates." U.S. Bureau of the Census, "ACS Controlled Estimates," https://ask.census.gov/cgi-bin/askcensus.cfg/php/enduser/std_adp.php?p_faqid=8014& p_sid=jzrwgzck&p_created=1233862845&p_sp=cF9zcmNoPSZwX3NvcnRfYnk9JnBfZ3J pZHNvcnQ9JnBfcm93X2NudD0mcF9wcm9kcz0mcF9jYXRzPSZwX3B2PSZwX2N2PSZ wX3BhZ2U9MQ!!&p_search_text=intercensal%20population%20estimates.

The PEP produces the official annual estimates of the resident population for the total United States, states and the District of Columbia, counties, incorporated places and minor civil divisions, and metropolitan areas. Estimates by basic population characteristics—age, sex, race, and Hispanic or non-Hispanic ethnicity—are available yearly for the nation, states and the District of Columbia, and counties. The estimates are benchmarked to the most recent decennial census and rely mainly on administrative records, such as birth and death records from the National Center for Health Statistics, Medicare enrollment data, and Internal Revenue Service tax return data on addresses, to update the census numbers. U.S. Bureau of the Census, "Population Estimates," *http://www.census.gov/ popes t/estimates.html.*

[17] U.S. Bureau of the Census, *American Community Survey, Design and Methodology* (Washington: GPO, 2009), p. 2-1.

[18] Ibid., p. 2-2.

[19] Ibid.

[20] Ibid.

[21] Ibid.

[22] The Bureau classifies living quarters as either housing units, by far the dominant type, or group quarters (GQs). A group-quarters facility is "owned or managed by an entity or organization providing housing and/or services for the residents. These services may include custodial or medical care, as well as other types of assistance, and residency is commonly restricted to those receiving these services." Ibid., p. 8-1.

The ACS does not include certain types of group quarters: "domestic violence shelters, soup kitchens, regularly scheduled mobile food vans, targeted nonsheltered outdoor locations, crews of commercial maritime vessels, natural disaster shelters, and dangerous encampments." They are excluded due to "[c]oncerns about privacy and the operational feasibility of repeated interviewing for a continuing survey, rather than once a decade for a census ...." "ACS estimates of the total population," however, "are controlled to be consistent with the Population Estimates Program estimate of the GQ resident population from all GQs, even those excluded from the ACS." Ibid., p. 4-9.

[23] ACS group-quarters data collection differs from the mail-out, mail-back operation used for most housing units. Group-quarters data are gathered by field representatives, who "may obtain the facility information by conducting either a personal visit or a telephone interview with the GQ contact." This interview determines whether the field representative "samples all, some, or none of the residents at a sampled facility for person-level interviews." Ibid., p. 8-1.

[24] Ibid., p. 2-2.

[25] Ibid., p. 2-3.

[26] Ibid.

[27] See Charles H. Alexander, "Still Rolling: Leslie Kish's 'Rolling Samples' and the American Community Survey," *Survey Methodology*, vol. 28, no. 1 (June 2002), p. 36.

[28] U.S. Bureau of the Census, *American Community Survey, Design and Methodology* (Washington: GPO, 2009), p. 2- 3.

[29] The 11 reports are available on the Bureau's website. See U.S. Bureau of the Census, *Meeting 21st Century Demographic Data Needs—Implementing the American Community Survey*, http://www.census.gov/acs/www/library/ by_series/implementing_the_acs/. The topics include assessments of ACS operational feasibility and survey quality; and comparisons of ACS with 2000 census demographic, social, economic, and housing characteristics.

[30] U.S. Bureau of the Census, *American Community Survey, Design and Methodology* (Washington: GPO, 2009), p. 2- 3.

[31] Ibid.

[32] "Sampling error," as the Bureau has explained, "is the difference between an estimate based on a sample and the corresponding value that would be obtained if the estimate were based on the entire population. ... Measures of the magnitude of sampling error, such as the variance and the standard error (the square root of the variance), reflect the variation in the estimates over all possible samples that could have been selected from the population using the same sampling methodology." Ibid., p. 12-1.

[33] Ibid., p. 2-4.

[34] Ibid., p. 2-3.

[35] U.S. Congress, Conference Committee, *Making Further Continuing Appropriations for the Fiscal Year 2003, and for Other Purposes* (Consolidated Appropriations Resolution, 2003), conference report to accompany H.J.Res. 2, 108th Cong., 1st sess., H.Rept. 108-10 (Washington: GPO, 2003), p. 689.

[36] Also in 2005, the Puerto Rico Community Survey, the ACS-equivalent there, expanded to all 78 Puerto Rican municipios. The present report discusses only the ACS in the 50 states and the District of Columbia.

[37] U.S. Bureau of the Census, *American Community Survey, Design and Methodology* (Washington: GPO, 2009), pp. 2- 1 and 2-4.

[38] U.S. Bureau of the Census, "American FactFinder," http://factfinder.census.gov/home/saff/main.html?_lang=en. Besides providing ready access to numerous ACS data tables, the site has a Download Center for "experienced users who need ... larger amounts of data than are available through other parts of American FactFinder." U.S. Bureau of the Census, "American FactFinder, Download Center," http://factfinder.census.gov/servlet/Download DatasetServlet?_lang=en.

[39] U.S. Bureau of the Census, *American Community Survey, Design and Methodology* (Washington: GPO, 2009), p. 2- 4.

[40] Ibid.

[41] U.S. Bureau of the Census, "American Community Survey, 2008 Release Schedule," http://www.census.gov/acs/ www/data _documentation/2008_release_schedule/.

[42] U.S. Bureau of the Census, "Quick Guide to the American Community Survey (ACS) Products in American FactFinder," p. 3, http://factfinder.census.gov/home/saff/aff_acs2009_ quickguide.pdf. See this guide for detailed information about the types of data available from the ACS, how the data are presented, and how best to access and use them. Another Bureau publication, specifically for congressional readers, is *A Compass for Understanding and Using American Community Survey Data: What Congress Needs to Know* (Washington: GPO, 2008).

[43] U.S. Bureau of the Census, "Quick Guide to the American Community Survey (ACS) Products in American FactFinder," p. 1, http://factfinder.census.gov/home/saff/aff_acs2009_ quickguide.pdf.

[44] Ibid., p. 3.

[45] Ibid., p. 1.

[46] Ibid., pp.

[47] Ibid., p. 13.
Nonsampling error, the other component of total survey error, includes "errors that occur during data collection (for example, nonresponse error, response error, and interviewer error) or data capture ...." U.S. Bureau of the Census, *American Community Survey, Design and Methodology* (Washington: GPO, 2009), glossary, p. 11.

[48] U.S. Bureau of the Census, "Quick Guide to the American Community Survey (ACS) Products in American FactFinder," p. 13, http://factfinder.census.gov/home/saff/aff_acs2009_ quickguide.pdf.

[49] U.S. Bureau of the Census, "Policy on New Content for the American Community Survey," p. 1, http://www.census.gov/acs/www/Downloads/operations

[50] 5 C.F.R. part 1320.

[51] U.S. Bureau of the Census, "Policy on New Content for the American Community Survey," p. 2, http://www.census.gov/acs/www/Downloads/operations

[52] Ibid., p. 3.

[53] Ibid., p. 2.

[54] See U.S. Bureau of the Census, "Questions on the Form and Why We Ask," *http://www. census.gov/acs/www/* about_the_survey/questions_and_why_we_ask/.

[55] See U.S. Bureau of the Census, "About the American Community Survey," *http://www. census.gov/acs/www/* about_the_survey/american_community_survey/.

[56] U.S. Department of Commerce, Bureau of the Census, "American Community Survey 5-Year Data Products," 74 *Federal Register* 9785, March 6, 2009. See also U.S. Department of Commerce, Bureau of the Census, "American Community Survey 5-Year Data Product Plans; Final Notice," 75 *Federal Register* 57254, September 20, 2010.

[57] U.S. Department of Commerce, Bureau of the Census, "American Community Survey 5-Year Data Products," 74 *Federal Register* 9786, March 6, 2009.

[58] See Andrew Reamer, Fellow, Brookings Institution Metropolitan Policy Program, "Re: Request for Comments on the American Community Survey 5-Year Data Products," April 20, 2009, in U.S. Bureau of the Census, "Comments Sent to the Census Bureau about *Federal Register* Notice," http://www.census.gov/acs/www/about_the_survey/ operations _ and_administration/.

[59] The Bureau defines "disclosure avoidance" as "statistical methods used in the tabulation of data prior to releasing data products to ensure the confidentiality of responses." U.S. Bureau of the Census, *American Community Survey, Design and Methodology* (Washington: GPO, 2009), glossary, p. 6.

[60] A "census tract" refers to "a small, relatively permanent statistical subdivision of a county delineated by a local committee of census data users for the purpose of presenting data. Census tract boundaries normally follow visible features, but may follow governmental unit boundaries and other nonvisible features; they always nest within counties. Designed to be relatively homogeneous units with respect to population characteristics, economic status, and living conditions at the time of establishment, census tracts average about 4,000 inhabitants." Ibid., glossary, p. 4.

[61] "A block group," in Bureau terminology, "is a cluster of blocks having the same first digit of their four-digit identifying number within a census tract." A block "is the smallest geographic entity for which the Census Bureau tabulates decennial census data. Many blocks correspond to individual city blocks bounded by streets, but blocks— especially in rural areas—may include many square miles and may have some boundaries that are not streets." Ibid., glossary, p. 3.

[62] Constance F. Citro and Graham Kalton, eds., *Using the American Community Survey: Benefits and Challenges* (Washington: National Academies Press, 2007), pp. 2, 4, and 5.

[63] U.S. Government Accountability Office, *American Community Survey: Key Unresolved Issues*, GAO-05-82, October 2004, p. 21.

[64] U.S. Bureau of the Census, *Meeting 21st Century Demographic Data Needs—Implementing the American Community Survey*; Report 3, *Testing the Use of Voluntary Methods*, December 2003, Appendix 4, http://www.census.gov/acs/www/library/by_ series/implementing_the_acs/.

[65] U.S. Bureau of the Census, "Housing Unit Estimates," http://factfinder.census. gov/servlet/DTTable?_bm=y&-geo_id=01000US&-ds_name=PEP2009_EST&-_lang= en&-mt_name=PEP_2009_EST_G2009_T002&-format=&- CONTEXT=dt.

[66] U.S. Office of Management and Budget, *Budget of the U.S. Government, Appendix, Fiscal Year 2011* (Washington: GPO, 2010), p. 210.

[67] Making further continuing appropriations for FY20 11, and for other purposes; H.J.Res. 101; P.L. 111-290. The act amends the Continuing Appropriations Act, 2011 (P.L. 111-242; 124 Stat. 2607) to extend specified FY20 11 continuing appropriations from December 3, 2010, through December 18, 2010.

[68] CRS Report R41 161, *Commerce, Justice, Science, and Related Agencies: FY2011 Appropriations*, coordinated by Nathan James, Oscar R. Gonzales, and Jennifer D. Williams, pp. 1, 11, and 12.

[69] Constance F. Citro, Daniel L. Cork, and Janet L. Norwood, eds., *The 2000 Census: Counting Under Adversity* (Washington: National Academies Press, 2004).

[70] As previously noted, the "mail return rate" is the percentage of questionnaires completed and returned from "occupied housing units with deliverable addresses." U.S. Government Accountability Office, *2010 Census: Census Bureau Needs Procedures for Estimating the Response Rate and Selecting for Testing Methods to Increase Response Rate*, GAO-08-1012, September 2008, footnote 6, p. 6.

[71] Constance F. Citro, Daniel L. Cork, and Janet L. Norwood, eds., *The 2000 Census: Counting Under Adversity* (Washington: National Academies Press, 2004), p. 100.

[72] U.S. Bureau of the Census, "2008 American Community Survey Sampling Memorandum Series ACS08-S-28," September 14, 2009.

[73] GAO has pointed out that the mail response rates in the ACS analysis "are comparable to the Bureau's definition of mail return rates for the decennial census in that vacant and nonexistent housing units are excluded from the denominator in the calculation." U.S. Government Accountability Office, *2010 Census: Census Bureau Needs Procedures for Estimating the Response Rate and Selecting for Testing Methods to Increase Response Rate*, GAO-08- 1012, September 2008, p. 14.

[74] U.S. Bureau of the Census, "2008 American Community Survey Sampling Memorandum Series ACS08-S-28," September 14, 2009, p. 6.

[75] Ibid.

The Bureau eventually closes much of the gap between questionnaires sent out and those mailed back. For example, the estimated total ACS response rate in 2008, after nonresponse follow-up, was 98%. Ibid., p. 5. In the 2000 census, to cite another example, the Bureau received 98.5% of the long forms it expected to receive from households and retained 93.2% of forms received. Constance F. Citro, Daniel L. Cork, and Janet L. Norwood, eds., *The 2000 Census: Counting Under Adversity* (Washington: National Academies Press, 2004), pp. 29 1-292.

[76] See, as examples, August Gribbin, "Census Bureau offers to find long-form alternative by '03," *Washington Times*, April 6, 2000, p. A8; D'Vera Cohn, "Census Complaints Hit Home," *Washington Post*, May 4, 2000, p. A9; August Gribbin, "Criticism of census form sparks bureau to re-look," *Washington Times*, April 11, 2000, p. A4; Steven A. Holmes, "Low Response to Long Form Causes Worry About Census," *New York Times*, April 7, 2000, p. A18.

[77] According to a nationwide survey of 1,933 people during the week of April 2, 2000, by InterSurvey of Menlo Park, CA, 47% of respondents who received the long form viewed the questions as "too intrusive; census should not ask." The highest proportions of respondents, 53% and 32%, respectively, viewed the income and disability questions as "too personal." The margin of error was plus or minus three percentage points. The poll results were cited in D'Vera Cohn, "Census Complaints Hit Home," *Washington Post*, May 4, 2000, p. A9.

[78] PBS broadcast the "Nosy Census" segment on March 30, 2000.

[79] CBS broadcast the Andy Rooney commentary on March 26, 2000.

[80] Opening remarks of Subcommittee Chairman Dan Miller in U.S. Congress, House Committee on Government Reform, Subcommittee on the Census, *Oversight of the 2000 Census: Mail-Back Response Rates and Status of Key Operations*, hearing, 106th Cong., 2nd sess., April 5, 2000, no. 106-186 (Washington: GPO, 2001), pp. 2-3.

[81] As the Bureau Director at the time observed during an ACS hearing, "Long form questions" are neither "less, nor more, intrusive because they are asked in the ACS rather than the decennial environment, but the environments are wholly different. It matters whether 20 million housing units are asked long form questions in one intense timeframe or whether those questions are asked in a series of monthly surveys." Testimony of then-Census Bureau Director Kenneth Prewitt in U.S. Congress, House Committee on Government Reform, Subcommittee on the Census, *The American Community Survey—A Replacement for the Census Long Form?*, hearing, 106th Cong., 2nd sess., July 20, 2000, no. 106-246 (Washington: GPO, 2001), p. 31.

[82] For examples of recent media reports, see Jon Rutter, "Census Survey a Little Too Intrusive for Some," Lancaster, PA, Online.com News, November 15, 2010; Mark Davis, "Census Wants to Know More, Way Too Much More, Critics of Survey Say," *Atlanta Journal-Constitution*, September 5, 2010, p. 1B; John Derbyshire, "Count Me Out," *National Review*, vol. 57, no. 2 (February 2005), p. 56; Kathleen Hennessey, "GOP Takes on Census Critics," *Los Angeles Times*, April 14, 2010, p. A11; "Questions on Census Survey 'Exceptionally Intrusive'," ABC 27 News, WHTM, Harrisburg, York, Lancaster, and Lebanon, PA, November 5, 2010; and William M. Dowd, "What? Why Me?" *Times Union*, June 14, 2009, p. B1.

[83] Ibid.

[84] U.S. Bureau of the Census, "Policy on New Content for the American Community Survey," p. 2, http://www.census.gov/acs/www/Downloads/operations

[85] Commerce is the Bureau's parent department.

[86] U.S. Bureau of the Census, *Meeting 21st Century Demographic Data Needs—Implementing the American Community Survey*; Report 3, *Testing the Use of Voluntary Methods*, December 2003, p. 1, http://www.census.gov/acs/ www/library/by_series/implementing_the_acs/.

[87] Ibid., pp. v and 1.

[88] Consolidated Appropriations Resolution, 2003, P.L. 108-7; 117 Stat. 11.

[89] U.S. Congress, Conference Committee, *Making Further Continuing Appropriations for the Fiscal Year 2003, and for Other Purposes* (Consolidated Appropriations Resolution, 2003), conference report to accompany H.J.Res. 2, 108th Cong., 1st sess., H.Rept. 108-10 (Washington: GPO, 2003), p. 689.

[90] U.S. Bureau of the Census, Meeting 21st Century Demographic Data Needs—Implementing the American Community Survey; Report 3, Testing the Use of Voluntary Methods, December 2003, and Report 11, Testing Voluntary Methods—Additional Results, December 2004, http://www.census.gov/acs/www/library/by_series/ implementing_ the_acs/.

[91] U.S. Bureau of the Census, *Meeting 21st Century Demographic Data Needs—Implementing the American Community Survey*; Report 3, *Testing the Use of Voluntary Methods*, December 2003, p. 1, http://www.census.gov/acs/ www/library/by_series/implementing_the_acs/.

[92] U.S. Bureau of the Census, Meeting 21st Century Demographic Data Needs—Implementing the American Community Survey; Report 11, Testing Voluntary Methods – Additional Results, December 2004, p. v, http://www.census.gov/acs/www/library/by_series/ implementing_the_acs/.

[93] U.S. Bureau of the Census, *Meeting 21st Century Demographic Data Needs—Implementing the American Community Survey*; Report 3, *Testing the Use of Voluntary Methods*, December 2003, p. 2, http://www.census.gov/acs/ www/library/by_series/implementing_the_acs/.

[94] The other mandatory treatment tested mail-out material that the Bureau had revised to clarify the nature and purpose of the survey. Ibid., p. 2.

[95] The other voluntary treatment "explained more directly that the survey was voluntary." Ibid., pp. 2-3.

[96] Ibid., p. 2.

[97] Ibid., p. 3.

[98] The Bureau defines "other relatives" as household members "related to the householder by birth, marriage, or adoption, but not specifically included in any other relationship category. Can include grandchildren, parents, in-laws, cousins, etc." See *http://factfinder. census. gov/home/en/epss/glossary_o.html*.

[99] U.S. Bureau of the Census, *Meeting 21st Century Demographic Data Needs—Implementing the American Community Survey*; Report 3, *Testing the Use of Voluntary Methods*, December 2003, p. 3, http://www.census.gov/acs/ www/library/by_series/implementing_the_acs/.

[100] Ibid., pp. 1 and 3.

[101] Ibid., p. 3.

[102] This rate refers to the percentage of questionnaires returned from all occupied housing units included in the mail-out phase. Ibid., p. 6.

[103] Ibid.

[104] Ibid., p. 7.

[105] Ibid., p. 8.

[106] Ibid.

[107] Ibid.

[108] Ibid., p. v.

[109] Ibid., p. 9.

[110] Ibid., p. 16.

[111] Ibid., pp. 16-17.

[112] Ibid., p. 17.

[113] See CRS Report R40551, *The 2010 Decennial Census: Background and Issues*, by Jennifer D. Williams.

[114] U.S. Bureau of the Census, "American Community Survey, Subjects Included in the American Community Survey," http://www.census.gov/acs/www/guidance

In: The American Community Survey ...   ISBN: 978-1-61324-362-6
Editors: B. M. Russo and A. D. Haffner   ©2011 Nova Science Publishers, Inc.

Chapter 2

POVERTY: 2008 AND 2009

United States Census Bureau

INTRODUCTION

This report is one of a series produced to highlight results from the 2009 American Community Survey (ACS). It presents poverty estimates based on data from the 2008 and the 2009 ACS. The report compares national and state level poverty rates and summarizes the distribution of income-to-poverty ratios for each state and the District of Columbia.

The ACS also provides poverty estimates for counties, places, and other localities.

HIGHLIGHTS

- In the 2009 ACS, 14.3 percent of the U.S. population had income below their respective poverty thresholds. The number of people in poverty increased to 42.9 million.
- Thirty-one states saw increases in both the number and percentage of people in poverty between the 2008 and the 2009 ACS.
- No state had a statistically significant decline in either the number in poverty or the poverty rate.

- In the 2009 ACS, 18.9 percent of people in the United States had income less than 125 percent of their poverty threshold, compared to 17.6 percent in the 2008 ACS.
- The percent of people with income less than 50 percent of their poverty threshold increased from 5.6 percent in the 2008 ACS to 6.3 in the 2009 ACS.

How Poverty Is Measured

Poverty status is determined by comparing annual income to a set of dollar values called thresholds that vary by family size, number of children, and age of householder. If a family's before tax money income is less than the dollar value of their threshold, then that family and every individual in it are considered to be in poverty. For people not living in families, poverty status is determined by comparing the individual's income to his or her threshold.

The poverty thresholds are updated annually to allow for changes in the cost of living using the Consumer Price Index (CPI-U). They do not vary geographically.

The ACS is a continuous survey, and people respond throughout the year. Since income is reported for the previous 12 months, the appropriate poverty threshold for each family is determined by multiplying the base-year poverty threshold (1982) by the average of monthly CPI values for the 12 months preceding the survey month.

For more information, see "How Poverty Is Calculated in the ACS" at <www.census.gov/hhes/www/poverty nitions.html>.

The estimates contained in this report are based on the 2008 and 2009 ACS samples. The ACS is conducted every month with income data collected for the 12 months preceding the interview. Because the survey is continuous, adjacent ACS years have income reference months in common. For these reasons, comparing the 2008 ACS with the 2009 ACS is not an exact comparison of the economic conditions in 2008 with those in 2009. Comparisons should be interpreted with care.[1] For more information on the ACS sample design and other topics visit <www.census.gov/acs /www>.

Figure 1.
Percentage of People in Poverty in the Past 12 Months by State and Puerto Rico: 2009

Percentage of people living below poverty level
- 16.0 or more
- 13.0 to 15.9
- 11.0 to 12.9
- Less than 11.0

United States = 14.3 percent

Sources: U.S. Census Bureau, American Community Survey, 2009, Puerto Rico Community Survey, 2009.

Figure 1. Percentage of People in Poverty in the Past 12 Months by State and Puerto Rico: 2009.

POVERTY

The 2009 ACS data indicate an estimated 14.3 percent of the U.S. population had income below their poverty threshold in the past 12 months. This is 1.0 percentage point higher than the 13.3 percent poverty rate estimated for the 2008 ACS. The estimated number of people in poverty increased by 3.5 million to 42.9 million in the 2009 ACS.[2]

The map displays the variation in poverty rates by state for the 2009 ACS. The table presented at the end of this report shows the number and the percentage of people in poverty by state in the 2008 and 2009 ACS.

Poverty rates from the 2009 ACS for the 50 states and the District of Columbia ranged from a low of 8.5 percent in New Hampshire to a high of 21.9 percent in Mississippi.[3]

Only five states had estimated poverty rates lower than 10 percent—Alaska, Connecticut, Maryland, New Hampshire, and New Jersey. On the

other side of the distribution five states had estimated poverty rates at or above
1 7 percent in 2009— Alabama, Arkansas, Kentucky, Mississippi, and West
Virginia.

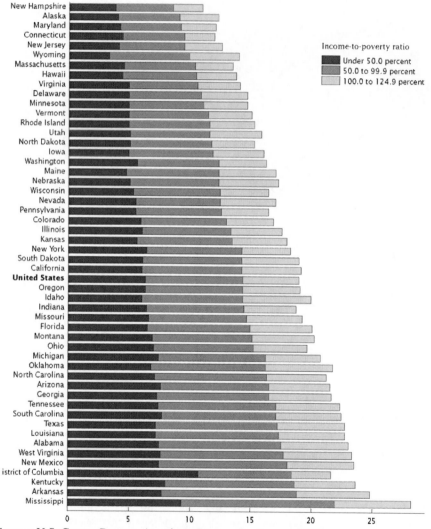

Source: U.S. Census Bureau, American Community Survey, 2009.

Figure 2. Percentage of People by Income-to-Poverty Ratio in the Past 12 Months by
State: 2009.

Thirty-one states experienced increases in both the number and percentage of people in poverty between the 2008 ACS and the 2009 ACS. No state had a statistically significant decline in either the number in poverty or the poverty rate.

Seventeen states and the District of Columbia saw no statistically significant differences in either the number of people in poverty or the poverty rate from the 2008 ACS to the 2009 ACS—Alaska, Connecticut, Delaware, Iowa, Louisiana, Maine, Massachusetts, Mississippi, Montana, New Mexico, North Dakota, Oklahoma, Rhode Island, Vermont, Virginia, West Virginia, and Wyoming.

DEPTH OF POVERTY

The poverty rate is an estimate of the proportion of people with family or personal income below the appropriate poverty threshold. Another measure, the income-topoverty ratio, gauges how close a family's income is to their poverty threshold. It measures the depth of poverty for those with income below their threshold and the proximity to poverty for those with income above their threshold.

WHAT IS THE AMERICAN COMMUNITY SURVEY?

The American Community Survey (ACS) is a nationwide survey designed to provide communities with reliable and timely demographic, social, economic, and housing data for the nation, states, congressional districts, counties, places, and other localities every year. It has an annual sample size of about 3 million addresses across the United States and Puerto Rico and includes both housing units and group quarters (e.g., nursing facilities and prisons). The ACS is conducted in every county throughout the nation, and every municipio in Puerto Rico, where it is called the Puerto Rico Community Survey. Beginning in 2006, ACS data for 2005 were released for geographic areas with populations of 65,000 and greater. For information on the ACS sample design and other topics, visit <*www.census. gov* /acs/www>.

In this report the income-to-poverty ratio is reported as a percentage. To illustrate, a family or individual with income equal to twice their poverty threshold has an incometo-poverty ratio of 200 percent. A family or individual with income equal to one-half of their poverty threshold has an income-to-poverty ratio of 50 percent.

The 2009 ACS data indicate that 18.9 percent of people in the United States had an annual income-to-poverty ratio less than 1 25 percent. This compares to 1 7.6 percent of people in the 2008 ACS. Similarly, in the 2009 ACS 6.3 percent of people had income-to-poverty ratios less than 50 percent, compared to 5.6 percent in the 2008 ACS.

At the state level, the share of the population with income-to-poverty ratios less than 125 percent ranged from a low of 10.9 percent in New Hampshire to a high of 28.2 percent in Mississippi in the 2009 ACS. The proportion of people with income-to-poverty ratios less than 50 percent ranged from a low of 3.3 percent in Wyoming to a high of 1 0.7 percent in the District of Columbia.[4]

SOURCE AND ACCURACY

Data presented in this report are based on people and households that responded to the ACS in 2008 and 2009. The resulting estimates are representative of the entire population. All comparisons presented in this report have taken sampling error into account and are significant at the 90 percent confidence level unless otherwise noted. Due to rounding, some details may not sum to totals. For information on sampling and estimation methods, confidentiality protection, and sampling and nonsampling errors, please see the "2009 ACS Accuracy of the Data" document located at <www. census. gov/acs/www/Downloads/data_documentation/Accuracy/ACS_Accuracy_of_ Data_2009.pdf>.

Number and Percentage of People in Poverty in the Past 12 Months by State and Puerto Rico: 2008 and 2009

Area	Below poverty in 2008				Below poverty in 2009				Change in poverty (2009 less 2008)			
	Number[1]	Margin of error[2] (±)	Percentage[1]	Margin of error[2] (±)	Number[1]	Margin of error[2] (±)	Percentage[1]	Margin of error[2] (±)	Number[1]	Margin of error[2] (±)	Percentage[1]	Margin of error[2] (±)
United States	39,328,443	248,194	13.3	0.1	42,868,163	236,589	14.3	0.1	*3,539,720	342,892	*1.0	0.1
Alabama.	711,205	21,859	15.7	0.5	804,683	22,895	17.5	0.5	*93,478	31,655	*1.8	0.7
Alaska	55,129	5,348	8.2	0.8	61,653	5,417	9.0	0.8	6,524	7,612	0.8	1.1
Arizona	950,189	29,215	14.9	0.5	1,069,897	28,715	16.5	0.4	*119,708	40,964	*1.6	0.6
Arkansas	481,121	19,455	17.3	0.7	527,378	17,322	18.8	0.6	*46,257	26,049	*1.5	0.9
California	4,813,999	72,549	13.4	0.2	5,128,708	60,936	14.2	0.2	*314,709	94,745	*0.8	0.3
Colorado	552,563	22,029	11.4	0.5	634,387	21,625	12.9	0.4	*81,824	30,869	*1.5	0.6
Connecticut	316,619	14,899	9.3	0.4	320,554	16,151	9.4	0.5	3,935	21,973	0.1	0.6
Delaware	88,253	6,813	10.4	0.8	93,251	9,829	10.8	1.1	4,998	11,960	0.4	1.4
District of Columbia	98,670	7,369	17.6	1.3	104,901	9,224	18.4	1.6	6,231	11,807	0.8	2.1
Florida	2,384,852	39,547	13.3	0.2	2,707,925	39,754	14.9	0.2	*323,073	56,075	*1.6	0.3
Georgia	1,376,646	31,633	14.6	0.3	1,574,649	36,922	16.5	0.4	*198,003	48,620	*1.9	0.5
Hawaii	115,828	9,217	9.2	0.7	131,007	9,277	10.4	0.7	*15,179	13,077	*1.2	1.0
Idaho	191,704	13,448	12.9	0.9	216,115	12,490	14.3	0.8	*24,411	18,353	*1.4	1.2

(Continued)

Area	Below poverty in 2008				Below poverty in 2009				Change in poverty (2009 less 2008)			
	Number[1]	Margin of error[2] (±)	Percentage[1]	Margin of error[2] (±)	Number[1]	Margin of error[2] (±)	Percentage[1]	Margin of error[2] (±)	Number[1]	Margin of error[2] (±)	Percentage[1]	Margin of error[2] (±)
Illinois	1,546,407	28,381	12.3	0.2	1,677,093	37,391	13.3	0.3	*130,686	46,942	*1.0	0.4
Indiana	803,514	20,242	13.0	0.3	896,972	23,765	14.4	0.4	*93,458	31,217	*1.4	0.5
Iowa	335,311	13,188	11.6	0.5	342,934	13,024	11.8	0.4	7,623	18,535	0.2	0.6
Kansas	308,031	13,298	11.3	0.5	365,033	15,162	13.4	0.6	*57,002	20,167	*2.1	0.7
Kentucky	718,092	21,593	17.3	0.5	777,295	21,970	18.6	0.5	*59,203	30,805	*1.3	0.7
Louisiana	748,410	24,921	17.4	0.6	755,460	23,513	17.3	0.5	7,050	34,263	-0.1	0.8
Maine	159,028	8,250	12.4	0.6	157,685	8,398	12.3	0.7	-1,343	11,773	-0.1	0.9
Maryland	442,095	16,444	8.0	0.3	505,286	18,824	9.1	0.3	*63,191	24,995	*1.1	0.5
Massachusetts	632,381	20,615	10.1	0.3	654,983	20,720	10.3	0.3	22,602	29,228	0.2	0.5
Michigan	1,417,701	24,516	14.5	0.3	1,576,704	30,948	16.2	0.3	*159,003	39,481	*1.7	0.4
Minnesota	498,502	15,279	9.8	0.3	563,006	17,470	11.0	0.3	*64,504	23,209	*1.2	0.5
Mississippi	606,203	24,657	21.4	0.9	624,360	17,712	21.9	0.6	18,157	30,359	0.5	1.1
Missouri	768,925	20,620	13.4	0.4	849,009	24,710	14.6	0.4	*80,084	32,184	*1.2	0.6
Montana	136,364	9,051	14.5	1.0	143,028	9,517	15.1	1.0	6,664	13,134	0.6	1.4
Nebraska	185,957	8,918	10.8	0.5	214,765	9,539	12.3	0.6	*28,808	13,059	*1.5	0.8
Nevada	296,858	16,528	11.6	0.6	321,940	18,092	12.4	0.7	*25,082	24,505	0.8	0.9

(Continued)

Area	Below poverty in 2008				Below poverty in 2009				Change in poverty (2009 less 2008)			
	Number[1]	Margin of error[2] (±)	Percentage[1]	Margin of error[2] (±)	Number[1]	Margin of error[2] (±)	Percentage[1]	Margin of error[2] (±)	Number[1]	Margin of error[2] (±)	Percentage[1]	Margin of error[2] (±)
New Hampshire	96,041	8,115	7.5	0.6	109,213	8,221	8.5	0.6	*13,172	11,551	*1.0	0.9
New Jersey	752,514	22,729	8.8	0.3	799,099	26,131	9.4	0.3	*46,585	34,633	*0.6	0.4
New Mexico	332,449	15,052	17.1	0.8	353,594	19,626	18.0	1.0	21,145	24,733	0.9	1.3
New York	2,616,642	35,663	13.8	0.2	2,691,757	43,874	14.2	0.2	*75,115	56,540	*0.4	0.3
North Carolina	1,309,342	35,177	14.6	0.4	1,478,214	29,213	16.3	0.3	*168,872	45,725	*1.7	0.5
North Dakota	74,258	5,334	12.1	0.9	72,342	4,796	11.7	0.8	−1,916	7,173	−0.4	1.2
Ohio	1,495,292	32,053	13.4	0.3	1,709,971	33,382	15.2	0.3	*214,679	46,279	*1.8	0.4
Oklahoma	554,406	18,504	15.7	0.5	577,956	18,136	16.2	0.5	23,550	25,910	0.5	0.7
Oregon	499,670	16,704	13.4	0.4	534,594	17,909	14.3	0.5	*34,924	24,490	*0.9	0.7
Pennsylvania	1,472,577	26,492	12.3	0.2	1,516,705	25,949	12.5	0.2	*44,128	37,084	0.2	0.3
Rhode Island	121,924	8,493	12.0	0.8	116,378	8,258	11.5	0.8	−5,546	11,846	−0.5	1.2
South Carolina	681,131	23,104	15.7	0.5	753,739	21,608	17.1	0.5	*72,608	31,634	*1.4	0.7
South Dakota	93,920	6,797	12.1	0.9	111,305	8,178	14.2	1.0	*17,385	10,634	*2.1	1.4
Tennessee	950,605	27,031	15.7	0.4	1,052,144	23,735	17.1	0.4	*101,539	35,973	*1.4	0.6
Texas	3,791,569	53,287	16.0	0.2	4,150,242	58,989	17.2	0.2	*358,673	79,494	*1.2	0.3
Utah	257,081	13,922	9.5	0.5	316,217	14,867	11.5	0.5	*59,136	20,368	*2.0	0.8

(Continued)

Area	Below poverty in 2008				Below poverty in 2009				Change in poverty (2009 less 2008)			
	Number[1]	Margin of error[2] (±)	Percentage[1]	Margin of error[2] (±)	Number[1]	Margin of error[2] (±)	Perentage[1]	Margin of error[2] (±)	Number[1]	Margin of error[2] (±)	Percentage[1]	Margin of error[2] (±)
Vermont	63,918	4,921	10.7	0.8	68,246	5,148	11.4	0.9	4,328	7,122	0.7	1.2
Virginia	771,424	24,154	10.3	0.3	802,578	26,888	10.5	0.4	31,154	36,144	0.2	0.5
Washington	731,115	22,092	11.4	0.3	804,237	23,667	12.3	0.4	*73,122	32,376	*0.9	0.5
West Virginia	301,530	13,055	17.1	0.7	313,419	11,866	17.7	0.7	11,889	17,642	0.6	1.0
Wisconsin	570,583	16,590	10.4	0.3	683,408	19,384	12.4	0.4	*112,825	25,514	*2.0	0.5
Wyoming	49,895	4,656	9.6	0.9	52,144	5,517	9.8	1.0	2,249	7,219	0.2	1.4
Puerto Rico	1,754,250	28,052	44.9	0.7	1,764,635	24,829	45.0	0.6	10,385	37,462	0.1	1.0

* Statistically different at the 90 percent confidence level.

[1] Poverty status is determined for individuals in housing units and noninstitutional group quarters. The poverty universe excludes children under age 15 who are not related to the householder, people living in institutional group quarters, and people living in college dormitories or military barracks.

[2] Data are based on a sample and are subject to sampling variability. A margin of error is a measure of an estimate's variability. The larger the margin of error in relation to the size of the estimate, the less reliable the estimate. This number when added to or subtracted from the estimate forms the 90 percent confidence interval.

Sources: U.S. Census Bureau, American Community Surveys, 2008 and 2009, Puerto Rico Community Surveys, 2008 and 2009.

NOTES

The Census Bureau also publishes poverty estimates based on the Current Population Survey's Annual Social and Economic Supplement (CPS ASEC). Following the standard specified by the Office of Management and Budget (OMB) in Statistical Policy Directive 14, data from the CPS ASEC are used to estimate the official national poverty rate, which can be found in the report *Income, Poverty, and Health Insurance Coverage in the United States: 2009*, available at <www .census.gov/prod/2010pubs/p60 -238.pdf>.

For information on poverty estimates from the ACS and how they differ from those based on the CPS ASEC, see "Differences Between the Income and Poverty Estimates From the American Community Survey and the Annual Social and Economic Supplement to the Current Population Survey" at <www.census.gov/hhes /www/poverty/about/datasou rces /index.html>.

End Notes

[1] For a discussion of this and related issues see Hogan, Howard, "Measuring Population Change Using the American Community Survey," *Applied Demography in the 21st Century*, eds., Steven H. Murdock and David A. Swanson, Springer Netherlands, 2008.
[2] The poverty universe is a subset of the total population covered by the ACS. Specifically, the universe excludes children younger than age 15 who are not related to the householder, people living in institutional group quarters, and those living in college dormitories or military barracks.
[3] New Hampshire's 2009 ACS poverty rate was not statistically different from the poverty rates for Alaska (9.0 percent) and Maryland (9.1 percent).
[4] Wyoming's 2009 ACS estimate for the proportion of people with income-to-poverty ratios less than 50 percent was not statistically different from the estimates for Alaska or New Hampshire.

In: The American Community Survey ...   ISBN: 978-1-61324-362-6
Editors: B. M. Russo and A. D. Haffner   ©2011 Nova Science Publishers, Inc.

Chapter 3

HOUSEHOLD INCOME FOR STATES: 2008 AND 2009

United States Census Bureau

INTRODUCTION

This report presents data on median household income at the national and state levels based on the 2008 and 2009 American Community Surveys (ACS).[1] The data are presented first in tabular form and then displayed on maps. The ACS provides detailed estimates of demographic, social, economic, and housing characteristics for states, congressional districts, counties, places, and other localities every year. A description of the ACS is provided in the text box "What Is the American Community Survey?"

In the 2009 ACS, information on income was collected between January and December 2009 and people were asked about income for the previous 12 months (the income reference period), yielding a total income time span covering 23 months (January 2008 to November 2009).[2] Therefore, adjacent ACS years have income reference months in common and comparing 2009 economic conditions with those in 2008 will not be precise.[3]

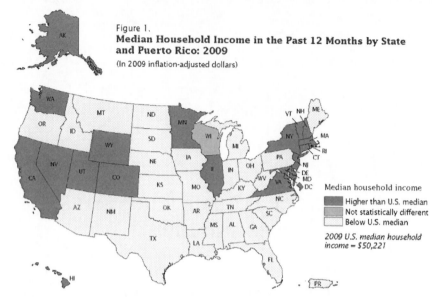

Figure 1.
Median Household Income in the Past 12 Months by State and Puerto Rico: 2009
(In 2009 inflation-adjusted dollars)

Median household income

Higher than U.S. median
Not statistically different
Below U.S. median

2009 U.S. median household income = $50,221

Sources: U.S. Census Bureau, American Community Survey, 2009, Puerto Rico Community Survey, 2009.

Figure 1. Median Household Income in the Past 12 Months by State and Puerto Rico: 2009.

Household Income: Includes income of the householder and all other people 15 years and older in the household, whether or not they are related to the householder.

Median: The point that divides the household income distribution into halves, one half with income above the median and the other with income below the median. The median is based on the income distribution of all households, including those with no income.

Gini Index: Summary measure of income inequality. The Gini Index varies from 0 to 1, 0 indicating perfect equality where there is a proportional distribution of income. A 1 indicates perfect inequality where one person has all the income and no one else has any.

MEDIAN HOUSEHOLD INCOME

Real median household income in the United States fell between the 2008 and 2009 ACS— decreasing by 2.9 percent from $51,726 to $50,221.

State estimates in the 2009 ACS ranged from $69,272 in Maryland to $36,646 in Mississippi.[4] The median household incomes were lower than the U.S. median in 29 states and higher in 20 states and the District of Columbia. Wisconsin had a median household income of $49,993, which was not significantly diff erent from the U.S. median.

Real median household income increased between the 2008 ACS and the 2009 ACS in one state. North Dakota's median rose 5.1 percent from $45,497 in 2008 to $47,827. This compares to increases in two states between the 2007 and the 2008 ACS. Between the 2006 and 2007 ACS there were increases in 33 states.

Real median household income decreased between the 2008 and the 2009 ACS in 34 states. Pennsylvania (1.4 percent) was among the smallest percent decreases, and Michigan (6.2 percent) was among the largest percent decreases. Between the 2007 and the 2008 ACS there were decreases in eight states. These decreases ranged from 1.5 percent to 4.0 percent. Only one state, Michigan (1.2 percent), had a decrease between the 2006 and the 2007 ACS.

In 15 states and the District of Columbia, the real median household income in the 2009 ACS was not statistically diff erent from that in the 2008 ACS.

GINI INDEX OF INCOME INEQUALITY

The Gini Index in 2009 for the United States was 0.469. Gini Indexes by state ranged from 0.532 (District of Columbia) to 0.402 (Alaska).[5] Three states as well as the District of Columbia had a Gini Index higher than the United States—Connecticut, New York, and Texas. Eleven states had a Gini Index which was not statistically diff erent from the U.S. Index. There were 36 states with Gini Indexes significantly lower than the U.S. Index.

The Gini Index increased in three states (Maryland, Nebraska, and New Hampshire) from 2008 to 2009 showing increasing inequality in the distribution of income. The Gini Index also decreased in three states (California, Montana, and Wyoming) from 2008 to 2009, which shows more equality in the distribution of income for these states. There were forty-four states that showed no change in Gini Index from 2008 to 2009. The United States had a Gini Index of 0.469 in the 2008 ACS and 2009 ACS.[6]

SOURCE AND ACCURACY

Data presented in this report are based on people and households that responded to the ACS in 2008 and 2009. The resulting estimates are representative of the entire population. All comparisons presented in this report have taken sampling error into account and are significant at the 90 percent confidence level unless otherwise noted. Due to rounding, some details may not sum to totals. For information on sampling and estimation methods, confidentiality protection, and sampling and nonsampling errors, please see the "2009 ACS Accuracy of the Data" document located at <www.census.gov/acs/www /Downloads/data_documentation /Accu racy/ACS_Accu racy_of _Data_2009.pdf>.

Figure 2.
Gini Index of Income Inequality in the Past 12 Months by State and Puerto Rico: 2009
(In 2009 inflation-adjusted dollars)

Gini Index

■ Higher than U.S. index
▒ Not statistically different
□ Below U.S. index

2009 U.S. Index = 0.469

Sources: U.S. Census Bureau, American Community Survey, 2009, Puerto Rico Community Survey, 2009.

Figure 2. Gini Index of Income Inequality in the Past 12 Months by State and Puerto Rico: 2009.

Median Household Income and Gini Index in the Past 12 Months by State and Puerto Rico: 2008 and 2009
(In 2009 inflation-adjusted dollars. Data are limited to the household population and exclude the population living in institutions, college dormitories, and other group quarters)

Area	2008 median household income (dollars)		2009 median household Income (dollars)		Change in median income — Percent		2008 Gini coefficients		2009 Gini coefficients		Change in Gini coefficients	
	Estimate	Margin of error[1] (±)	Estimate	Margin of error[1] (±)	Estimate	Margin of error[1] (±)	Estimate	Margin of error[1] (±)	Estimate	Margin of error[1] (±)	Estimate	Margin of error[1] (±)
United States	**51,726**	**73**	**50,221**	**74**	***-2.9**	**0.2**	**0.469**	**0.001**	**0.469**	**0.002**	**–**	**0.002**
Alabama	42,408	542	40,489	528	*-4.5	1.7	0.467	0.006	0.471	0.005	0.004	0.008
Alaska	67,413	2,295	66,953	2,331	-0.7	4.8	0.406	0.015	0.402	0.014	-0.004	0.020
Arizona	50,489	542	48,745	484	*-3.5	1.4	0.453	0.004	0.451	0.005	-0.002	0.006
Arkansas	38,778	652	37,823	629	*-2.5	2.3	0.459	0.007	0.461	0.006	0.002	0.009
California	60,625	251	58,931	274	*-2.8	0.6	0.473	0.003	0.467	0.002	*-0.006	0.003
Colorado	57,030	646	55,430	704	*-2.8	1.7	0.456	0.005	0.453	0.005	-0.003	0.007
Connecticut	68,283	983	67,034	993	-1.8	2.0	0.485	0.006	0.480	0.006	-0.005	0.009
Delaware	58,173	1,472	56,860	1,744	-2.3	3.9	0.442	0.011	0.434	0.010	-0.008	0.014
District of Columbia	57,654	2,445	59,290	1,710	2.8	5.3	0.540	0.013	0.532	0.010	-0.008	0.016
Florida	47,452	354	44,736	290	*-5.7	0.9	0.472	0.004	0.469	0.003	-0.003	0.005
Georgia	50,328	443	47,590	414	*-5.4	1.2	0.468	0.005	0.469	0.004	0.001	0.006
Hawaii	67,384	1,992	64,098	1,574	*-4.9	3.7	0.425	0.010	0.425	0.009	–	0.013
Idaho	47,248	905	44,926	953	*-4.9	2.7	0.422	0.009	0.421	0.008	-0.001	0.012
Illinois	55,671	407	53,966	404	*-3.1	1.0	0.467	0.004	0.469	0.004	0.002	0.005

(Continued)

Area	2008 median household income (dollars)		2009 median household Income (dollars)		Change in median income Percent		2008 Gini coefficients		2009 Gini coefficients		Change in Gini coefficients	
	Estimate	Margin of error1 (±)	Estimate	Margin of error1 (±)	Estimate	Margin of error1 (±)	Estimate	Margin of error1 (±)	Estimate	Margin of error1 (±)	Estimate	Margin of error1 (±)
Indiana	47,657	521	45,424	455	*-4.7	1.4	0.438	0.005	0.434	0.004	-0.004	0.006
Iowa	48,559	600	48,044	426	-1.1	1.5	0.429	0.005	0.431	0.005	0.002	0.007
Kansas	49,686	571	47,817	670	*-3.8	1.7	0.442	0.006	0.444	0.005	0.002	0.008
Kentucky	41,299	472	40,072	535	*-3.0	1.7	0.468	0.006	0.464	0.005	-0.004	0.008
Louisiana	43,288	652	42,492	629	-1.8	2.1	0.478	0.006	0.473	0.006	-0.005	0.008
Maine	46,331	810	45,734	935	-1.3	2.7	0.434	0.008	0.432	0.008	-0.002	0.012
Maryland	69,844	755	69,272	696	-0.8	1.5	0.438	0.005	0.448	0.004	*0.010	0.006
Massachusetts	64,941	703	64,081	680	-1.3	1.5	0.472	0.004	0.468	0.005	-0.004	0.007
Michigan	48,246	455	45,255	358	*-6.2	1.2	0.451	0.003	0.453	0.004	0.002	0.005
Minnesota	56,767	513	55,616	546	*-2.0	1.3	0.444	0.005	0.439	0.004	-0.005	0.006
Mississippi	37,749	698	36,646	695	*-2.9	2.6	0.479	0.007	0.470	0.008	-0.009	0.010
Missouri	46,654	377	45,229	519	*-3.1	1.4	0.448	0.005	0.450	0.004	0.002	0.006
Montana	43,443	1,176	42,322	1,073	-2.6	3.6	0.447	0.010	0.431	0.009	*-0.016	0.013
Nebraska	49,342	756	47,357	804	*-4.0	2.2	0.427	0.006	0.440	0.007	*0.013	0.009
Nevada	56,137	805	53,341	981	*-5.0	2.2	0.432	0.008	0.433	0.006	0.001	0.010
New Hampshire	63,650	1,598	60,567	1,385	*-4.8	3.2	0.418	0.007	0.431	0.009	*0.013	0.012
New Jersey	69,938	638	68,342	659	*-2.3	1.3	0.462	0.004	0.465	0.004	0.003	0.005
New Mexico	43,177	938	43,028	1,033	-0.3	3.2	0.459	0.007	0.453	0.007	-0.006	0.009

(Continued)

Area	2008 median household income (dollars)		2009 median household Income (dollars)		Change in median income — Percent		2008 Gini coefficients		2009 Gini coefficients		Change in Gini coefficients	
	Estimate	Margin of error[1] (±)	Estimate	Margin of error[1] (±)	Estimate	Margin of error[1] (±)	Estimate	Margin of error[1] (±)	Estimate	Margin of error[1] (±)	Estimate	Margin of error[1] (±)
New York.	55,486	433	54,659	396	*-1.5	1.0	0.505	0.003	0.502	0.003	-0.003	0.005
North Carolina	46,244	438	43,674	375	*-5.6	1.2	0.463	0.004	0.464	0.004	0.001	0.006
North Dakota	45,497	1,018	47,827	995	*5.1	3.2	0.450	0.012	0.450	0.013	–	0.018
Ohio	47,428	288	45,395	350	*-4.3	0.9	0.450	0.003	0.453	0.003	0.003	0.004
Oklahoma	42,624	646	41,664	502	*-2.3	1.9	0.456	0.005	0.460	0.005	0.004	0.007
Oregon	49,714	651	48,457	623	*-2.5	1.8	0.447	0.005	0.443	0.005	-0.004	0.007
Pennsylvania	50,245	274	49,520	286	*-1.4	0.8	0.458	0.003	0.460	0.003	0.002	0.004
Rhode Island	54,877	1,705	54,119	1,522	-1.4	4.1	0.460	0.014	0.457	0.011	-0.003	0.017
South Carolina	44,053	589	42,442	565	*-3.7	1.8	0.463	0.006	0.462	0.005	-0.001	0.008
South Dakota	46,008	1,133	45,043	1,214	-2.1	3.6	0.448	0.013	0.452	0.015	0.004	0.019
Tennessee	43,311	375	41,725	439	*-3.7	1.3	0.471	0.005	0.467	0.005	-0.004	0.007
Texas	49,453	279	48,259	244	*-2.4	0.7	0.475	0.002	0.474	0.003	-0.001	0.004
Utah	56,304	772	55,117	803	*-2.1	2.0	0.411	0.007	0.414	0.008	0.003	0.010
Vermont	52,207	1,064	51,618	950	-1.1	2.7	0.432	0.012	0.428	0.009	-0.004	0.016
Virginia	61,064	462	59,330	482	*-2.8	1.1	0.460	0.004	0.456	0.003	-0.004	0.005
Washington	57,536	529	56,548	528	*-1.7	1.3	0.443	0.005	0.439	0.004	-0.004	0.006
West Virginia	37,677	915	37,435	707	-0.6	3.1	0.453	0.009	0.463	0.008	0.010	0.012

(Continued)

Area	2008 median household income (dollars)		2009 median household Income (dollars)		Change in median income		2008 Gini coefficients		2009 Gini coefficients		Change in Gini coefficients	
					Percent							
	Estimate	Margin of error[1] (±)	Estimate	Margin of error[1] (±)	Estimate	Margin of error[1] (±)	Estimate	Margin of error[1] (±)	Estimate	Margin of error[1] (±)	Estimate	Margin of error[1] (±)
Wisconsin	51,942	348	49,993	405	*-3.8	1.0	0.426	0.004	0.432	0.004	0.006	0.006
Wyoming	52,931	1,838	52,664	1,877	-0.5	5.0	0.444	0.020	0.415	0.014	*-0.029	0.025
Puerto Rico	18,318	338	18,314	327	–	2.6	0.541	0.007	0.532	0.007	-0.009	0.009

* Statistically different at the 90 percent confidence level. – Represents or rounds to zero.

[1] Data are based on a sample and are subject to sampling variability. A margin of error is a measure of an estimate's variability. The larger the margin of error in relation to the size of the estimate, the less reliable the estimate. This number when added to and subtracted from the estimate forms the 90 percent confidence interval.

Sources: U.S. Census Bureau, American Community Surveys, 2008 and 2009, Puerto Rico Community Surveys, 2008 and 2009.

End Notes

[1] The text of this report discusses data for the United States, including the 50 states and the District of Columbia. Data for the Commonwealth of Puerto Rico, collected with the Puerto Rico Community Survey, are shown in Figure 1, Figure 2, and a table.

[2] All income data are infl ation adjusted to 2009 dollars. "Real" refers to income after adjusting for inflation.

[3] For a discussion of this and related issues, see Hogan, Howard, "Measuring Population Change Using the American Community Survey," *Applied Demography in the 21st Century*, eds., Steven H. Murdock and David A. Swanson, Springer Netherlands, 2008.

[4] The median household income for Maryland was not statistically diff erent from the median household income for New Jersey and Alaska. The median household income for Mississippi was not statistically diff erent from the median household income for West Virginia.

[5] The Gini Index for Alaska was not statistically diff erent from the Gini Index for Wyoming and Utah.

[6] See <www.census.gov/prod/2010pubs /acsbr09-1 .pdf> for more information on poverty publications.

In: The American Community Survey ...   ISBN: 978-1-61324-362-6
Editors: B. M. Russo and A. D. Haffner   ©2011 Nova Science Publishers, Inc.

Chapter 4

MEN'S AND WOMEN'S EARNINGS FOR STATES AND METROPOLITAN STATISTICAL AREAS: 2009

United States Census Bureau

INTRODUCTION

This report presents data on men's and women's earnings at the national, state, and metropolitan levels based on the 2009 American Community Survey (ACS). "Earnings" are defined as the sum of wages, salary, and net self-employment income and do not include other income sources such as property income, government cash transfers, or other types of cash income. Estimates are restricted to full-time, year-round workers 16 years or older. To be considered a "year-round" worker, an individual must have worked 50 or more weeks in the past 12 months, including paid time off for vacation or sick leave. To be considered "full-time" an individual must have worked 35 or more hours per week in the weeks they worked in the past 12 months.

In the 2009 ACS, information on earnings was collected between January 2009 and December 2009. Respondents were asked about income from the previous 12 months. As a result, the 2009 ACS reference periods span a total of 23 months (January 2008 to November 2009).[1]

MEN'S AND WOMEN'S EARNINGS

For full-time, year-round workers, the 2009 ACS median earnings for women were 78.2 percent of men's earnings—$35,549 compared with $45,485. As compared with 2008, median earnings for men were up from $45,161, median earnings for women were up from $35,104, and the ratio of women's earnings to men's earnings was up from 77.7.[2,3]

Women's earnings were lower than men's earnings in each of the 50 states and in the District of Columbia. Women's earnings were higher than men's in Puerto Rico.

In the District of Columbia and eight states—Arizona, California, Florida, Maryland, New York, Nevada, North Carolina, and Texas—the women's-to-men's earnings ratios were 80 percent or more and statistically higher than the national ratio of 78.2.[4]

At 88.2 percent, the District of Columbia was among the highest ratios of women's to men's earnings. Wyoming, at 65.5 percent, was among the lowest.[5]

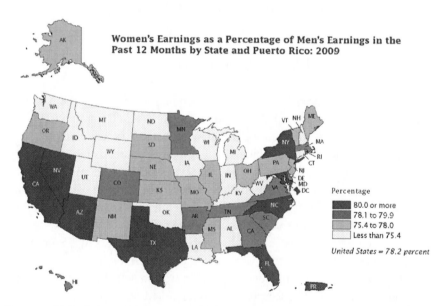

Women's Earnings as a Percentage of Men's Earnings in the Past 12 Months by State and Puerto Rico: 2009

Percentage

- ■ 80.0 or more
- ■ 78.1 to 79.9
- □ 75.4 to 78.0
- □ Less than 75.4

United States = 78.2 percent

Sources: U.S. Census Bureau, American Community Survey, 2009, Puerto Rico Community Survey, 2009.

Women's Earnings as a Percentage of Men's Earnings in the Past 12 Months by State and Puerto Rico: 2009.

Table 1. Median Earnings in the Past 12 Months of Full-Time, Year-Round Workers 16 and Older by Sex and Women's Earnings as a Percentage of Men's Earnings by State and Puerto Rico: 2009 (In 2009 inflation-adjusted dollars)

| Area | Median earnings (dollars) | | | | Women's earnings as a percentage of men's earnings | |
| | Men | | Women | | | |
	Estimate	Margin of error[1] (±)	Estimate	Margin of error[1] (±)	Estimate	Margin of error[1] (±)
United States	45,485	128	35,549	79	78.2	0.3
Alabama	41,331	481	30,658	499	74.2	1.5
Alaska	51,019	1,369	39,017	1,013	76.5	2.9
Arizona	41,916	446	34,651	551	82.7	1.6
Arkansas	36,465	826	28,640	493	78.5	2.2
California	48,389	232	40,019	276	82.7	0.7
Colorado	47,983	446	38,058	420	79.3	1.1
Connecticut	59,387	663	43,900	974	73.9	1.8
Delaware	48,038	1,287	37,645	1,435	78.4	3.7
District of Columbia	61,993	2,965	54,698	3,599	88.2	7.2
Florida	39,122	244	32,109	253	82.1	0.8
Georgia	42,667	537	33,665	457	78.9	1.5
Hawaii	45,911	2,055	35,977	979	78.4	4.1
Idaho	40,440	762	29,122	715	72.0	2.2
Illinois	49,336	323	37,841	281	76.7	0.8

Table 1. (Continued)

| Area | Median earnings (dollars) | | | | Women's earnings as a percentage of men's earnings | |
	Men		Women			
	Estimate	Margin of error[1] (±)	Estimate	Margin of error[1] (±)	Estimate	Margin of error[1] (±)
Indiana	43,631	483	31,762	298	72.8	1.1
Iowa	42,634	611	31,431	416	73.7	1.4
Kansas	42,494	794	32,341	548	76.1	1.9
Kentucky	40,748	527	30,481	498	74.8	1.6
Louisiana	44,174	679	29,350	407	66.4	1.4
Maine	42,156	862	32,314	676	76.7	2.2
Maryland	55,116	866	44,937	709	81.5	1.8
Massachusetts	56,902	923	45,062	627	79.2	1.7
Michigan	48,066	350	34,542	410	71.9	1.0
Minnesota	48,492	313	38,025	379	78.4	0.9
Mississippi	37,528	780	28,506	627	76.0	2.3
Missouri	41,660	442	31,993	334	76.8	1.1
Montana	39,830	926	28,461	741	71.5	2.5
Nebraska	39,516	608	30,562	561	77.3	1.9
Nevada	43,425	1,057	35,691	794	82.2	2.7
New Hampshire	50,837	726	37,527	950	73.8	2.1
New Jersey	57,738	569	44,166	572	76.5	1.2

Table 1. (Continued)

| Area | Median earnings (dollars) | | | | Women's earnings as a percentage of men's earnings | |
| | Men | | Women | | | |
	Estimate	Margin of error[1] (±)	Estimate	Margin of error[1] (±)	Estimate	Margin of error[1] (±)
New Mexico	39,562	950	30,578	734	77.3	2.6
New York	49,174	279	40,584	311	82.5	0.8
North Carolina	40,359	419	32,576	384	80.7	1.3
North Dakota	40,693	736	29,742	662	73.1	2.1
Ohio	44,563	431	33,616	304	75.4	1.0
Oklahoma	39,174	494	29,413	436	75.1	1.5
Oregon	44,572	836	34,121	550	76.6	1.9
Pennsylvania	46,747	473	35,301	385	75.5	1.1
Rhode Island	49,439	1,025	39,248	1,028	79.4	2.7
South Carolina	39,648	518	31,010	386	78.2	1.4
South Dakota	36,977	1,263	28,515	555	77.1	3.0
Tennessee	39,509	356	31,222	379	79.0	1.2
Texas	40,621	291	32,578	267	80.2	0.9
Utah	45,800	1,010	31,186	491	68.1	1.8
Vermont	45,234	1,305	35,276	1,439	78.0	3.9
Virginia	50,236	466	39,354	363	78.3	1.0
Washington	51,305	498	38,521	483	75.1	1.2

Table 1. (Continued)

Area	Median earnings (dollars)				Women's earnings as a percentage of men's earnings	
	Men		Women			
	Estimate	Margin of error[1] (±)	Estimate	Margin of error[1] (±)	Estimate	Margin of error[1] (±)
West Virginia	40,231	799	27,855	677	69.2	2.2
Wisconsin	44,812	401	33,611	382	75.0	1.1
Wyoming	47,828	1,270	31,308	1,216	65.5	3.1
Puerto Rico	19,906	450	20,563	420	103.3	3.2

[1] Data are based on a sample and are subject to sampling variability. A margin of error is a measure of an estimate's variability. The larger the margin of error in relation to the size of the estimate, the less reliable the estimate. This number when added to and subtracted from the estimate forms the 90 percent confi dence interval.

Sources: U.S. Census Bureau, American Community Survey, 2009, Puerto Rico Community Survey, 2009.

Table 2. Median Earnings in the Past 12 Months of Full-Time, Year-Round Workers 16 and Older by Metropolitan and Nonmetropolitan Areas by State and Puerto Rico: 2009 (In 2009 inflation-adjusted dollars)

| Area | Median earnings (dollars) | | | | | | Nonmetropolitan areas earnings as a percentage of metropolitan areas earnings | |
| | Total | | In metropolitan areas | | In nonmetropolitan areas | | | |
	Estimate	Margin of error[1] (±)	Estimate	Margin of error[1] (±)	Estimate	Margin of error[1] (±)	Estimate	Margin of error[1] (±)
United States	**40,409**	**65**	**41,735**	**67**	**33,555**	**133**	**80.4**	**0.3**
Alabama	36,731	457	38,008	348	32,542	970	85.6	2.7
Alaska	45,361	1,659	46,180	2,037	43,930	2,034	95.1	6.1
Arizona	38,573	275	38,801	297	35,184	1,203	90.7	3.2
Arkansas	32,365	423	34,266	634	29,769	471	86.9	2.1
California	44,313	280	44,450	288	38,989	1,526	87.7	3.5
Colorado	42,767	442	43,874	482	37,660	789	85.8	2.0
Connecticut	51,604	562	52,154	579	47,553	1,750	91.2	3.5
Delaware	42,458	1,063	44,701	1,366	36,443	2,159	81.5	5.4
District of Columbia	58,782	1,539	58,782	1,539	(NA)	(NA)	(NA)	(NA)
Florida	35,891	248	36,246	252	30,292	711	83.6	2.0
Georgia	38,531	304	39,936	348	30,756	480	77.0	1.4
Hawaii	40,461	784	41,898	962	37,402	1,110	89.3	3.4
Idaho	35,374	582	37,137	752	32,401	931	87.2	3.1

Table 2. (Continued)

Area	Median earnings (dollars)						Nonmetropolitan areas earnings as a percentage of metropolitan areas earnings	
	Total		In metropolitan areas		In nonmetropolitan areas			
	Estimate	Margin of error[1] (±)	Estimate	Margin of error[1] (±)	Estimate	Margin of error[1] (±)	Estimate	Margin of error[1] (±)
Illinois	43,407	340	45,106	415	34,794	616	77.1	1.5
Indiana	38,442	237	39,295	275	34,740	572	88.4	1.6
Iowa	37,825	348	39,763	519	35,113	445	88.3	1.6
Kansas	38,157	387	41,367	655	31,544	473	76.3	1.7
Kentucky	35,854	414	37,914	497	31,938	499	84.2	1.7
Louisiana	37,040	464	38,035	455	33,256	923	87.4	2.6
Maine	37,777	564	39,231	748	34,972	1,000	89.1	3.1
Maryland	50,271	342	50,628	340	42,586	2,054	84.1	4.1
Massachusetts	50,596	355	50,610	358	48,368	4,933	95.6	9.8
Michigan	41,081	276	42,455	338	35,109	621	82.7	1.6
Minnesota	43,088	378	46,648	523	36,047	440	77.3	1.3
Mississippi	32,220	436	35,122	834	30,086	702	85.7	2.9
Missouri	37,145	354	39,220	308	29,824	398	76.0	1.2
Montana	33,848	1,035	34,276	1,323	33,503	1,330	97.7	5.4
Nebraska	35,643	462	38,612	593	31,593	498	81.8	1.8
Nevada	39,580	516	39,478	501	40,707	2,057	103.1	5.4

Table 2. (Continued)

Area	Median earnings (dollars)						Nonmetropolitan areas earnings as a percentage of metropolitan areas earnings	
	Total		In metropolitan areas		In nonmetropolitan areas			
	Estimate	Margin of error[1] (±)	Estimate	Margin of error[1] (±)	Estimate	Margin of error[1] (±)	Estimate	Margin of error[1] (±)
New Hampshire	44,014	839	47,119	1,504	40,076	1,029	85.1	3.5
New Jersey	50,688	315	50,688	315	(NA)	(NA)	(NA)	(NA)
New Mexico	35,003	876	36,829	1,039	31,908	1,133	86.6	3.9
New York	45,169	327	46,428	342	36,032	700	77.6	1.6
North Carolina	36,796	355	38,395	356	32,362	389	84.3	1.3
North Dakota	35,571	709	36,490	1,092	34,597	889	94.8	3.7
Ohio	39,403	217	40,353	298	34,715	534	86.0	1.5
Oklahoma	34,700	434	36,437	563	31,327	613	86.0	2.1
Oregon	39,514	429	40,693	571	35,130	907	86.3	2.5
Pennsylvania	41,076	229	42,248	249	34,383	533	81.4	1.3
Rhode Island	44,927	1,133	44,927	1,133	(NA)	(NA)	(NA)	(NA)
South Carolina	35,392	523	36,448	564	31,628	650	86.8	2.2
South Dakota	32,370	619	33,104	1,040	31,780	703	96.0	3.7
Tennessee	35,637	341	37,583	310	30,425	473	81.0	1.4
Texas	37,409	218	38,087	182	31,467	341	82.6	1.0
Utah	39,404	408	39,549	464	38,171	1,173	96.5	3.2

Table 2. (Continued)

| | Median earnings (dollars) | | | | | | | Nonmetropolitan areas earnings as a percentage of metropolitan areas earnings | |
| | Total | | In metropolitan areas | | In nonmetropolitan areas | | | | |
	Estimate	Margin of error[1] (±)	Estimate	Margin of error[1] (±)	Estimate	Margin of error[1] (±)		Estimate	Margin of error[1] (±)
Vermont	40,319	920	44,538	2,106	38,697	762		86.9	4.4
Virginia	44,915	476	47,438	485	33,877	779		71.4	1.8
Washington	45,843	544	47,230	561	37,253	922		78.9	2.2
West Virginia	34,423	689	36,445	1,078	32,163	722		88.3	3.3
Wisconsin	39,718	239	41,125	324	35,886	453		87.3	1.3
Wyoming	39,871	1,449	37,619	1,705	41,417	2,040		110.1	7.4
Puerto Rico	20,261	358	20,345	360	18,651	1,143		91.7	5.8

(NA) Not available.

[1] Data are based on a sample and are subject to sampling variability. A margin of error is a measure of an estimate's variability. The larger the margin of error in relation to the size of the estimate, the less reliable the estimate. This number when added to and subtracted from the estimate forms the 90 percent confidence interval.

Sources: U.S. Census Bureau, American Community Survey, 2009, Puerto Rico Community Survey, 2009.

In Connecticut, Maryland, Massachusetts, New Hampshire, New Jersey, Washington, and the District of Columbia, median men's earnings were more than $50,000. Only the District of Columbia had median women's earnings above $50,000.

EARNINGS INSIDE AND OUTSIDE OF METROPOLITAN AREAS

The 2009 ACS median earnings were $41 ,735 for people who worked full-time, year-round and lived in metropolitan areas. For people who worked full-time, year- round and lived outside of metro areas, they were $33,555, or 80.4 percent of the earnings in metropolitan areas.

In 43 of the 48 states with both metropolitan and nonmetropolitan areas,[6] median earnings were higher in metropolitan areas than in nonmetropolitan areas.

In four states—Alaska, Massachusetts, Montana, and Nevada—the differences between median earnings for workers in metropolitan and non metropolitan areas were not statistically signifi cant. Earnings for nonmetropolitan workers were lower than earnings for metropolitan workers in Wyoming.

Seven states—Georgia, Illinois, Kansas, Minnesota, Missouri, New York, and Virginia—had nonmetropolitan-to-metropolitan- earnings ratios below the national ratio of 80.4. A total of 35 states had nonmetropolitan-to-metropolitan-earnings ratios above the national ratio.[7]

Wyoming was among the states with the highest ratios of earnings for non metropolitan workers to earnings of metropolitan workers at 110.1 percent.[8] Virginia—at 71.4 percent—was the lowest.

SOURCE AND ACCURACY

Data presented in this report are based on people and households that responded to the ACS in 2009. The resulting estimates are representative of the entire population. All comparisons presented in this report have taken sampling error into account and are signifi cant at the 90 percent confi dence level unless otherwise noted. Due to rounding, some details may not sum to totals. For information on sampling and estimation methods, confi dentiality protection, and sampling and nonsampling errors, please see the "2009 ACS Accuracy of the Data" document located at <www.census.gov/acs/www /Downloads/data_documentation/Accuracy/ACS_Accuracy_of _Data_2009.pdf>.

End Notes

[1] All income data are infl ation adjusted to 2009 dollars.

[2] 2008 data are available via the Census Bureau Web site's American Fact Finder tool at <factfi nder.census.gov>. Income data for data year 2008 are available in subject table S2002.

[3] In addition to varying by sex, earnings vary widely based on occupation. For more information, see Day, Jennifer Cheeseman and Jeff rey Rosenthal, 2009, "Detailed Occupations and Median Earnings: 2008," U.S. Census Bureau, <www.census.gov/hhes/www/ ioindex/reports .html>.

[4] The ratio of women's-to-men's earnings for the District of Columbia was not statistically different from those of Arizona, California, Florida, Maryland, Nevada, or New York.

[5] The ratio of women's-to-men's earnings for Wyoming was not statistically diff erent from those of Louisiana, Utah, and West Virginia.

[6] New Jersey, Rhode Island, and the District of Columbia do not contain any non- metropolitan areas.

[7] The difference between earnings for workers in metropolitan areas and nonmetropolitan areas was not statistically signifi cant from the national average in Delaware, Maryland, Nebraska, Pennsylvania, Tennessee, or Washington.

[8] The ratio of nonmetropolitan earnings to metropolitan earnings in Wyoming was not statistically diff erent from the ratio in Nevada.

In: The American Community Survey ...   ISBN: 978-1-61324-362-6
Editors: B. M. Russo and A. D. Haffner   ©2011 Nova Science Publishers, Inc.

Chapter 5

USUAL HOURS WORKED IN THE PAST 12 MONTHS FOR WORKERS 16 TO 64: 2008 AND 2009

United States Census Bureau

INTRODUCTION

Since the onset of the recession in December of 2007, work hours have trended downward because of increasing involuntary part-time work and a reduction in overtime hours.[1] These trends vary by metropolitan statistical area (metro area) and by type of employment.[2] This report will show where work-hour cuts have been most prevalent. It highlights changes in usual hours worked per week by sex, occupation, industry, and class of worker.

While work hours typically vary little from year to year, they tend to decline during periods of recession. They can also be a leading indicator of changes in employment, because employers may increase or decrease work hours for current employees prior to layoff s or hiring.[3] An increase in part-time work and a reduction in usual work hours are some of the indicators of underemployment, and as such, are important measures of the overall employment situation.[4]

Usual Hours: Usual hours refer to the usual number of hours worked during a week at all jobs held. Mean usual hours is obtained by dividing the aggregate number of hours worked by the total number of workers aged 16 to 64 who have worked within the past 12 months.

Occupation: Occupation describes the kind of work a person does on the job.

Industry: Industry describes the kind of business conducted by a person's employing organization. Individu-als provide descriptions of what is made, what is sold, or what service is provided by their employer.

Class of worker: Class of worker categorizes people according to the type of ownership of the employing organization.

Universe: Usual hours are provided for individuals aged 16 to 64 who have worked within the past 12 months. Individuals provide occupation, industry, and class of worker data for the person's job during the reference week. For those who worked at two or more jobs, the data refer to their primary job. For people who are not currently employed but report having a job within the last 12 months, the data refer to their last job.

CHANGE IN USUAL WORK HOURS

Work hours in the United States fell by about 36 minutes per week from 39.0 hours in 2008 to 38.4 hours in 2009. Work hours fell in 46 of the 50 largest U.S. metro areas. None of the 50 metro areas reported an increase in work hours.

Men experienced larger work-hour reductions than women. Men's work hours declined by 48 minutes per week, from 41.7 hours to 40.9 hours per week. Women's work hours declined by 24 minutes per week, from 36.1 hours to 35.7 hours per week. In addition to experiencing a larger reduction in work hours, men's work hours declined in a larger number of metro areas, falling in 43 metro areas compared with 19 for women.

Table 1. Usual Hours Worked in the Past 12 Months for Workers Aged 16 to 64 by Metropolitan Statistical Area: 2008 and 2009[1]

Area	2008		2009		Change in usual hours worked in minutes	Margin of error[2] (±)
	Estimate	Margin of error[2] (±)	Estimate	Margin of error[2] (±)		
United States	**39.0**	**0.1**	**38.4**	**0.1**	***-36**	**8**
Atlanta-Sandy Springs-Marietta, GA	39.9	0.2	39.1	0.2	*-48	17
Austin-Round Rock, TX	39.7	0.2	39.0	0.2	*-42	17
Baltimore-Towson, MD	39.3	0.2	38.8	0.2	*-30	17
Birmingham-Hoover, AL	39.9	0.2	39.2	0.3	*-42	22
Boston-Cambridge-Quincy, MA-NH	38.5	0.2	37.9	0.1	*-36	13
Buffalo-Niagara Falls, NY	37.4	0.3	36.9	0.3	*-30	25
Charlotte-Gastonia-Concord, NC-SC	39.8	0.3	39.2	0.2	*-36	22
Chicago-Naperville-Joliet, IL-IN-WI	38.9	0.1	38.3	0.1	*-36	8
Cincinnati-Middletown, OH-KY-IN	38.6	0.2	38.2	0.2	*-24	17
Cleveland-Elyria-Mentor, OH	38.5	0.2	37.6	0.2	*-54	17
Columbus, OH	39.0	0.2	38.4	0.3	*-36	22
Dallas-Fort Worth-Arlington, TX	40.5	0.2	39.8	0.1	*-42	13
Denver-Au rora-Broomfi eld, CO	39.4	0.2	39.0	0.2	*-24	17
Detroit-Warren-Livonia, MI	38.5	0.2	37.5	0.2	*-60	17

Table 1. (Continued)

Area	2008		2009		Change in usual hours worked in minutes	Margin of error[2] (±)
	Estimate	Margin of error[2] (±)	Estimate	Margin of error[2] (±)		
Hartford-West Hartford-East Hartford, CT	38.3	0.3	37.6	0.2	*-42	22
Houston-Sugar Land-Baytown, TX	41.0	0.2	40.3	0.2	*-42	17
Indianapolis-Carmel, IN	39.5	0.2	38.8	0.2	*-42	17
Jacksonville,FL	39.9	0.3	39.4	0.3	*-30	25
Kansas City, MO-KS	39.7	0.2	39.0	0.2	*-42	17
Las Vegas-Paradise, NV	39.7	0.3	38.9	0.2	*-48	22
Los Angeles-Long Beach-Santa Ana, CA	38.7	0.1	38.1	0.1	*-36	8
Louisville/Jefferson County, KY-IN	38.9	0.2	38.4	0.3	*-30	22
Memphis, TN-MS-AR	39.3	0.3	38.5	0.3	*-48	25
Miami-Fort Lauderdale-Pompano Beach, FL	39.5	0.2	38.8	0.1	*-42	13
Milwaukee-Waukesha-West Allis, WI	38.2	0.2	37.9	0.2	*-18	17
Minneapolis-St. Paul-Bloomington, MN-WI	38.2	0.1	37.8	0.3	*-24	19
Nashville-Davidson–Murfreesboro–Franklin, TN	39.4	0.2	39.0	0.2	*-24	17
New Orleans-Metairie-Kenner, LA	39.7	0.3	39.4	0.3	-18	25
New York-Northern New Jersey-Long Island, NY-NJ-PA	39.2	0.2	39.1	0.1	-6	13

Table 1. (Continued)

Area	2008		2009		Change in usual hours worked in minutes	Margin of error[2] (±)
	Estimate	Margin of error[2] (±)	Estimate	Margin of error[2] (±)		
Oklahoma City, OK.	39.7	0.2	39.1	0.2	*–36	17
Orlando–Kissimmee, FL	39.3	0.2	38.6	0.3	*–42	22
Philadelphia–Camden–Wilmington, PA-NJ-DE-MD	38.8	0.2	38.5	0.2	*–18	17
Phoenix–Mesa–Scottsdale, AZ	39.5	0.1	38.8	0.2	*–42	13
Pittsburgh,PA	38.5	0.2	38.1	0.2	*–24	17
Portland–Vancouver–Beaverton, OR-WA	38.4	0.2	37.6	0.2	*–48	17
Providence–New Bedford-Fall River, RI-MA	37.5	0.2	37.6	0.3	6	22
Raleigh-Cary,NC	39.7	0.3	39.0	0.3	*–42	25
Richmond, VA	39.4	0.3	38.5	0.3	*–54	25
Riverside–San Bernardino–Ontario, CA	38.5	0.2	37.6	0.2	*–54	17
Sacramento–Arden-Arcade–Roseville, CA	38.1	0.3	37.7	0.3	–24	25
St. Louis,MO-IL	38.3	0.2	38.0	0.2	*–18	17
Salt Lake City, UT	38.5	0.3	37.8	0.3	*–42	25
San Antonio, TX	39.8	0.2	39.2	0.3	*–36	22
San Diego–Carlsbad-San Marcos, CA	39.0	0.2	38.5	0.2	*–30	17
San Francisco–Oakland-Fremont, CA	38.5	0.2	38.1	0.2	*–24	17

Table 1. (Continued)

Area	2008		2009		Change in usual hours worked in minutes	Margin of error[2] (±)
	Estimate	Margin of error[2] (±)	Estimate	Margin of error[2] (±)		
San Jose-Sunnyvale-Santa Clara, CA	39.2	0.2	38.4	0.2	*–48	17
Seattle-Tacoma-Bellevue, WA	39.0	0.2	38.5	0.2	*–30	17
Tampa-St. Petersburg-Clearwater, FL	39.6	0.2	39.1	0.2	*–30	17
Virginia Beach-Norfolk-Newport News, VA-NC	39.8	0.3	39.2	0.3	*–36	25
Washington-Arlington-Alexandria, DC-VA-MD-WV	40.0	0.2	39.5	0.2	*–30	17

* Statistically different at the 90 percent confidence level.
[1] Fifty most populous metropolitan statistical areas based on population estimates as of July 1, 2009. Metropolitan statistical area boundaries defined by the Office of Management and Budget as of November 2008.
[2] Data are based on a sample and are subject to sampling variability. A margin of error is a measure of an estimate's variability. The larger the margin of error in relation to the size of the estimate, the less reliable the estimate. When added to and subtracted from the estimate, the margin of error forms the 90 percent confidence interval.

Sources: U.S. Census Bureau, American Community Surveys, 2008 and 2009.

Table 2. Usual Hours Worked in the Past 12 Months for Workers Aged 16 to 64 by Sex and by Metropolitan Statistical Area: 2008 and 2009[1]

Area	Male						Female					
	2008 Estimate	2008 Margin of error²(±)	2009 Estimate	2009 Margin of error²(±)	Change in usual hours worked in minutes	Margin of error²(±)	2008 Estimate	2008 Margin of error²(±)	2009 Estimate	2009 Margin of error²(±)	Change in usual hours worked in minutes	Margin of error²(±)
United States	**41.7**	**0.1**	**40.9**	**0.1**	***_48**	**8**	**36.1**	**0.1**	**35.7**	**0.1**	***_24**	**8**
Atlanta-Sandy Springs-Marietta, GA	42.3	0.2	41.2	0.2	*–66	17	37.3	0.2	36.8	0.2	*–30	17
Austin-Round Rock, TX	42.0	0.4	41.0	0.3	*–60	30	36.9	0.3	36.7	0.3	–12	25
Baltimore-Towson, MD	41.8	0.2	41.2	0.3	*–36	22	36.8	0.3	36.5	0.3	–18	25
Birmingham-Hoover, AL	42.7	0.4	41.6	0.3	*–66	30	36.9	0.4	36.5	0.4	–24	34
Boston-Cambridge-Quincy, MA-NH	41.6	0.2	40.8	0.2	*–48	17	35.3	0.2	34.9	0.2	*–24	17
Buffalo-Niagara Falls, NY	40.1	0.4	39.7	0.4	–24	34	34.6	0.4	34.1	0.3	–30	30
Charlotte-Gastonia-Concord, NC-SC	42.6	0.3	41.5	0.3	*–66	25	36.8	0.3	36.7	0.4	–6	30
Chicago-Naperville-Joliet, IL-IN-WI	41.5	0.2	40.6	0.2	*–54	17	36.0	0.1	35.7	0.2	*–18	13
Cincinnati-Middletown, OH-KY-IN	41.7	0.3	40.7	0.3	*–60	25	35.4	0.3	35.5	0.3	6	25

Table 2. (Continued)

Area	Male						Female					
	2008		2009		Change in usual hours worked in minutes	Margin of error² (±)	2008		2009		Change in usual hours worked in minutes	Margin of error² (±)
	Estimate	Margin of error² (±)	Estimate	Margin of error² (±)			Estimate	Margin of error² (±)	Estimate	Margin of error² (±)		
Cleveland-Elyria-Mentor, OH	41.5	0.3	40.2	0.3	*–78	25	35.3	0.3	35.0	0.3	–18	25
Columbus, OH	41.6	0.3	40.6	0.3	*–60	25	36.3	0.3	36.0	0.3	–18	25
Dallas-Fort Worth-Arlington, TX	42.8	0.2	41.9	0.2	*–54	17	37.6	0.2	37.3	0.2	*–1 8	17
Denver-Aurora-Broomfield, CO	41.8	0.2	41.2	0.2	*–36	17	36.7	0.3	36.4	0.3	–18	25
Detroit-Warren-Livonia, MI	41.3	0.2	40.2	0.2	*–66	17	35.4	0.2	34.8	0.2	*–36	17
Hartford-West Hartford-East Hartford, CT	40.9	0.4	40.5	0.3	–24	30	35.4	0.4	34.6	0.3	*–48	30
Houston-Sugar Land-Baytown, TX	43.5	0.2	42.4	0.2	*–66	17	37.8	0.2	37.6	0.3	–12	22
Indianapolis-Carmel, IN	42.1	0.3	41.4	0.3	*–42	25	36.6	0.3	36.0	0.3	*–36	25
Jacksonville, FL	42.0	0.4	41.6	0.3	–24	30	37.6	0.3	37.0	0.3	*–36	25
Kansas City, MO-KS	42.2	0.3	41.6	0.3	*–36	25	37.0	0.3	36.3	0.3	*–42	25
Las Vegas-Paradise, NV	41.3	0.3	40.4	0.3	*–54	25	37.8	0.3	36.9	0.3	*–54	25

Table 2. (Continued)

Area	Male						Female					
	2008		2009				2008		2009			
	Estimate	Margin of error² (±)	Estimate	Margin of error² (±)	Change in usual hours worked in minutes	Margin of error² (±)	Estimate	Margin of error² (±)	Estimate	Margin of error² (±)	Change in usual hours worked in minutes	Margin of error² (±)
Los Angeles-Long Beach-Santa Ana, CA	40.8	0.2	39.9	0.2	*–54	17	36.3	0.2	35.9	0.1	*–24	13
Louisville/Jefferson County, KY-IN	41.3	0.3	40.6	0.4	*–42	30	36.4	0.3	36.1	0.4	–18	30
Memphis, TN-MS-AR	41.3	0.4	40.6	0.5	*–42	38	37.2	0.4	36.5	0.4	*–42	34
Miami-Fort Lauderdale-Pompano Beach, FL	41.5	0.2	40.5	0.3	*–60	22	37.3	0.2	36.9	0.2	*–24	17
Milwaukee-Waukesha-West Allis, WI	40.9	0.3	40.4	0.3	*–30	25	35.4	0.3	35.3	0.3	–6	25
Minneapolis-St. Paul-Bloomington, MN-WI	40.7	0.2	40.0	0.2	*–42	17	35.5	0.2	35.3	0.2	–12	17
Nashville-Davidson—Murfreesboro—Franklin, TN	41.8	0.3	41.3	0.3	*–30	25	36.7	0.3	36.5	0.3	–12	25
New Orleans-Metairie-Kenner, LA	42.5	0.5	41.9	0.4	–36	38	36.9	0.4	36.8	0.4	–6	34
New York-Northern New Jersey-Long Island, NY-NJ-PA	41.8	0.2	41.6	0.2	–12	17	36.4	0.1	36.4	0.1	0	8

Table 2. (Continued)

Area	Male						Female					
	2008		2009		Change in usual hours worked in minutes	Margin of error²(±)	2008		2009		Change in usual hours worked in minutes	Margin of error²(±)
	Estimate	Margin of error²(±)	Estimate	Margin of error²(±)			Estimate	Margin of error²(±)	Estimate	Margin of error²(±)		
Oklahoma City, OK	42.2	0.4	41.5	0.3	*–42	30	36.9	0.3	36.4	0.4	–30	30
Orlando-Kissimmee, FL	41.1	0.4	40.2	0.3	*–54	30	37.2	0.3	36.9	0.3	–18	25
Philadelphia-Camden-Wilmington, PA-NJ-DE-MD	41.6	0.2	41.2	0.2	*–24	17	35.8	0.2	35.6	0.2	–12	17
Phoenix-Mesa-Scottsdale, AZ	41.3	0.2	40.6	0.2	*–42	17	37.3	0.3	36.6	0.3	*–42	25
Pittsburgh, PA	41.6	0.2	40.9	0.3	*–42	22	35.2	0.3	35.2	0.2	0	22
Portland-Vancouver-Beaverton, OR-WA	41.1	0.3	40.0	0.2	*–66	22	35.4	0.3	34.9	0.3	*–30	25
Providence-New Bedford-Fall River, RI-MA	40.6	0.4	40.5	0.3	–6	30	34.3	0.3	34.6	0.4	18	30
Raleigh-Cary, NC	42.0	0.4	41.3	0.4	*–42	34	37.1	0.5	36.4	0.4	*–42	38
Richmond, VA	41.9	0.4	40.6	0.4	*–78	34	36.8	0.4	36.3	0.4	–30	34
Riverside-San Bernardino-Ontario, CA	40.8	0.3	40.0	0.3	*–48	25	35.6	0.2	34.7	0.3	*–54	22
Sacramento-Arden-Arcade-Roseville, CA	40.3	0.3	39.6	0.3	*–42	25	35.6	0.3	35.5	0.3	–6	25

Table 2. (Continued)

Area	Male 2008 Estimate	Male 2008 Margin of error² (±)	Male 2009 Estimate	Male 2009 Margin of error² (±)	Male Change in usual hours worked in minutes	Male Margin of error² (±)	Female 2008 Estimate	Female 2008 Margin of error² (±)	Female 2009 Estimate	Female 2009 Margin of error² (±)	Female Change in usual hours worked in minutes	Female Margin of error² (±)
St. Louis,MO-IL	40.6	0.2	40.2	0.2	*–24	17	35.8	0.2	35.6	0.3	–12	22
Salt Lake City, UT	41.3	0.3	40.2	0.4	*–66	30	35.1	0.4	34.8	0.4	–18	34
San Antonio, TX	41.9	0.3	41.2	0.3	*–42	25	37.4	0.3	37.1	0.4	–18	30
San Diego-Carlsbad-San Marcos, CA	41.5	0.3	40.8	0.3	*–42	25	35.9	0.2	35.6	0.3	–18	22
San Francisco-Oakland-Fremont, CA	40.4	0.2	40.0	0.2	*–24	17	36.3	0.2	36.1	0.3	–12	22
San Jose-Sunnyvale-Santa Clara, CA	41.4	0.3	40.5	0.3	*–54	25	36.4	0.4	35.7	0.3	*–42	30
Seattle-Tacoma-Bellevue, WA	41.7	0.3	41.0	0.2	*–42	22	35.9	0.2	35.6	0.3	–18	22
Tampa-St. Petersburg-Clearwater, FL	41.6	0.3	41.0	0.3	*–36	25	37.4	0.3	37.1	0.3	–18	25

Table 2. (Continued)

Virginia Beach-Norfolk-Newport News, VA-NC	42.4	0.4	42.1	0.4	-18	34	36.9	0.3	36.2	0.5	*-42	35
Washington-Arlington-Alexandria, DC-VA-MD-WV	42.1	0.2	41.4	0.2	*-42	17	37.7	0.2	37.5	0.2	-12	17

[1] Fifty most populous metropolitan statistical areas based on population estimates as of July 1, 2009. Metropolitan statistical area boundaries defi ned by the Offi ce of Management and Budget as of November 2008.

[2] Data are based on a sample and are subject to sampling variability. A margin of error is a measure of an estimate's variability. The larger the margin of error in relation to the size of the estimate, the less reliable the estimate. When added to and subtracted from the estimate, the margin of error forms the 90 percent confi dence interval.

Sources: U.S. Census Bureau, American Community Surveys, 2008 and 2009.

USUAL WORK HOURS BY METROPOLITAN STATISTICAL AREA

In 2009, residents of Houston- Sugar Land-Baytown, TX, and Dallas-Fort Worth-Arlington, TX, worked the longest number of hours at 40.3 and 39.8 hours per week, respectively. Work hours were longest in Houston-Sugar Land-Baytown, TX, with men working 42.4 hours per week and women working 37.6 hours per week.[5]

Work hours were shortest in Buff alo-Niagara Falls, NY at 36.9 hours per week. Men worked the shortest number of hours in Sacramento–Arden-Arcade–Roseville, CA, at 39.6 hours per week while women worked the shortest number of hours in Buff alo-Niagara Falls, NY, at 34.1 hours per week.[6]

USUAL WORK HOURS BY OCCUPATION[7]

Workers in construction, extraction, maintenance, and repair occupations, production, transportation, and material moving occupations, and farming, fi shing, and forestry occupations experienced the largest decrease in work hours. In each of these occupations work hours declined by about an hour per week. Workers in sales and offi ce occupations and managerial, professional, and related occupations worked 24 minutes less in 2009.

USUAL WORK HOURS BY INDUSTRY[8]

Work hours declined by about 74 minutes per week in agriculture, forestry, fi shing, and hunting, and mining industries and by about 67 minutes per week in construction industries.[9] The smallest decrease in work hours was registered in the fi nance and insurance, and real estate and rental and leasing industries with a decrease of 5 minutes per week between 2008 and 2009.

USUAL WORK HOURS BY CLASS OF WORKER

Self-employed workers experienced a greater reduction in work hours between 2008 and 2009 than workers in other types of employment. Workers who were self-employed in their own unincorporated businesses worked 66 minutes less in 2009 while those self-employed in their own incorporated businesses worked 49 minutes less in 2009.[10] Government workers were the least likely to work reduced hours between 2008 and 2009 with a reduction of 1 7 minutes per week.[11]

Sources: U.S. Census Bureau, American Community Surveys, 2008 and 2009.

Usual Hours Worked in the Past 12 Months for Workers Aged 16 to 64 by Occupation, Industry, and Class of Worker.

SOURCE AND ACCURACY

Data presented in this report are based on people and households that responded to the ACS in 2008 and 2009. The resulting estimates are representative of the entire population. All comparisons presented in this report have taken sampling error into account and are signifi cant at the 90 percent confidence level unless otherwise noted. Due to rounding, some details may not sum to totals. For information on sampling and estimation methods, confi dentiality protection, and sampling and nonsampling errors, please see the "2009 ACS Accuracy of the Data" document located at <www.census.gov/acs/www /Downloads/data_documentation /Accu racy/ACS_Accu racy_of _Data_2009.pdf>.

End Notes

[1] Bureau of Labor Statistics. 2009. "The Employment Situation: January 2009." Available online at <www.bls.gov/news.release/archives /empsit_02062009.pdf>.

[2] For more information on metropolitan statistical areas please see <www.whitehouse. gov/ omb/assets .pdf>.

[3] Bureau of Labor Statistics. 2008. "Involuntary Part-Time Work on the Rise." *Issues in Labor Statistics*, December 2008.

[4] Underemployed individuals are those who wanted full-time jobs but worked less than 35 hours per week due to slack work (a reduction in hours in response to unfavorable business conditions) or because they were only able to fi nd part-time work.

[5] Work hours for men in Houston-Sugar Land-Baytown, TX, are not statistically different from work hours for men in Virginia Beach-Norfolk-Newport News, VA-NC. Work hours for women in Houston-Sugar Land- Baytown, TX, are not statistically diff erent from work hours for women in WashingtonArlington-Alexandria, DC-VA-MD-WV, Dallas- Fort Worth-Arlington, TX, and San Antonio, TX.

[6] Work hours for men in Sacramento– Arden-Arcade–Roseville, CA, are not statistically diff erent from work hours for men in Buff alo-Niagara Falls, NY, Los Angeles-Long Beach-Santa Ana, CA, and Riverside-San Bernardino-Ontario, CA. Work hours for women in Buffalo-Niagara Falls, NY, are not statistically different from work hours for women in Providence-New Bedford-Fall River, RI-MA.

[7] Occupational categories are based on the Standard Occupational Classifi cation 2000. For more information, see <www.bls.gov/soc>.

[8] Industry categories are based on the North American Industry Classifi cation System 2007. For more information, see <www.census.gov/naics>.

[9] The estimate for agriculture, forestry, fi shing, and hunting, and mining is not statistically diff erent from the estimate for construction.

[10] The estimates for self-employed in own not incorporated business workers and self-employed in own incorporated business workers are not statistically diff erent from the estimate for unpaid family workers.

[11] The estimate for government workers is not statistically diff erent from the estimate for unpaid family workers.

In: The American Community Survey ...   ISBN: 978-1-61324-362-6
Editors: B. M. Russo and A. D. Haffner   ©2011 Nova Science Publishers, Inc.

Chapter 6

PUBLIC TRANSPORTATION USAGE AMONG U.S. WORKERS: 2008 AND 2009

United States Census Bureau

INTRODUCTION

This report presents data from the 2008 and 2009 American Community Surveys (ACS) on the percentage of commuters who used public transportation to get to work in U.S. metropolitan statistical areas (metro areas).[1] The percentage of workers who usually travel to work using public transportation has remained at about 5 percent since the 1 990 Census.[2]

Public transportation accounts for a small percentage of commutes at the national level, but plays a more prominent role in several of the nation's largest metro areas, especially in densely populated communities. About 39 percent of all workers who usually travel to work using public transportation live in the New York-Northern New Jersey-Long Island, NY-NJ-PA Metro Area. In an eff ort to provide more transportation choices for Americans nationwide, investment in public transportation systems has been an integral component of several major   federal transportation programs in recent decades.

The ACS asks respondents about their usual means of transportation to work. "Public transportation" includes workers who used a bus, trolley, streetcar, subway or elevated rail, railroad, or ferryboat, and did not work at home. Respondents were to report their usual transportation method for the previous week, whether or not the information was consistent with their commuting activities for the majority of the year.

Workers are civilians and members of the Armed Forces, 16 years and older, who were at work the previous week. Persons on vacation or not at work the prior week are not included.

Means of transportation to work refers to the principal mode of travel that the worker usually used to get from home to work during the reference week. People who used diff erent means of transportation on diff erent days of the week were asked to specify the one they used most often. People who used more than one means of transportation to get to work each day were asked to report the one used for the longest distance during the work trip. Workers who worked at home are not included in this category. For more detailed defi nitions of these terms and other ACS terms, see the ACS subject defi - nitions list at <www.census.gov/acs /www/data_ documen tation /documentation_main/>.

PUBLIC TRANSPORTATION USAGE AMONG U.S. WORKERS: 2008 AND 2009

Among the nation's workers, 6.9 million commuted to work using public transportation in 2009. This is a reduction from 2008, when 7.2 million workers used public transportation to get to work. Table 2 lists ACS estimates of the number of workers who commuted by public transportation in the 50 largest metro areas, in 2008 and 2009, as well as the change over the year.[3] The national percentage of workers 16 years and over who used public transportation to commute to work in 2009 (5.0 percent) was not statistically diff erent from the percentage in 2008.

The New York-Northern New Jersey-Long Island, NY-NJ-PA Metro Area had the highest percentage of workers who commuted by public transportation (30.5 percent). It was followed by the San Francisco-Oakland-Fremont, CA Metro Area, where 14.6 percent of workers commuted by public transportation.[4] The percentage of workers who commuted by public transportation exceeded 10 percent in only 5 of the 366 metro areas in 2009.[5] In Los Angeles, the nation's second largest metro area, about 6 percent of workers commuted by public transportation. Also fall-ing within the category of 5 to 10 percent were several college towns, including Ithaca, NY, and

Ames, IA. For the majority of metro areas, including several large metro areas such as Detroit-Warren-Livonia, MI, the public transportation usage rate among workers did not exceed 2 percent. The map provides a visual illustration of the percentage of workers who commuted by public transportation for all metro areas in 2009.

Table 2 shows comparisons between the 50 largest metro areas in 2008 and 2009. Ten experienced a statistically signifi cant decline in the number of public transportation commuters, and two (Seattle-Tacoma-Bellevue, WA, and Washington-Arlington-Alexandria, DC-VA-MD-WV) experienced a statistically signifi cant increase in the number of public transit commuters.[6] The 2009 estimates were not statistically diff erent from the 2008 estimates in the remainder of the metro areas. Boston-CambridgeQuincy, MA-NH; Seattle-TacomaBellevue, WA; and WashingtonArlington-Alexandria, DC-VA-MD-WV, were the only three metro areas that experienced a statistically signifi cant increase in the percentage of workers who commuted by public transportation, and four metro areas experienced a statistically signifi cant decline in the percentage of public transportation commuters.[7]

Table 1 shows the top 15 metro areas ranked by the number of workers who commuted by public transportation in 2009. The New York-Northern New Jersey-Long Island, NY-NJ-PA Metro Area had the highest number of workers who used public transportation in 2009, at 2.7 million workers. The Chicago-Naperville-Joliet, IL-IN-WI Metro Area and the Washington-Arlington-Alexandria, DC-VA-MD-WV Metro Area had the second and third highest number of workers who used public transportation, at 506,000 and 405,000 workers, respectively. All except 4 of the metro areas included in this list were among the 15 largest metro areas in 2009.8

SOURCE AND ACCURACY

Data presented in this report are based on people and households that responded to the ACS in 2008 and 2009. The resulting estimates are representative of the entire population. All comparisons presented in this report have taken sampling error into account and are signifi cant at the 90 percent confi - dence level unless otherwise noted. Due to rounding, some details may not sum to totals. For information on sampling and estimation methods, confi dentiality protection, and sampling and nonsampling errors, please see the "2009 ACS Accuracy of the Data" document located at

<www.census.gov/acs /www/Down loads/data _documentation/Accuracy/ ACS _Accu racy_of_Data_2009.pdf>.

For more information about the public transportation usage or other commuting characteristics of U.S. workers, go to the U.S.Census Bureau's Journey to Work and Migration Statistics Branch Web site, at <www. census.gov /popu lation/www/socdemo /journey.html>, or contact the Journey to Work and Migration Statistics Branch at 301 -763-2454.

Table 1. Top 15 U.S. Metropolitan Statistical Areas Ranked by Number of Workers Age 16 and Older Who Commuted to Work by Public Transportation: 2009

Rank	Metropolitan statistical area	Used public transportation	
		Number	Percent
1	New York-Northern New Jersey-Long Island, NY-NJ-PA	2,673,447	30.5
2	Chicago-Naperville-Joliet, IL-IN-WI	506,221	11.5
3	Washington-Arlington-Alexandria, DC-VA-MD-WV	404,829	14.1
4	Los Angeles-Long Beach-Santa Ana, CA	360,028	6.2
5	San Francisco-Oakland-Fremont, CA	304,111	14.6
6	Boston-Cambridge-Quincy, MA-NH	283,582	12.2
7	Philadelphia-Camden-Wilmington, PA-NJ-DE-MD	256,987	9.3
8	Seattle-Tacoma-Bellevue, WA	147,955	8.7
9	Atlanta-Sandy Springs-Marietta, GA	92,326	3.7
10	Miami-Fort Lauderdale-Pompano Beach, FL	85,771	3.5
11	Baltimore-Towson, MD	82,119	6.2
12	Minneapolis-St. Paul-Bloomington, MN-WI	78,837	4.7
13	Portland-Vancouver-Beaverton, OR-WA	63,877	6.1
14	Pittsburgh,PA	62,928	5.8
15	Houston-Sugar Land-Baytown, TX	60,547	2.2

Source: U.S. Census Bureau, American Community Survey, 2009.

Percentage of Workers Who Commuted by Public Transportation by Metropolitan Statistical Area: 2009

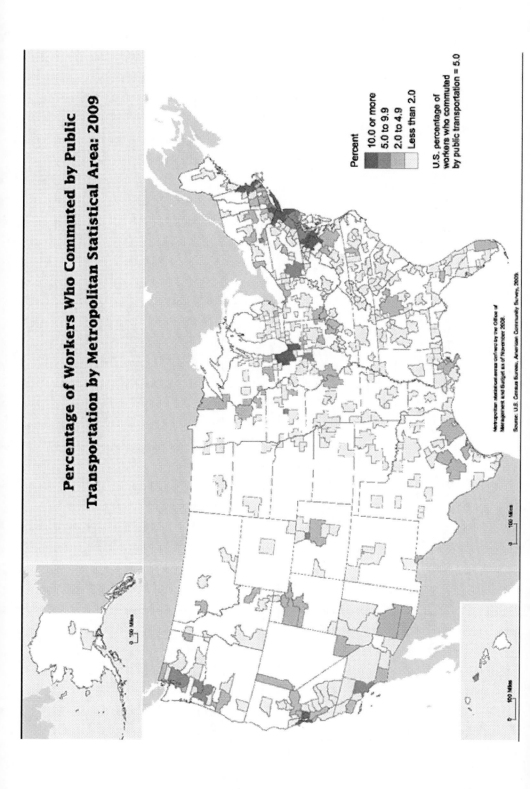

Percent

- 10.0 or more
- 5.0 to 9.9
- 2.0 to 4.9
- Less than 2.0

U.S. percentage of workers who commuted by public transportation = 5.0

Metropolitan statistical areas defined by the Office of Management and Budget as of November 2008.

Source: U.S. Census Bureau, American Community Survey, 2009.

Table 2. Public Transportation Usage for the 50 Largest Metropolitan Statistical Areas[1]: 2008 and 2009
(Estimates and percents are for members of the Armed Forces and civilians who were at work last week and used public transportation to get to work)

Metropolitan area	2008 public transportation				2009 public transportation				Change in public transportation usage (2009 less 2008)			
	Estimate	Margin of error[1] (±)	Percent	Margin of error[1] (±)	Estimate	Margin of error[1] (±)	Percent	Margin of error[1] (±)	Estimate	Margin of error[1] (±)	Percent	Margin of error[1] (±)
United States	7,186,530	46,249	5.0	0.1	6,922,424	42,396	5.0	0.1	−264,106	62,741	–	–
Atlanta-Sandy Springs-Marietta, GA	93,756	6,365	3.6	0.2	92,326	7,995	3.7	0.3	−1,430	10,219	0.1	0.4
Austin-Round Rock, TX	25,526	3,000	3.0	0.3	24,113	3,638	2.8	0.4	−1,413	4,716	−0.2	0.5
Baltimore-Towson, MD	88,056	5,544	6.5	0.4	82,119	5,132	6.2	0.4	−5,937	7,555	−0.3	0.6
Birmingham-Hoover, AL	4,569	1,229	0.9	0.2	3,360	1,063	0.7	0.2	−1,209	1,625	−0.2	0.3
Boston-Cambridge-Quincy, MA-NH	272,917	9,327	11.6	0.4	283,582	10,583	12.2	0.4	10,665	14,106	*0.6	0.6
Buffalo-Niagara Falls, NY	18,162	2,484	3.4	0.5	18,676	2,417	3.6	0.5	514	3,466	0.2	0.6
Charlotte-Gastonia-Concord, NC-SC	19,800	2,823	2.3	0.3	15,417	2,246	1.9	0.3	*−4,383	3,608	*−0.4	0.4

Table 2. (Continued)

Metropolitan area	2008 public transportation				2009 public transportation				Change in public transportation usage (2009 less 2008)			
	Estimate	Margin of error[1] (±)	Percent	Margin of error[1] (±)	Estimate	Margin of error[1] (±)	Percent	Margin of error[1] (±)	Estimate	Margin of error[1] (±)	Percent	Margin of error[1] (±)
Chicago-Naperville-Joliet, IL-IN-W	522,547	13,047	11.3	0.3	506,221	12,311	11.5	0.3	−16,326	17,938	0.2	0.4
Cincinnati-Middletown, OH-KY-IN	27,069	2,968	2.6	0.3	24,649	3,022	2.4	0.3	−2,420	4,236	−0.1	0.4
Cleveland-Elyria-Mentor, OH	38,435	3,216	3.9	0.3	35,493	3,565	3.8	0.4	−2,942	4,802	−0.1	0.5
Columbus, OH	15,070	2,138	1.7	0.2	11,897	2,160	1.4	0.3	*−3,173	3,039	−0.3	0.3
Dallas-Fort Worth-Arlington, TX	51,351	3,823	1.6	0.1	46,452	3,818	1.5	0.1	−4,899	5,403	−0.1	0.2
Denver-Aurora-Broomfi eld, CO	64,420	5,296	4.9	0.4	59,240	4,326	4.6	0.3	−5,180	6,838	−0.2	0.5
Detroit-Warren-Livonia, MI	34,107	3,304	1.7	0.2	28,939	3,422	1.6	0.2	*−5,168	4,757	−0.1	0.3
Hartford-West Hartford-East Hartford, CT	15,172	2,183	2.5	0.4	16,445	2,112	2.8	0.4	1,273	3,038	0.3	0.5
Houston-Sugar Land-Baytown, TX	71,908	5,349	2.6	0.2	60,547	4,929	2.2	0.2	*−11,361	7,274	*−0.4	0.3

Table 2. (Continued)

Metropolitan area	2008 public transportation				2009 public transportation				Change in public transportation usage (2009 less 2008)			
	Estimate	Margin of error[1] (∓)	Percent	Margin of error[1] (∓)	Estimate	Margin of error[1] (∓)	Percent	Margin of error[1] (∓)	Estimate	Margin of error[1] (∓)	Percent	Margin of error[1] (∓)
Indianapolis-Carmel, IN	10,277	2,000	1.2	0.2	8,310	1,678	1.0	0.2	−1,967	2,611	−0.2	0.3
Jacksonville, FL	7,660	1,733	1.2	0.3	7,343	1,730	1.2	0.3	−317	2,449	–	0.4
Kansas City, MO-KS	15,231	2,189	1.5	0.2	12,348	2,226	1.2	0.2	−2,883	3,122	−0.3	0.3
Las Vegas-Paradise, NV	33,140	4,234	3.7	0.5	27,834	2,590	3.2	0.3	*−5,306	4,963	−0.5	0.5
Los Angeles-Long Beach-Santa Ana, CA	380,484	12,110	6.4	0.2	360,028	13,185	6.2	0.2	*−20,456	17,903	−0.2	0.3
Louisville/Jefferson County, KY-IN	13,066	2,113	2.2	0.3	13,724	2,520	2.4	0.4	658	3,289	0.2	0.6
Memphis, TN-MS-AR	7,300	1,660	1.2	0.3	8,212	1,624	1.5	0.3	912	2,322	0.2	0.4
Miami-Fort Lauderdale-Pompano Beach, FL	93,277	6,184	3.7	0.2	85,771	6,434	3.5	0.3	−7,506	8,924	−0.2	0.4
Milwaukee-Waukesha-West Allis, WI	28,407	3,108	3.6	0.4	27,437	3,195	3.7	0.4	−970	4,457	–	0.6

Table 2. (Continued)

Metropolitan area	2008 public transportation				2009 public transportation				Change in public transportation usage (2009 less 2008)			
	Estimate	Margin of error[1] (±)	Percent	Margin of error[1] (±)	Estimate	Margin of error[1] (±)	Percent	Margin of error[1] (±)	Estimate	Margin of error[1] (±)	Percent	Margin of error[1] (±)
Minneapolis-St. Paul-Bloomington, MN-WI	83,771	4,355	4.8	0.2	78,837	4,762	4.7	0.3	-4,934	6,453	-0.1	0.4
Nashville-Davidson—Murfreesboro—Franklin, TN	7,896	1,443	1.0	0.2	8,829	1,622	1.2	0.2	933	2,171	0.1	0.3
New Orleans-Metairie-Kenner, LA	13,470	2,776	2.6	0.5	14,390	2,175	2.7	0.4	920	3,527	–	0.7
New York-Northern New Jersey- Long Island, NY-NJ-PA	2,755,897	24,847	30.4	0.3	2,673,447	26,566	30.5	0.3	*-82,450	36,374	0.1	0.4
Oklahoma City, OK	2,957	1,155	0.5	0.2	2,466	921	0.4	0.2	-491	1,477	-0.1	0.3
Orlando-Kissimmee, FL	15,214	2,209	1.5	0.2	17,368	2,816	1.8	0.3	2,154	3,579	0.3	0.4
Philadelphia-Camden-Wilmington, PA-NJ-DE-MD	257,961	9,317	9.3	0.3	256,987	10,409	9.3	0.4	-974	13,970	–	0.5
Phoenix-Mesa-Scottsdale, AZ	50,744	5,020	2.6	0.3	42,855	4,394	2.3	0.2	*-7,889	6,671	-0.3	0.3

Table 2. (Continued)

Metropolitan area	2008 public transportation				2009 public transportation				Change in public transportation usage (2009 less 2008)			
	Estimate	Margin of error[1] (∓)	Percent	Margin of error[1] (∓)	Estimate	Margin of error[1] (∓)	Percent	Margin of error[1] (∓)	Estimate	Margin of error[1] (∓)	Percent	Margin of error[1] (∓)
Pittsburgh, PA	65,071	4,227	5.8	0.4	62,928	3,767	5.8	0.3	–2,143	5,662	–	0.5
Portland-Vancouver-Beaverton, OR-A.	68,810	4,630	6.3	0.4	63,877	4,299	6.1	0.4	–4,933	6,318	–0.2	0.6
Providence-New Bedford-Fall River, RI-MA	21,389	2,459	2.7	0.3	20,534	2,518	2.7	0.3	–855	3,519	–	0.5
Raleigh-Cary, NC	5,702	1,454	1.0	0.3	5,231	1,328	1.0	0.2	–471	1,969	–0.1	0.4
Richmond, VA	12,514	2,152	2.0	0.4	11,676	2,003	2.0	0.3	–838	2,940	–	0.5
New York-Northern New Jersey-Long Island, NY-NJ-PA	2,755,897	24,847	30.4	0.3	2,673,447	26,566	30.5	0.3	*–82,450	36,374	0.1	0.4
Riverside-San Bernardino-Ontario, CA	31,211	4,078	1.8	0.2	28,913	3,469	1.8	0.2	–2,298	5,354	–	0.3
Sacramento-Arden-Arcade-Roseville, CA	27,158	2,665	2.8	0.3	24,632	3,254	2.7	0.4	–2,526	4,207	–0.1	0.4
St. Louis, MO-	38,115	3,827	2.8	0.3	33,881	3,215	2.6	0.2	–4,234	4,998	–0.2	0.4
Salt Lake City,	18,161	2,254	3.2	0.4	16,375	2,397	3.0	0.4	–1,786	3,290	–0.2	0.6
San Antonio, TX	23,335	3,098	2.5	0.3	21,342	3,492	2.3	0.4	–1,993	4,668	–0.2	0.5

Table 2. (Continued)

Metropolitan area	2008 public transportation				2009 public transportation				Change in public transportation usage (2009 less 2008)			
	Estimate	Margin of error[1] (±)	Percent	Margin of error[1] (±)	Estimate	Margin of error[1] (±)	Percent	Margin of error[1] (±)	Estimate	Margin of error[1] (±)	Percent	Margin of error[1] (±)
San Diego-Carlsbad- San Marcos, CA	48,489	4,521	3.4	0.3	43,289	3,659	3.1	0.3	−5,200	5,816	−0.3	0.4
San Francisco-Oakland-Fremont, CA	308,137	8,558	14.4	0.4	304,111	9,655	14.6	0.4	−4,026	12,902	0.2	0.6
San Jose-Sunnyvale-Santa Clara, CA	32,081	3,935	3.6	0.4	26,319	2,665	3.1	0.3	*−5,762	4,753	*−0.5	0.5
Seattle-Tacoma-Bellevue, WA	138,309	6,360	8.0	0.4	147,955	6,793	8.7	0.4	*9,646	9,306	*0.7	0.5
Tampa-St. Petersburg-Clearwater, FL	16,636	2,994	1.3	0.2	16,695	3,368	1.4	0.3	59	4,506	0.1	0.4
Virginia Beach-Norfolk-Newport News, VA-NC	18,283	3,098	2.2	0.4	11,973	2,256	1.4	0.3	*−6,310	3,833	*−0.7	0.5

Table 2. (Continued)

Metropolitan area	2008 public transportation				2009 public transportation				Change in public transportation usage (2009 less 2008)			
	Estimate	Margin of error[1] (±)	Percent	Margin of error[1] (±)	Estimate	Margin of error[1] (±)	Percent	Margin of error[1] (±)	Estimate	Margin of error[1] (±)	Percent	Margin of error[1] (±)
Washington-Arlington-Alexandria, DC-VA-MD-WV	387,332	10,326	13.4	0.4	404,829	12,540	14.1	0.4	*17,497	16,244	*0.8	0.6

– Represents or rounds to zero.

[1] Fifty most populous metropolitan statistical areas based on population estimates as of July 1, 2009. Metropolitan statistical area boundaries defi ned by the Offi ce of Management and Budget as of November 2008.

[2] Data are based on a sample and are subject to sampling variability. A margin of error is a measure of an estimate's variability. The larger the margin of error in relation to the size of the estimate, the less reliable the estimate. When added to and subtracted from the estimate, the margin of error forms the 90 percent confi dence interval.

Sources: U.S. Census Bureau, American Community Surveys, 2008 and 2009.

End Notes

[1] For more information on metropolitan statistical areas, please see <www.whitehouse.gov/omb /assets .pdf>.

[2] Percent public transportation usage for 1990 and 2000 was 5.12 and 4.57, respectively.

[3] The margins of error for estimates in Table 2 were calculated using an unrounded standard error.

[4] The percentage of public transportation commuters in the San Francisco-OaklandFremont, CA Metro Area was not statistically different from that of the Washington Arlington-Alexandria, DC-VA-MD-WV Metro Area.

[5] For the following metro areas, the percentage of workers who commuted by public transportation in 2009 exceeded and was statistically diff erent from 10 percent: Boston-Cambridge-Quincy, MA-NH; ChicagoNaperville-Joliet, IL-IN-WI; New York-Northern New Jersey-Long Island, NY-NJ-PA; San Francisco-Oakland-Fremont, CA; and Washington-Arlington-Alexandria, DC-VA-MDWV.

[6] The following metro areas experienced a statistically signifi cant decline in the number of public transportation commuters: Charlotte-Gastonia-Concord, NC-SC; Columbus, OH; Detroit-Warren-Livonia, MI; Houston-Sugar Land-Baytown, TX; Las Vegas- Paradise, NV; Los Angeles-Long Beach-Santa Ana, CA; New York-Northern New Jersey-Long Island, NY-NJ-PA; Phoenix-Mesa-Scottsdale, AZ; San Jose-Sunnyvale-Santa Clara, CA; and Virginia Beach-Norfolk-Newport News, VA-NC.

[7] The following metro areas experienced a statistically signifi cant decline in the percentage of public transportation commuters: Charlotte-Gastonia-Concord, NC-SC; Houston- Sugar Land-Baytown, TX; San Jose-SunnyvaleSanta Clara, CA; and Virginia Beach-Norfolk-Newport News, VA-NC.

[8] The following metro areas were not included among the 1 5 largest in 2009: Baltimore-Towson, MD; Minneapolis-St. Paul- Bloomington, MN-WI; Pittsburgh, PA; and Portland-Vancouver-Beaverton, OR-WA.

In: The American Community Survey ...   ISBN: 978-1-61324-362-6
Editors: B. M. Russo and A. D. Haffner   ©2011 Nova Science Publishers, Inc.

Chapter 7

PROPERTY VALUE: 2008 AND 2009

United States Census Bureau

INTRODUCTION

This report presents data on property value at the national level and for metropolitan statistical areas (metro areas) based on the 2008 and 2009 American Community Surveys (ACS).[1] The value of property is an important component in measuring neighborhood quality, housing aff ordability, and wealth. These data provide socioeconomic information not captured by household income and comparative information about metro housing markets.

The change in property values provides insight into the many countervailing pressures evident in metro housing markets throughout the nation. Record number of foreclosures, high levels of unemployment, and borrowers owing more on their mortgages than their homes are worth continued to depress housing markets while federal initiatives such as the first-time homebuyer tax credit and low mortgage interest rates attempted to provide some much needed stability.[2] The maps and table that accompany this report identify median property values in 2009 and percentage changes of property values between 2008 and 2009 for metro areas.

In the ACS, value is the owner's estimate of how much the property (house and lot, mobile home and lot, or condominium unit) would sell for if it were for sale.

Median value means that one-half of all homes were worth more and one-half were worth less. Median value estimates for 2008 were infl ation-adjusted to 2009 dollars.[3]

PROPERTY VALUE

In 2009, the median property value for owner-occupied homes in the United States was $185,200. Of all 366 metro areas, the median property values ranged from $76,100 in McAllen-EdinburgMission, TX, to $638,300 in San JoseSunnyvale-Santa Clara, California. Median property values were significantly below the national median in 247 metro areas while 107 had median property values significantly higher than the national median. Twelve metro areas were not significantly diff erent from the national median.

Among the 50 most populous metro areas, 20 metro areas had lower median property values and 29 had higher median property values than the national median. One metro area (Jacksonville, FL) was not significantly diff erent from the national median

Five of the ten highest median property values among the fifty most populous metro areas were located in California: San Jose-Sunnyvale-Santa Clara ($638,300), San Francisco-OaklandFremont ($591,600), Los Angeles-Long Beach-Santa Ana ($463,600), San DiegoCarlsbad-San Marcos ($417,700), and Sacramento–Arden-Arcade–Roseville ($298,000). The remaining five Metro Areas with the highest median property values were New York, Northern New Jersey-Long Island, NY-NJ-PA ($439,500); Washington Arlington-Alexandria, DC-VA-MD-WV ($387,900); Boston-Cambridge, Quincy, MA-NH ($369,200); SeattleTacoma-Bellevue, WA ($355,400); and Baltimore-Towson, MD ($299,200).[4]

The lowest median property value of the 50 most populous metro areas was Buff alo-Niagara Falls, NY ($116,000). Pittsburgh, PA, had the second lowest median property value at $1 20,600. Oklahoma City, OK ($1 23,400) and San Antonio, TX ($1 25,800) followed, though they were not significantly diff erent from one another. Rounding out the bottom five with a median property value of $1 35,800 was Memphis, TN-MS-AR.

CHANGE IN PROPERTY VALUE

Between 2008 and 2009, median property value decreased in the United States by 5.8 percent. The percentage change in the 366 metro areas ranged from a decline of 34.0 percent in Merced, CA, to an increase of 1 9.7 percent in Hattiesburg, MS. One hundred thirty-three metro areas experienced a decrease in median property value. Of these 133 metro areas, 54 had a percentage decrease that was lower than the national percentage decline of – 5.8 percent. Only 13 of the metro areas experienced an increase in median property value between 2008 and 2009.

Among the 50 most populous metro areas, none experienced a significant percentage increase in median property value. However, 1 5 had a percentage decrease in median property value significantly lower than the national percentage decline of –5.8 percent.

Of the 50 most populous metro areas with a percentage change in median property value of –9 percent or lower, 6 metro areas were located in California and 4 metro areas were located in Florida. Riverside-San Bernardino-Ontario, CA (–25.8 percent) and Las Vegas- Paradise, NV (–25.7 percent) had the largest percentage decreases in median property value between 2008 and 2009, though they were not significantly diff erent from one another.

SOURCE AND ACCURACY

Data presented in this report are based on people and households that responded to the ACS in 2008 and 2009. The resulting estimates are representative of the entire population. All comparisons presented in this report have taken sampling error into account and are significant at the 90 percent confidence level unless otherwise noted. Due to rounding, some details may not sum to totals. For information on sampling and estimation methods, confidentiality protection, and sampling and nonsampling errors, please see the "2009 ACS Accuracy of the Data" document located at <*www.census.gov/ acs/www/Downloads/data_documentation/Accu*racy/ACS_Accuracy_of Data_ 2009.pdf>.

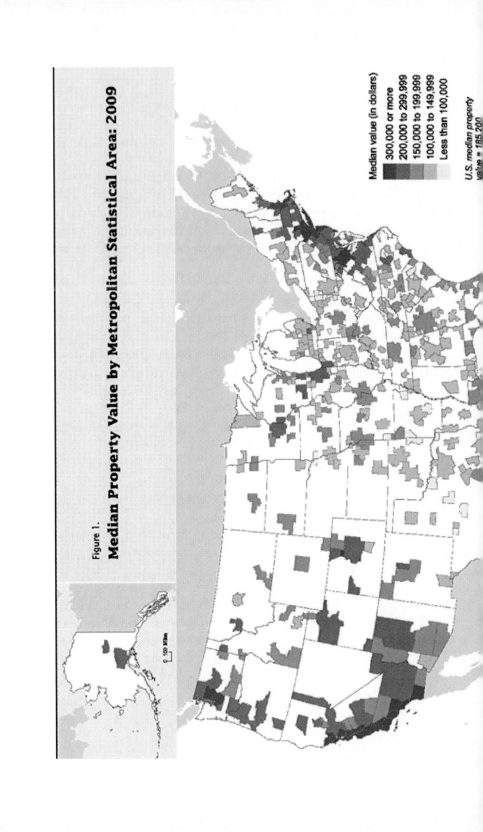

Figure 1.

Median Property Value by Metropolitan Statistical Area: 2009

Median value (in dollars)

300,000 or more
200,000 to 299,999
150,000 to 199,999
100,000 to 149,999
Less than 100,000

U.S. median property
value = 185,200

Figure 2.

Change in Median Property Value by Metropolitan Statistical Area: 2008 to 2009

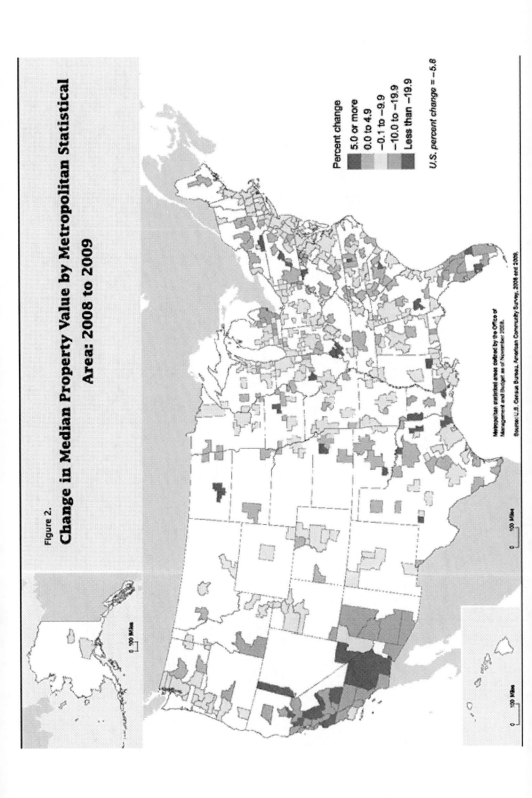

Percent change

5.0 or more
0.0 to 4.9
−0.1 to −9.9
−10.0 to −19.9
Less than −19.9

U.S. percent change = −5.8

Metropolitan statistical areas defined by the Office of
Management and Budget as of November 2008.

Source: U.S. Census Bureau, American Community Survey, 2008 and 2009.

0   100 Miles

0   100 Miles

0   100 Miles

Median Property Value by Metropolitan Statistical Area:[1] 2008 and 2009
(In 2009 inflation-adjusted dollars. Data are limited to owner-occupied housing units)

Area	2008 median property value (dollars)		2009 median property value (dollars)		Percent change in median property value (2009 less 2008)	
	Estimate	Margin of error[2] (±)	Estimate	Margin of error[2] (±)	Estimate	Margin of error[2] (±)
United States	**196,700**	**341**	**185,200**	**329**	***–5.8**	**0.2**
Atlanta-Sandy Springs-Marietta,	198,400	1,579	187,300	1,972	*–5.6	1.2
Austin-Round Rock, TX	187,800	2,840	189,300	2,947	0.8	2.2
Baltimore-Towson, MD	310,700	3,667	299,200	3,137	*–3.7	1.5
Birmingham-Hoover, AL	146,500	3,104	142,000	2,986	*–3.1	2.9
Boston-Cambridge-Quincy, MA-NH	382,600	2,760	369,200	2,200	*–3.5	0.9
Buffalo-Niagara Falls, NY	116,600	1,717	116,000	1,587	–0.5	2.0
Charlotte-Gastonia-Concord, NC-SC	178,900	3,629	173,800	2,055	*–2.9	2.3
Chicago-Naperville-Joliet, IL-IN-WI	268,100	1,460	249,600	1,600	*–6.9	0.8
Cincinnati-Middletown, OH-KY-IN	160,600	1,627	156,400	1,537	*–2.6	1.4
Cleveland-Elyria-Mentor, OH	152,500	1,441	147,400	1,784	*–3.3	1.5
Columbus, OH	165,900	1,628	162,700	1,690	*–1.9	1.4
Dallas-Fort Worth-Arlington, TX	148,100	1,066	149,700	1,306	1.1	1.1
Denver-Aurora-Broomfield, CO	249,700	2,294	248,500	2,142	–0.5	1.3
Detroit-Warren-Livonia, MI	164,000	947	139,900	1,679	*–14.7	1.1
Hartford-West Hartford-East Hartford, CT	266,000	3,538	259,700	2,978	*–2.4	1.7
Houston-Sugar Land-Baytown, TX	141,600	1,264	139,800	1,368	–1.3	1.3
Indianapolis-Carmel, IN	146,900	1,590	146,300	1,658	–0.4	1.6

(Continued)

Area	2008 median property value (dollars)		2009 median property value (dollars)		Percent change in median property value (2009 less 2008)	
	Estimate	Margin of error[2] (±)	Estimate	Margin of error[2] (±)	Estimate	Margin of error[2] (±)
Jacksonville,FL	203,300	3,841	185,000	3,330	*-9.0	2.4
Kansas City, MO-KS	161,500	1,417	158,500	1,634	*-1.9	1.3
Las Vegas-Paradise, NV	272,000	3,429	202,100	3,459	*-25.7	1.6
Los Angeles-Long Beach-Santa Ana, CA	550,200	3,556	463,600	2,804	*-15.7	0.7
Louisville/Jefferson County, KY-IN	146,600	2,172	145,400	2,055	-0.8	2.0
Memphis, TN-MS-AR	139,800	2,897	135,800	2,935	-2.9	2.9
Miami-Fort Lauderdale-Pompano Beach, FL	273,600	2,290	227,400	2,024	*-16.9	1.0
Milwaukee-Waukesha-West Allis, WI	211,300	2,188	207,100	2,738	*-2.0	1.6
Minneapolis-St. Paul-Bloomington, MN-WI	246,300	1,245	234,000	1,159	*-5.0	0.7
Nashville-Davidson-Murfreesboro-Franklin, TN	173,000	2,493	175,100	2,189	1.2	1.9
New Orleans-Metairie-Kenner, LA	183,600	3,227	181,500	2,695	-1.1	2.3
New York-Northern New Jersey-Long Island, NY-NJ-PA	459,200	1,772	439,500	1,722	*-4.3	0.5
Oklahoma City, OK	122,000	2,051	123,400	2,070	1.1	2.4
Orlando-Kissimmee, FL	231,900	2,537	191,600	3,082	*-17.4	1.6
Philadelphia-Camden-Wilmington, PA-NJ-DE-MD	253,900	1,917	248,100	1,727	*-2.3	1.0
Phoenix-Mesa-Scottsdale, AZ	243,000	1,894	196,300	2,507	*-19.2	1.2
Pittsburgh,PA	119,100	1,282	120,600	1,443	1.3	1.6
Portland-Vancouver-Beaverton, OR-WA	305,600	4,285	287,900	2,890	*-5.8	1.6
Providence-New Bedford-Fall River, RI-MA	295,200	2,617	274,700	2,818	*-6.9	1.3

(Continued)

Area	2008 median property value (dollars)		2009 median property value (dollars)		Percent change in median property value (2009 less 2008)	
	Estimate	Margin of error[2] (±)	Estimate	Margin of error[2] (±)	Estimate	Margin of error[2] (±)
Raleigh-Cary,NC	207,400	4,182	203,700	4,388	–1.8	2.9
Richmond, VA	239,900	2,917	230,400	2,578	*–4.0	1.6
Riverside-San Bernardino-Ontario, CA	329,800	2,968	244,800	2,559	*–25.8	1.0
Sacramento–Arden-Arcade–Roseville, CA	350,500	3,096	298,000	3,509	*–15.0	1.3
St. Louis,MO-IL	163,800	1,470	160,500	1,265	*–2.0	1.2
Salt Lake City, UT	254,500	4,084	243,900	3,049	*–4.2	1.9
San Antonio, TX	125,700	2,305	125,800	2,403	0.1	2.7
San Diego-Carlsbad-San Marcos, CA	479,800	4,272	417,700	5,353	*–12.9	1.4
San Francisco-Oakland-Fremont, CA	669,100	4,924	591,600	5,792	*–11.6	1.1
San Jose-Sunnyvale-Santa Clara, CA	719,700	8,074	638,300	7,474	*–11.3	1.4
Seattle-Tacoma-Bellevue, WA	378,900	2,830	355,400	2,611	*–6.2	1.0
Tampa-St. Petersburg-Clearwater, FL	193,500	1,873	166,000	1,514	*–14.2	1.1
Virginia Beach-Norfolk-Newport News, VA-NC	257,300	3,130	249,600	2,939	*–3.0	1.6
Washington-Arlington-Alexandria, DC-VA-MD-WV	426,500	2,866	387,900	2,520	*–9.1	0.9

* Statistically different at the 90 percent confidence level.

[1] Fifty most populous metropolitan statistical areas based on population estimates as of July 1, 2009. Metropolitan statistical areas defined by the Office of Management and Budget as of November 2008.

[2] Data are based on a sample and are subject to sampling variability. A margin of error is a measure of an estimate's variability. The larger the margin of error in relation to the size of the estimate, the less reliable the estimate. When added to and subtracted from the estimate, the margin of error forms the 90 percent confidence interval.

Sources: U.S. Census Bureau, American Community Surveys, 2008 and 2009.

End Notes

[1] For more information on metro areas, please see <www.whitehouse.gov/omb/assets *.pdf*>.

[2] For a more in-depth discussion of this and related issues see Joint Center for Housing Studies of Harvard University, State of the Nation's Housing 2010, <www.jchs.harvard.edu/son/index.htm>.

[3] For more information on property value, please see <www.census.gov/acs/ www/ UseData/Def.htm>.

[4] The median property values of Sacramento–Arden-Arcade–Roseville, CA Metro Area and Baltimore-Towson, MD Metro Area are not significantly diff erent from one another.

In: The American Community Survey ...   ISBN: 978-1-61324-362-6
Editors: B. M. Russo and A. D. Haffner   ©2011 Nova Science Publishers, Inc.

Chapter 8

RENTAL HOUSING MARKET CONDITION MEASURES: 2009

United States Census Bureau

INTRODUCTION

This report presents data from the 2009 American Community Survey (ACS) on rental market conditions, including share of occupied housing, housing costs, housing cost "burden," and vacancy rate at the national level and for metropolitan statistical areas (metro areas).[1]

Rental housing is catapulting to the top of the national housing agenda, The past 30 years have witnessed a housing policy that has been focused on promoting homeownership. The large gap between the number of renting households and the units that they can aff ord will only grow as foreclosures persist and home mortgages become increasingly scarce for all but the most qualified buyers.[2] Consequently, rental housing is getting a second look as an important component of a national housing policy.[3] A high rental vacancy rate coupled with a low share of homes that are renter-occupied generally implies more housing choices available for renting households. The share of burdened households can be lower in such markets. Conversely, a low rental vacancy rate in a market with a high percentage of renter households can signify a tighter rental market, fewer housing choices, and more aff ordability problems, particularly for low-income households. In these markets, the shares of burdened renters are often higher.

Gross rent: The monthly amount of rent plus the estimated average monthly cost of utilities (electricity, gas, water, and sewer) and fuels (oil, coal, kerosene, wood, etc.).

Gross rent as a percentage of income: The ratio of gross rent to household income. It is used as a measure of housing aff ordability by policymakers and as a determinant of eligibility for federal housing programs and is often referred to as housing cost burden.

For this report, a renting household is considered "burdened" if the household is required to spend 35 percent or more of its income on housing costs.

Rental vacancy rate: The proportion of the rental inventory that is vacant "for rent." It is computed by dividing the number of vacant units "for rent" by the sum of renter-occupied units, vacant units "for rent," and vacant units that have been rented but not yet occupied, and then multiplying by 100.

RENTAL HOUSING MARKET MEASURES

Housing Costs

In 2009, median gross rent in the metro areas in the United States ranged from $495 in the Johnstown, PA Metro Area and the Wheeling, WV-OH Metro Area to $1,414 in the San Jose-SunnyvaleSanta Clara, CA Metro Area compared with the national median of $842. Among the 366 metro areas, 247 (67.5 percent) had a median gross rent below the national median, 68 (1 8.6 percent) had a median gross rent above the national median and 51 (13.9 per-cent) were not statistically diff erent from the national median.

A comparison of all metro areas to the national median masks the tighter rental conditions faced by renters living in higher density metro areas. Out of the 50 most populous metro areas, the average renter household in 27 (54 percent) spent more on rent than the national median, those in 1 7 (34 percent) spent less than the national median, and those in 6 (12 percent) were not statistically diff erent from the national median.

Among the 50 most populous metro areas, the Pittsburgh, PA Metro Area had the lowest median gross rent ($643). Pittsburgh, PA, was followed by the Metro Areas: Buff alo-Niagara Falls, NY; Louisville/Jeff erson County, KY-IN; Cincinnati-Middletown, OH-KY-IN; Oklahoma City, OK; and Cleveland-Elyria-Mentor, OH, where rents were between $652 and $706. The St. Louis, MO-IL Metro Area rounded out the most aff ordable markets with a median gross rent of $732.

The San Jose-Sunnyvale-Santa Clara, CA Metro Area, with a gross rent of $1,414 was the most expensive rental market among the 50 most populous metro areas. Following San Jose-Sunnyvale-Santa Clara, CA was the San Francisco-OaklandFremont, CA Metro Area and the Washington-Arlington-Alexandria, DC-VA-MD-WV Metro Area, both with median gross rent of $1,303. The fourth highest median gross rent was in the San DiegoCarlsbad-San Marcos, CA Metro Area ($1,224); the fifth highest median gross rent was in the Los Angeles-Long Beach-Santa Ana, CA Metro Area ($1,197). Rounding out the top seven most expensive Metro Areas are New York-Northern New Jersey-Long Island, NY-NJ-PA ($1,125) and Boston-CambridgeQuincy, MA-NH ($1,123), which were not significantly diff erent from each other.

Renter Burden

Nationwide, nearly 2 in 5 renter households (42.5 percent) were burdened by housing costs consuming 35 percent or more of their incomes. Housing cost burdens ranged from a low of 23.2 percent of renting households in the Casper, WY Metro Area to a high of 62.7 percent of renting households in the College Station-Bryan, TX Metro Area, which could be due to a large student population. Renters living in 196 of the 366 metro areas (53.6 percent) mirrored the nation, with no statistical diff erence between their shares of burdened renters and the national 42.5 percent share. Ninety-one metro areas (24.9 percent) had shares of burdened renters that were significantly lower than the nation's 42.5 percent share; while the shares of burdened renters living in 79 metro areas (21 .6 percent) were significantly higher than the share of burdened renters nationwide.

Despite the high gross rents faced by renters living in the 50 most populous metro areas, their incomes appear to have compensated making them less likely to be burdened by high shelter costs. Shares of burdened renters living in 18 of the metro areas (36 percent) were lower than the nation. In 1 3 metro areas (26 percent) shares were higher than the nation. Nineteen (38 percent) had shares of burdened renters that were not significantly diff erent from the nation.

Some of the heaviest burdens in the 50 most populous metro areas were borne by renters in Florida and California, states hard hit by the housing market-led recession. In Miami-Fort Lauderdale-Pompano Beach, FL, more than one-half (54.3 percent) of renting households were burdened. In Orlando-Kissimmee, FL, 50.8 percent of renters were burdened. The share in Orlando-Kissimmee, FL, while lower than the share of burdened renters in Miami-Fort Lauderdale- Pompano Beach, FL, did not diff er from the shares of burdened renters in New Orleans-Metairie-Kenner, LA (49.7 percent) or Riverside-San Bernardino-Ontario, CA (48.7 percent).

Rental Vacancy Rate

Nationwide, the rental vacancy rate was 8.4 percent. The rates in the nation's metro areas ranged from 0.5 percent in the Logan, UT-ID Metro Area to 33.4 percent in the Myrtle Beach-North Myrtle Beach- Conway, SC Metro Area. Excess rental inventory was less likely to plague metro areas than the national rental housing market as a whole, with 1 07 (29.2 percent) of all metro areas having a rental vacancy rate below the national rental vacancy rate and 72 (19.7 percent) having vacancy rates above the national rate. Vacancy rates in 187 (51.1 percent) were not statistically diff erent from the 8.4 percent national rate.

Unlike all metropolitan statistical areas combined, the 50 most populous metro areas did not compare as favorably to the nation's rental housing market when vacancy rates are used as a barometer. Of the 50 most populous metropolitan statistical areas, 21 metro areas (42 percent) had rental vacancy rates above the national rate while 1 5 (30 percent) had rental vacancy rates below the national rate. The rental vacancy rates in 14 of the 50 most populous metro areas (28 percent) were not significantly diff erent from the nation's vacancy rate.

Figure 1.

Percent of Renters Spending 35 Percent or More of Household Income for Gross Rent by Metropolitan Statistical Area: 2009

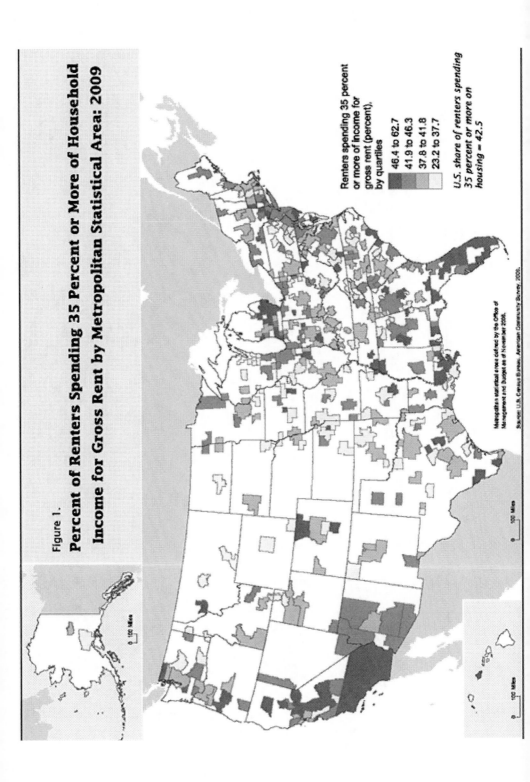

Renters spending 35 percent or more of income for gross rent (percent), by quartiles

- 46.4 to 62.7
- 41.9 to 46.3
- 37.8 to 41.8
- 23.2 to 37.7

U.S. share of renters spending 35 percent or more on housing = 42.5

Metropolitan statistical areas defined by the Office of Management and Budget as of November 2008.

Source: U.S. Census Bureau, American Community Survey 2009.

0 100 Miles

0 100 Miles

0 100 Miles

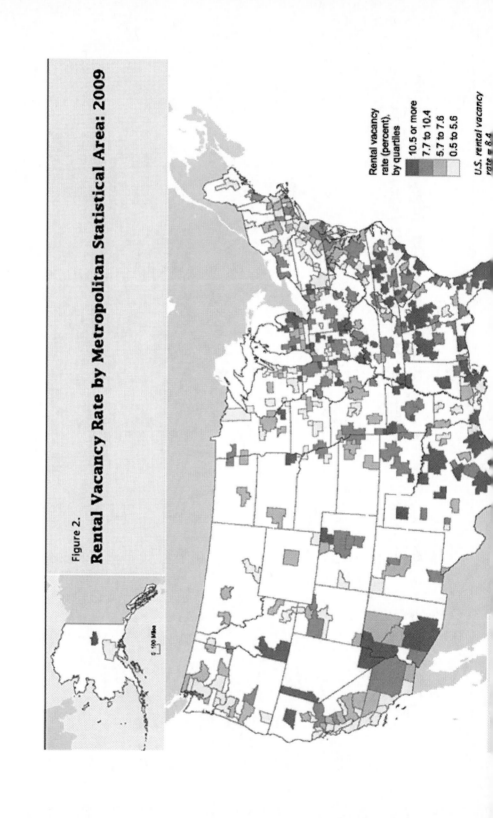

Figure 2.

Rental Vacancy Rate by Metropolitan Statistical Area: 2009

0 100 Miles

Rental vacancy
rate (percent),
by quartiles

10.5 or more
7.7 to 10.4
5.7 to 7.6
0.5 to 5.6

U.S. rental vacancy
rate = 8.4

Twelve of the fifty most populous metro areas had double digit rental vacancy rates. These Metro Areas are: Jacksonville, FL; Atlanta-Sandy Springs-Marietta, GA; Memphis, TNMS-AR; Phoenix-Mesa-Scottsdale, AZ; Tampa-St. Petersburg- Clearwater, FL; Orlando-Kissimmee, FL; Houston-Sugarland-Baytown, TX; Las Vegas-Paradise, NV; Dallas- Fort Worth-Arlington, TX; San Antonio, TX; Miami-Fort Lauderdale- Pompano Beach, FL; and DetroitWarren-Livonia, MI.

San Jose-Sunnyvale-Santa Clara, CA (3.4 percent) and Milwaukee-Waukesha-West Allis, WI (4.3 per-cent) had the lowest rental vacancy rates, but were not statistically diff erent from each other. While the rental vacancy rate in MilwaukeeWaukesha-West Allis, WI, did not diff er from New York-Northern New Jersey-Long Island, NY-NJ-PA (5.0 percent); San Diego-CarlsbadSan Marcos, CA (5.0 percent); and Seattle-Tacoma-Bellevue, WA (5.1), the rental vacancy rate in San JoseSunnyvale-Santa Clara, CA, was significantly lower than the rental vacancy rates in the remaining 48 of the 50 most populous metro areas.

For more information, the U.S. Census Bureau and the Department of Housing and Urban Development also publish renter share of occupied housing, housing costs for renters, renter burden, and rental vacancy rates for the United States and selected metropolitan statistical areas in the *American Housing Survey (AHS)*. The Current Population Survey (CPS)/Housing Vacancy Survey (HVS) is the official source of the rental vacancy rate and share of renter-occupied housing units for the United States, the 50 states, and the 75 largest metro areas. The housing cost data available from the HVS are limited to asking rents for vacant rental units in the United States. HVS does not purport to measure housing cost burden.

Rental Market Conditions Measures by Metropolitan Statistical Area:[1] 2009

Area	Renter occupied (percent)		Median gross rent (dollars)		Share of renters spending 35 percent or more of income for gross rent (percent)		Rental vacancy rate (percent)	
	Estimate	Margin of error[2] (±)	Estimate	Margin of error[2] (±)	Estimate	Margin of error[2] (±)	Estimate	Margin of error[2] (±)
United States	**34.13**	**0.1**	**842**	**2**	**42.48**	**0.1**	**8.43**	**0.1**
Atlanta-Sandy Springs-Marietta, GA	31.52	0.5	912	8	43.04	1.2	13.96	0.9
Austin-Round Rock, TX	41.34	1.0	909	14	41.55	1.8	7.78	1.0
Baltimore-Towson, MD	31.99	0.7	1,048	17	44.58	1.6	8.23	0.9
Birmingham-Hoover, AL	29.53	1.1	758	12	45.47	2.4	11.75	1.8
Boston-Cambridge-Quincy, MA-NH	36.56	0.5	1,123	12	38.76	1.1	5.56	0.6
Buffalo-Niagara Falls, NY.	33.42	0.9	663	11	45.58	2.2	8.01	1.3
Charlotte-Gastonia-Concord, NC-SC	33.09	0.9	793	12	38.79	1.9	8.91	1.2
Chicago-Naperville-Joliet, IL-IN-WI	33.03	0.4	900	7	43.26	0.8	8.73	0.5
Cincinnati-Middletown, OH-KY-IN.	31.79	0.7	686	13	40.46	1.9	10.89	1.1
Cleveland-Elyria-Mentor, OH	33.61	0.7	695	11	44.03	1.7	9.69	0.9
Columbus, OH	36.77	0.8	757	12	38.57	1.7	10.40	1.1
Dallas-Fort Worth-Arlington, TX	37.79	0.5	846	6	38.97	1.0	12.12	0.6

(Continued)

Area	Renter occupied (percent)		Median gross rent (dollars)		Share of renters spending 35 percent or more of income for gross rent (percent)		Rental vacancy rate (percent)	
	Estimate	Margin of error² (±)	Estimate	Margin of error² (±)	Estimate	Margin of error² (±)	Estimate	Margin of error² (±)
Denver-Aurora-Broomfield, CO	34.40	0.8	876	13	41.65	1.4	7.75	1.0
Detroit-Warren-Livonia, MI	27.96	0.5	783	8	47.04	1.3	11.05	0.9
Hartford-West Hartford-East Hartford, CT	30.34	0.9	917	17	43.00	2.1	7.85	1.3
Houston-Sugar Land-Baytown, TX	37.74	0.5	848	7	40.52	1.1	12.27	0.7
Indianapolis-Carmel, IN	33.63	0.9	750	13	39.83	1.8	9.50	1.3
Jacksonville,FL	32.16	1.0	903	21	44.68	2.5	14.09	1.5
Kansas City, MO-KS	32.05	0.8	763	12	36.10	1.9	10.31	1.2
Las Vegas-Paradise, NV	43.12	0.9	1,034	19	43.03	1.6	12.15	1.3
Los Angeles-Long Beach-Santa Ana, CA	49.27	0.4	1,197	8	47.27	0.6	5.29	0.3
Louisville/Jefferson County, KY-IN	31.45	1.2	675	9	38.95	2.4	9.84	1.2
Memphis, TN-MS-AR	36.14	1.1	765	11	47.19	2.2	13.87	1.6
Miami-Fort Lauderdale-Pompano Beach, FL	35.39	0.5	1,077	11	54.35	1.2	11.75	0.7
Milwaukee-Waukesha-West Allis, WI	37.65	0.8	766	10	42.42	1.6	4.28	0.9

(Continued)

Area	Renter occupied (percent)		Median gross rent (dollars)		Share of renters spending 35 percent or more of income for gross rent (percent)		Rental vacancy rate (percent)	
	Estimate	Margin of error[2] (±)	Estimate	Margin of error[2] (±)	Estimate	Margin of error[2] (±)	Estimate	Margin of error[2] (±)
Minneapolis-St. Paul-Bloomington, MN-WI	27.57	0.6	840	12	41.27	1.5	5.91	0.7
Nashville-Davidson–Murfreesboro–Franklin, TN	32.24	0.9	784	14	39.22	2.4	10.23	1.5
New Orleans-Metairie-Kenner, LA	34.41	1.0	890	14	49.71	2.5	11.07	1.5
New York-Northern New Jersey-Long Island, NY-NJ-PA	47.29	0.3	1,125	5	42.93	0.5	5.04	0.2
Oklahoma City, OK	34.67	0.9	689	15	41.77	2.5	8.02	1.2
Orlando-Kissimmee, FL	33.87	0.9	982	10	50.75	1.9	12.91	1.2
Philadelphia-Camden-Wilmington, PA-NJ-DE-MD	30.43	0.5	912	10	43.32	1.0	8.91	0.7
Phoenix-Mesa-Scottsdale, AZ	33.65	0.6	912	12	43.07	1.5	13.58	0.9
Pittsburgh,PA	29.84	0.7	643	9	38.19	1.3	5.61	0.9
Portland-Vancouver-Beaverton, OR-WA	37.92	0.8	876	9	41.38	1.4	5.60	0.9
Providence-New Bedford-Fall River, RI-MA	36.08	0.8	844	17	39.33	1.8	7.25	1.0
Raleigh-Cary,NC	31.48	1.1	842	12	37.63	2.4	11.44	1.9

(Continued)

Area	Renter occupied (percent)		Median gross rent (dollars)		Share of renters spending 35 percent or more of income for gross rent (percent)		Rental vacancy rate (percent)	
	Estimate	Margin of error[2] (±)	Estimate	Margin of error[2] (±)	Estimate	Margin of error[2] (±)	Estimate	Margin of error[2] (±)
Richmond, VA	31.00	1.1	901	20	42.67	2.2	7.78	1.4
Riverside-San Bernardino-Ontario, CA	34.14	0.7	1,084	14	48.70	1.4	8.14	0.8
Sacramento–Arden-Arcade–Roseville, CA	38.40	0.8	998	16	46.76	1.7	8.02	1.0
St. Louis,MO-IL	29.31	0.7	732	9	41.21	1.6	6.54	0.9
Salt Lake City, UT..	30.59	1.2	835	19	41.29	2.5	8.08	1.7
San Antonio, TX	34.99	0.9	765	12	39.20	2.0	11.89	1.3
San Diego-Carlsbad-San Marcos, CA	44.82	0.6	1,224	14	48.05	1.3	5.05	0.5
San Francisco-Oakland-Fremont, CA	44.46	0.6	1,303	16	40.20	1.1	5.46	0.6
San Jose-Sunnyvale-Santa Clara, CA	41.12	1.0	1,414	21	37.37	1.7	3.40	0.7
Seattle-Tacoma-Bellevue, WA.	38.23	0.6	1,015	13	38.76	1.3	5.13	0.7
Tampa-St. Petersburg-Clearwater, FL	32.14	0.8	908	13	45.52	1.6	13.44	1.1
Virginia Beach-Norfolk-Newport News, VA-NC	36.84	0.9	984	19	41.03	1.9	6.16	1.0

(Continued)

Area	Renter occupied (percent)		Median gross rent (dollars)		Share of renters spending 35 percent or more of income for gross rent (percent)		Rental vacancy rate (percent)	
	Estimate	Margin of error[2] (±)	Estimate	Margin of error[2] (±)	Estimate	Margin of error[2] (±)	Estimate	Margin of error[2] (±)
Washington–Arlington–Alexandria, DC-VA-MD-WV	33.99	0.5	1,303	11	38.14	1.0	6.95	0.6

[1] Fifty most populous metropolitan statistical areas based on population estimates as of July 1, 2009. Metropolitan statistical area boundaries defined by the Office of Management and Budget as of November 2008.

[2] Data are based on a sample and are subject to sampling variability. A margin of error is a measure of an estimate's variability. The larger the margin of error in relation to the size of the estimate, the less reliable the estimate. When added to and subtracted from the estimate, the margin of error forms the 90 percent confidence interval.

Source: U.S. Census Bureau, American Community Survey, 2009.

SOURCE AND ACCURACY

Data presented in this report are based on people and households that responded to the ACS in 2009. The resulting estimates are representative of the entire population. All comparisons presented in this report have taken sampling error into account and are significant at the 90 percent confidence level unless otherwise noted. Due to rounding, some details may not sum to totals. For information on sampling and estimation methods, confidentiality protection, sampling and nonsampling errors, please see the "2009 ACS Accuracy of the Data" document located at <www.census.gov/acs/www /Downloads/data _docu mentation/Accuracy/ACS_Accuracy_of_Data_ 2009. pdf>.

End Notes

[1] For a detailed explanation of the metropolitan statistical areas in this report, go to <www. whitehouse.gov/omb/assets .pdf>.

[2] Fannie Mae in a February 26, 2010, letter to lenders entitled "An Introduction to Fannie Mae's Loan Quality Initiative" outlines rigid procedures to which lenders wishing to sell it mortgages must adhere, including borrower disclosure of all liabilities on the final loan application, as well as new emphasis on providing sound monthly debt to income ratios at the time of the delivery of the mortgage to Fannie Mae.

[3] The Dodd-Frank Wall Street Reform and Consumer Protection Act requires the Obama Administration to develop a proposal for housing reform by early 2011, including restructuring Fannie Mae and Freddie Mac, The U.S. Department of Housing and Urban Development (HUD) expects that the promotion of rental housing will be a cornerstone of the proposal. In a July 21, 2010, article in *The Washington Post*, HUD Secretary Shaun Donovan stated "While we continue to promote aff ordable homeownership, for many Americans renting will continue to be the only or preferred option."

In: The American Community Survey ...   ISBN: 978-1-61324-362-6
Editors: B. M. Russo and A. D. Haffner   ©2011 Nova Science Publishers, Inc.

Chapter 9

FOOD STAMP/SUPPLEMENTAL NUTRITION ASSISTANCE PROGRAM (SNAP) RECEIPT IN THE PAST 12 MONTHS FOR HOUSEHOLDS BY STATE: 2008 AND 2009

United States Census Bureau

INTRODUCTION

This report presents data on food stamp/SNAP receipt for the past 12 months at the national and state levels based on the 2008 and 2009 American Community Surveys (ACS). The data in this report are for households, not individuals. If any person living at the sample address at the time of the interview received food stamps/SNAP, the household is included in the count. Respondents were asked to report any spells of food stamp/SNAP receipt for the past 12 months.

FOOD STAMP/SNAP RECEIPT IN 2009

In 2009, the American Recovery and Reinvestment Act (ARRA) was signed into law as a direct result of the economic downturn. The ARRA provided increased food stamp/SNAP benefits to low-income families.

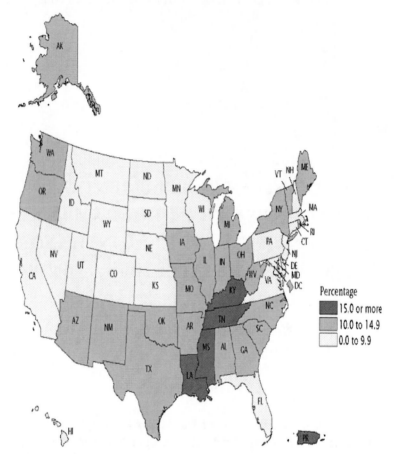

Sources: U.S. Census Bureau, American Community Survey, 2009, Puerto Rico
Community Survey, 2009.

Figure 1. Percentage Receiving Food Stamps/Supplemental Nutrition Assistance
(SNAP) for Households by State and Puerto Rico: 2009.

In 2009, 11.7 million households reported receiving food stamp/ SNAP
benefits during the past 12 months. Among the states with the highest food
stamp/SNAP participation were Louisiana (17.4 percent), Tennessee (15.3
percent), and Kentucky (15.1 percent).[1]

The Food Stamp Act of 1977 defines this federally-funded program as
one intended to "permit low-income households to obtain a more nutritious
diet" (from Title XIII of Public Law 95-113, The Food Stamp Act of 1977,
declaration of policy). Food purchasing power is increased by providing

eligible households with coupons or cards that can be used to purchase food. The Food and Nutrition Service (FNS) of the U.S. Department of Agriculture (USDA) administers the Food Stamp Program through state and local welfare offices. The Food Stamp Program is the major national income support program to which all low-income and low-resource households, regardless of household characteristics, are eligible.

The questions on participation in the Food Stamp Program were designed to identify households in which one or more of the current members received food stamps during the past 12 months.

In 2008, the Food Stamp Program was renamed the Supplemental Nutrition Assistance Program (SNAP).

Although not statistically different when compared with some other states, states with the lowest food stamp/SNAP participation rates included Colorado (6.1 percent), New Jersey (5.5 percent), and Wyoming (5.2 percent).

FOOD STAMP/SNAP RECEIPT IN 2008 AND 2009

In 2009, 10.3 percent of all households reported receipt of food stamps/SNAP, a 19.8 percent increase over the 2008 figure of 8.6 percent. No states experienced a decline in food stamps/SNAP receipt between 2008 and 2009. Forty-six states, the District of Columbia, and Puerto Rico experienced an increase in food stamp/ SNAP receipt. The only states that did not experience a statistically significant increase were Hawaii, Maine, Montana, and North Dakota.

Although not statistically different from several other states, the food stamp/SNAP receipt increased by 32.4 percent in Florida, 32.2 percent in New Hampshire, and 31.3 percent in Nevada between 2008 and 2009.

Altogether, there were eight states in which the increase in food stamp/SNAP receipt was larger than the national increase of 1 9.8 percent, and eleven states with increases that were smaller than the national increase (Figure 2).

SOURCE AND ACCURACY

Data presented in this report are based on people and households that responded to the ACS in 2008 and 2009. The resulting estimates are representative of the entire population. All comparisons presented in this report have taken sampling error into account and are significant at the 90 percent confidence level unless otherwise noted. Due to rounding, some details may not sum to totals. For information on sampling and estimation methods, confidentiality protection, and sampling and nonsampling errors, please see the "2009 ACS Accuracy of the Data" document located at <www.census. gov/acs /www/Down loads/data _documentation/Accuracy/ACS_Accu racy_ of_ Data_2009.pdf>.

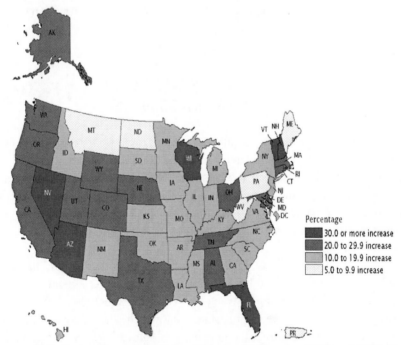

Sources: U.S. Census Bureau, American Community Surveys, 2008 and 2009, Puerto Rico Community Surveys, 2008 and 2009.

Figure 2. Percent Change in Food Stamp/Supplemental Nutrition Assistance (SNAP) Receipt for Households by State and Puerto Rico: 2008 and 2009.

Food Stamp/Supplemental Nutrition Assistance program (SNAP) Receipt in the past 12 Months for Households by State and puerto Rico: 2008 and 2009

Area	Food stamp/SNAP receipt in 2008				Food stamp/SNAP receipt in 2009				Change in food stamp/SNAP receipt			
	Estimate	Margin of error[1] (±)	Percentage	Margin of error[1] (±)	Estimate	Margin of error[1] (±)	Percentage	Margin of error[1] (±)	Estimate	Margin of error[1] (±)	Percentage	Margin of error[1] (±)
United States	9,770,597	49,238	8.6	0.1	11,707,519	48,656	10.3	0.1	1,936,922	69,223	*19.8	0.8
Alabama	186,630	6,756	10.3	0.4	235,122	7,393	12.7	0.4	48,492	10,015	*26.0	6.0
Alaska	18,825	1,815	7.9	0.8	23,699	2,465	10.0	1.0	4,874	3,061	*25.9	17.9
Arizona	186,071	8,165	8.2	0.4	244,136	9,376	10.7	0.4	58,065	12,433	*31.2	7.7
Arkansas	140,865	5,668	12.6	0.5	157,428	5,591	14.0	0.5	16,563	7,962	*11.8	6.0
California	624,731	12,717	5.1	0.1	754,865	13,278	6.2	0.1	130,134	18,386	*20.8	3.3
Colorado	95,111	5,109	5.0	0.3	116,941	5,077	6.1	0.3	21,830	7,203	*23.0	8.5
Connecticut	87,102	4,342	6.6	0.3	107,127	4,818	8.1	0.4	20,025	6,486	*23.0	8.3
Delaware	24,322	2,269	7.4	0.7	30,371	2,804	9.3	0.9	6,049	3,607	*24.9	16.4
District of Columbia	27,032	2,188	10.8	0.9	32,032	2,737	12.8	1.1	5,000	3,505	*18.5	13.9
Florida	504,043	12,589	7.1	0.2	667,567	13,808	9.6	0.2	163,524	18,685	*32.4	4.3
Georgia	320,790	9,125	9.2	0.3	378,962	8,892	10.9	0.2	58,172	12,741	*18.1	4.4
Hawaii	31,443	2,688	7.2	0.6	34,900	3,005	7.8	0.7	3,457	4,032	11.0	13.5
Idaho	43,218	3,610	7.6	0.6	49,288	3,365	8.8	0.6	6,070	4,935	*14.0	12.3
Illinois	416,101	9,487	8.7	0.2	486,801	10,413	10.2	0.2	70,700	14,086	*17.0	3.7
Indiana	226,864	7,639	9.1	0.3	267,661	8,452	10.8	0.3	40,797	11,392	*18.0	5.4
Iowa	107,115	4,585	8.8	0.4	123,219	5,166	10.0	0.4	16,104	6,908	*15.0	6.9

(Continued)

Area	Food stamp/SNAP receipt in 2008				Food stamp/SNAP receipt in 2009				Change in food stamp/SNAP receipt			
	Estimate	Margin of error[1] (±)	Percent-age	Margin of error[1] (±)	Estimate	Margin of error[1] (±)	Percent-age	Margin of error[1] (±)	Estimate	Margin of error[1] (±)	Percent-age	Margin of error[1] (±)
Kansas	78,258	4,192	7.0	0.4	91,291	3,873	8.3	0.3	13,033	5,707	*16.7	8.0
Kentucky	230,001	7,352	13.6	0.4	255,794	6,607	15.1	0.4	25,793	9,884	*11.2	4.6
Louisiana	264,816	7,863	16.3	0.5	293,164	8,739	17.4	0.5	28,348	11,756	*10.7	4.7
Maine	73,984	3,725	13.6	0.7	78,873	4,202	14.5	0.8	4,889	5,616	6.6	7.8
Maryland	114,870	5,947	5.5	0.3	147,415	5,156	7.0	0.3	32,545	7,871	*28.3	8.0
Massachusetts	191,055	6,347	7.7	0.3	233,115	7,834	9.4	0.3	42,060	10,083	*22.0	5.8
Michigan	465,280	7,882	12.2	0.2	555,220	11,569	14.5	0.3	89,940	13,998	*19.3	3.2
Minnesota	114,501	4,499	5.5	0.2	131,783	5,803	6.3	0.3	17,282	7,343	*15.1	6.8
Mississippi	144,994	5,437	13.2	0.5	164,624	6,259	15.0	0.6	19,630	8,290	*13.5	6.1
Missouri	260,372	7,236	11.2	0.3	293,576	7,316	12.5	0.3	33,204	10,290	*12.8	4.2
Montana	30,432	2,454	8.1	0.6	32,887	2,497	8.8	0.7	2,455	3,501	8.1	12.0
Nebraska	46,895	3,290	6.7	0.5	58,665	4,203	8.2	0.6	11,770	5,337	*25.1	12.5
Nevada	49,855	3,780	5.2	0.4	65,473	4,578	6.8	0.5	15,618	5,937	*31.3	13.5
New Hampshire	26,652	2,735	5.3	0.5	35,223	2,786	7.0	0.5	8,571	3,904	*32.2	17.1
New Jersey	150,029	5,640	4.8	0.2	174,459	7,059	5.5	0.2	24,430	9,035	*16.3	6.4
New Mexico	66,800	3,776	9.0	0.5	79,217	4,267	10.7	0.6	12,417	5,698	*18.6	9.3
New York	754,459	15,087	10.6	0.2	891,528	14,154	12.4	0.2	137,069	20,687	*18.2	3.0
North Carolina	343,177	9,370	9.5	0.3	401,614	10,150	11.0	0.3	58,437	13,814	*17.0	4.4
North Dakota	19,628	2,044	7.1	0.7	21,168	1,953	7.6	0.7	1,540	2,827	7.8	15.0

(Continued)

Area	Food stamp/SNAP receipt in 2008				Food stamp/SNAP receipt in 2009				Change in food stamp/SNAP receipt			
	Estimate	Margin of error[1] (±)	Percentage	Margin of error[1] (±)	Estimate	Margin of error[1] (±)	Percentage	Margin of error[1] (±)	Estimate	Margin of error[1] (±)	Percentage	Margin of error[1] (±)
Ohio	448,544	8,996	9.9	0.2	569,270	10,381	12.6	0.2	120,726	13,737	*26.9	3.4
Oklahoma	153,347	6,231	10.9	0.4	172,416	5,857	12.1	0.4	19,069	8,551	*12.4	6.0
Oregon	172,176	6,884	11.7	0.5	215,791	6,686	14.5	0.4	43,615	9,596	*25.3	6.3
Pennsylvania	440,743	9,088	9.0	0.2	477,892	8,088	9.7	0.2	37,149	12,166	*8.4	2.9
Rhode Island	31,478	2,873	7.9	0.7	40,499	3,277	10.0	0.8	9,021	4,358	*28.7	15.7
South Carolina	183,087	6,987	10.8	0.4	214,770	7,924	12.4	0.4	31,683	10,564	*17.3	6.2
South Dakota	26,809	2,328	8.4	0.7	30,705	2,768	9.7	0.8	3,896	3,617	*14.5	14.3
Tennessee	311,518	7,894	12.8	0.3	375,597	9,373	15.3	0.4	64,079	12,254	*20.6	4.3
Texas	798,173	14,044	9.5	0.2	979,499	13,447	11.5	0.2	181,326	19,444	*22.7	2.7
Utah	48,124	3,314	5.6	0.4	62,314	3,714	7.2	0.4	14,190	4,977	*29.5	11.8
Vermont	21,845	1,842	8.7	0.7	28,433	1,982	11.3	0.8	6,588	2,706	*30.2	14.2
Virginia	194,281	7,634	6.6	0.3	232,617	6,911	7.8	0.2	38,336	10,298	*19.7	5.9
Washington	221,475	7,459	8.7	0.3	282,907	8,024	11.1	0.3	61,432	10,955	*27.7	5.6
West Virginia	96,909	4,521	12.9	0.6	106,391	4,809	14.2	0.6	9,482	6,600	*9.8	7.1
Wisconsin	147,187	5,285	6.5	0.2	192,121	5,720	8.5	0.3	44,934	7,788	*30.5	6.1
Wyoming	8,580	1,380	4.1	0.7	11,089	1,735	5.2	0.8	2,509	2,217	*29.2	29.0
Puerto Rico	392,827	7,766	33.1	0.6	415,075	6,823	35.1	0.5	22,248	10,338	*5.7	2.7

* Statistically different at the 90 percent confidence level .

[1] Data are based on a sample and are subject to sampling variability . A margin of error is a measure of an estimate's variability . The larger the margin of error in relation to the size of the estimate, the less reliable the estimate . When added to and subtracted from the estimate, the margin of error forms the 90 percent confidence interval .

Sources: U.S. Census Bureau, American Community Surveys, 2008 and 2009, Puerto Rico Community Surveys, 2008 and 2009 .

End Notes

[1] Tennessee's and Kentucky's 2009 ACS food stamp/SNAP participation rates were not statistically different from Mississippi's (15.0 percent) or Maine's (14.5 percent). Tennessee and Kentucky were not statistically different from each other.

In: The American Community Survey ...   ISBN: 978-1-61324-362-6
Editors: B. M. Russo and A. D. Haffner   ©2011 Nova Science Publishers, Inc.

Chapter 10

LABOR FORCE PARTICIPATION RATE FOR SELECTED AGE GROUPS: 2008 AND 2009

United States Census Bureau

The recent economic downturn has affected the labor force participation of men and women of all ages and education levels.[1] Recent college graduates have had difficulty obtaining jobs,[2] while older workers are returning to work or continuing to work in order to bolster their diminished retirement savings.[3] Some younger workers may enroll in school or stay in school due to diminished job prospects, while others may end their job search out of frustration.[4] The recession has also had an impact on workers in the prime working age group of 25 to 54, particularly for men and especially for those with less education. The largest job losses have been in male-dominated industries such as construction and manufacturing, whereas female-dominated industries such as healthcare have fared relatively better over the course of the recession.[5] As a result of men bearing the brunt of the job losses, women are entering the labor force to supplement family income when their spouses have either lost their jobs or have had their work hours reduced.[6] Consequently, workers of all ages and education levels will be competing for jobs within a smaller job market pool.

Labor force participation rate: The labor force participation rate represents the proportion of the population that is in the labor force. For example, if there are 100 people in the population 16 years and over, and 64 of them are in the labor force, then the labor force participation rate for the population 16 years and over would be 64 percent.

Civilian labor force: Consists of people classified as employed or unemployed.

Labor force: All people classified in the civilian labor force plus members of the U.S. Armed Forces (people on active duty with the U.S. Army, Air Force, Navy, Marine Corps, or Coast Guard).

Employed: This category includes all civilians 16 years old and over who either (1) were "at work," that is, those who did any work at all during the reference week as paid employees, worked in their own business or profession, worked on their own farm, or worked 15 hours or more as unpaid workers on a family farm or in a family business; or (2) were "with a job but not at work," that is, those who did not work during the reference week but had jobs or businesses from which they were temporarily absent due to illness, bad weather, industrial dispute, vacation, or other personal reasons.

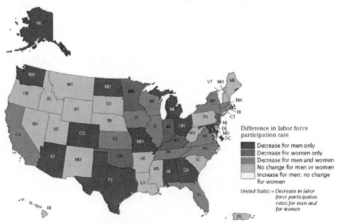

Sources: U.S. Census Bureau, American Community Surveys, 2008 and 2009, Puerto Rico Community Surveys, 2008 and 2009.

Labor Force Participation Rate Change by State: 2008 to 2009; Men and Women Aged 16 to 24.

Excluded from the employed are people whose only activ-ity consisted of work around the house or unpaid volunteer work for religious, charitable, and similar organizations; also excluded are all institutionalized people and people on active duty in the U.S. Armed Forces.

For men aged 16 to 24, the national labor force participation rate decreased 2.3 percentage points from 61 .5 percent in 2008 to 59.2 percent in 2009. For women this age, the national labor force participation rate decreased 1 .7 percentage points from 60.4 percent to 58.7 percent. For these men and women, the drop in labor force participation rate was related both to discouraged workers dropping out of the labor force[7] and to an increase in school enrollment rates. Between 2008 and 2009, school enrollment increased nationally for this age group from 60.1 percent to 60.6 percent.[8] Of the ten states that had an increase in school enrollment between 2008 and 2009, six had decreases in labor force participation (see Table 1).

There were 20 states for which the labor force participation rate for men aged 16 to 24 and for women aged 16 to 24 did not change from 2008 to 2009 (see map). For 1 2 states and the District of Columbia, the male labor force participation rate decreased while the female rate did not change. There were five states (Indiana, Kentucky, Minnesota, New Jersey, and Oklahoma) that experienced a decrease in labor force participation rate for women and not for men. There were 12 states that had a decrease in the labor force participation rates for men and for women.

Vermont was the only state with an increase in male labor force partici-pation rate; its rate for women did not change.

For men aged 25 to 54, the national labor force participation rate decreased from 88.5 percent in 2008 to 87.9 percent in 2009, while women in this group experienced an increase from 77.0 percent to 77.1 percent. The drop in the male labor force participation rate for this age group was related to large job losses in male-dominated industries, such as construction and manu-facturing, and the subsequent withdrawal of men in these industries from the labor force. This, in turn, may have contributed to the rise in women this age entering or returning to the labor force to off set losses in household income after, for example, a husband's job loss or reduction in hours worked.[9] Women also faced better job prospects as a result of possessing education levels, such as advanced degrees, required to attain and hold on to jobs in today's evolving economy.

For men 55 years and older, the national labor force participation rate remained unchanged (at 45.2 percent) from 2008 to 2009, while the rate for women increased from 32.8 percent to 33.2 percent.[10] These results were partly related to older workers staying at their existing jobs longer, or returning to the work force, or both.

**Table 1. Percent Change in Labor Force Participation
Rate and School Enrollment Rate From 2008 to 2009
for Those Aged 16 to 24**

State	Change in labor force participation rate	Change in school enrollment rate
Arizona	−2.65	1.75
California	−2.56	1.10
Florida	−2.36	1.81
Georgia	−2.33	1.56
Maryland	−2.28	1.81
Virginia	−3.01	1.67

Sources: U.S. Census Bureau, American Community Surveys, 2008 and 2009.

SOURCE AND ACCURACY

Data presented in this report are based on people and households that responded to the ACS in 2008 and 2009. The resulting estimates are representative of the entire population. All comparisons presented in this report have taken sampling error into account and are significant at the 90 percent confidence level unless otherwise noted.

Due to rounding, some details may not sum to totals. For information on sampling and estimation methods, confidentiality protection, and sampling and nonsampling errors, please see the "2009 ACS Accuracy of the Data" document located at <www.census.gov/acs /www/Down loads/data _docu mentation/Accuracy/ACS _Accu racy_of_Data_2009.pdf>.

Table 2. Labor Force Participation Rate by State and Age: 2008 and 2009; Men Only (In percent)

Area	2008						2009						Change from 2008 to 2009					
	16 to 24		25 to 54		55 and older		16 to 24		25 to 54		55 and older		16 to 24		25 to 54		55 and older	
	Rate	M.O.E.	Rate	M.O.E.	Rate	M.O.E.	Rate	M.O.E.	Rate	M.O.E.	Rate	M.O.E.	Rate	M.O.E.	Rate	M.O.E.	Rate	M.O.E.
United States	**61.5**	**0.2**	**88.5**	**0.1**	**45.2**	**0.1**	**59.2**	**0.2**	**87.9**	**0.1**	**45.2**	**0.1**	***-2.3**	**0.3**	***-0.6**	**0.1**	**–**	**0.2**
Alabama	61.2	1.8	85.3	0.6	40.8	0.9	58.5	1.6	84.8	0.6	40.8	0.8	*-2.7	2.4	-0.5	0.8	–	1.2
Alaska	71.0	3.1	88.3	1.5	54.6	2.6	63.9	4.0	87.8	1.4	54.6	2.1	*-7.1	5.1	-0.5	2.1	–	3.4
Arizona	63.7	1.4	87.4	0.5	39.9	0.8	59.8	1.3	86.0	0.6	39.8	0.8	*-3.9	1.9	*-1.4	0.8	-0.2	1.2
Arkansas	63.2	2.0	84.0	0.9	38.5	1.0	61.7	2.4	84.3	0.8	39.7	1.1	-1.5	3.1	0.3	1.2	1.2	1.5
California	58.4	0.5	88.5	0.2	45.9	0.4	55.4	0.5	88.1	0.2	46.4	0.4	*-3.0	0.7	*-0.4	0.3	*0.6	0.5
Colorado	68.4	1.2	91.2	0.5	51.2	0.9	65.9	1.2	89.7	0.5	51.1	0.8	*-2.5	1.7	*-1.5	0.7	-0.1	1.2
Connecticut	63.0	1.9	90.4	0.5	51.6	1.0	59.6	1.7	90.4	0.6	52.0	0.9	*-3.4	2.6	–	0.7	0.3	1.4
Delaware	62.9	3.4	89.3	1.1	43.1	1.8	59.1	3.8	89.0	1.2	43.9	2.0	-3.8	5.1	-0.3	1.6	0.7	2.7
District of Columbia	50.2	4.2	88.0	1.8	45.9	3.3	42.2	4.6	87.4	1.6	49.8	3.1	*-8.0	6.2	-0.6	2.4	3.9	4.5
Florida	60.4	0.8	87.5	0.3	38.6	0.4	57.8	0.8	87.0	0.4	38.8	0.4	*-2.6	1.1	*-0.5	0.5	0.3	0.6
Georgia	57.7	1.0	87.8	0.5	47.7	0.7	54.7	1.2	86.7	0.5	45.7	0.8	*-3.0	1.6	*-1.1	0.7	*-2.0	1.1
Hawaii	62.4	2.9	89.4	1.1	46.5	1.5	60.5	2.9	89.7	1.1	47.3	1.2	-1.9	4.1	0.3	1.5	0.8	1.9
Idaho	67.5	2.7	92.0	1.0	43.8	1.4	65.7	2.9	88.6	0.9	43.3	1.2	-1.8	3.9	*-3.4	1.3	-0.5	1.9
Illinois	62.3	1.0	89.9	0.3	46.9	0.5	60.5	1.0	89.3	0.4	47.2	0.5	*-1.8	1.4	*-0.6	0.5	0.3	0.7
Indiana	62.5	1.2	88.9	0.4	46.1	0.6	60.9	1.4	88.4	0.5	46.1	0.7	-1.7	1.8	-0.5	0.6	0.1	0.9
Iowa	72.1	1.4	91.8	0.5	49.3	0.7	68.9	2.0	91.5	0.6	48.4	0.8	*-3.2	2.4	-0.3	0.8	-0.9	1.1
Kansas	71.2	1.6	91.2	0.5	50.9	1.0	66.8	1.9	89.8	0.6	49.5	0.9	*-4.4	2.4	*-1.4	0.8	*-1.3	1.3
Kentucky	63.0	1.5	82.7	0.6	37.8	0.9	61.2	1.5	83.0	0.6	39.4	0.9	-1.8	2.1	0.3	0.9	*1.5	1.2
Louisiana	60.0	2.0	84.0	0.6	43.1	1.1	59.2	1.7	84.9	0.7	43.7	1.0	-0.8	2.6	0.9	1.0	0.6	1.5

Table 2. (Continued)

Area	2008						2009						Change from 2008 to 2009					
	16 to 24		25 to 54		55 and older		16 to 24		25 to 54		55 and older		16 to 24		25 to 54		55 and older	
	Rate	M.O.E.	Rate	M.O.E.	Rate	M.O.E.	Rate	M.O.E.	Rate	M.O.E.	Rate	M.O.E.	Rate	M.O.E.	Rate	M.O.E.	Rate	M.O.E.
Maine	63.0	2.5	87.9	1.0	45.1	1.3	64.6	2.4	87.9	0.9	44.8	1.3	1.5	3.5	–	1.4	-0.3	1.8
Maryland	62.3	1.4	90.5	0.5	52.4	0.8	59.4	1.7	89.8	0.5	52.9	1.0	*-2.9	2.2	*-0.7	0.7	0.4	1.3
Massachusetts	62.7	1.2	89.8	0.5	49.6	0.9	59.2	1.2	89.7	0.5	49.9	0.7	*-3.4	1.7	-0.2	0.6	0.3	1.2
Michigan	61.5	0.9	86.4	0.4	39.7	0.5	59.6	1.1	85.5	0.5	39.3	0.5	*-1.9	1.5	*-0.9	0.6	-0.4	0.8
Minnesota	68.8	1.5	92.9	0.4	48.9	0.7	68.4	1.1	92.3	0.4	47.7	0.6	-0.4	1.8	*-0.7	0.5	*-1.2	1.0
Mississippi	55.2	2.1	83.6	0.9	40.7	1.3	52.3	2.2	81.6	0.9	40.1	1.3	-2.9	3.1	*-2.0	1.3	-0.7	1.9
Missouri	65.5	1.2	88.5	0.5	43.6	0.8	63.1	1.2	87.1	0.6	43.6	0.7	*-2.4	1.7	*-1.4	0.7	–	1.1
Montana.	65.7	3.6	88.7	1.0	45.7	1.8	62.1	4.0	86.4	1.2	46.0	1.7	-3.6	5.3	*-2.3	1.6	0.3	2.5
Nebraska	73.0	2.0	92.6	0.7	52.6	1.2	70.7	1.9	91.9	0.8	51.8	1.2	-2.3	2.8	-0.6	1.0	-0.7	1.7
Nevada	65.0	2.2	91.0	0.8	47.1	1.3	63.7	1.9	91.0	0.7	47.6	1.3	-1.4	2.8	–	1.0	0.5	1.9
New Hampshire	66.8	2.5	92.8	0.8	51.6	1.8	65.0	2.7	91.1	0.9	52.5	1.4	-1.9	3.7	*-1.7	1.3	1.0	2.3
New Jersey	57.7	1.1	91.1	0.4	49.9	0.7	56.8	1.2	90.7	0.3	50.3	0.7	-0.9	1.7	-0.4	0.5	0.4	1.0
New Mexico	60.4	2.5	84.2	1.1	41.7	1.4	60.3	2.7	84.1	1.2	41.7	1.4	-0.1	3.7	-0.1	1.6	-0.1	2.0
New York	54.2	0.8	87.8	0.3	44.9	0.5	51.4	0.7	87.6	0.3	45.4	0.4	*-2.8	1.0	-0.3	0.5	0.5	0.6
North Carolina	62.1	1.3	88.2	0.4	44.8	0.6	59.4	1.2	87.9	0.4	43.5	0.5	*-2.6	1.8	-0.3	0.6	*-1.3	0.8
North Dakota	73.8	2.5	92.5	0.9	48.2	1.8	66.3	3.1	93.0	0.9	48.2	1.5	*-7.5	4.0	0.5	1.3	0.4	2.4
Ohio.	64.0	0.8	88.3	0.4	43.9	0.5	60.4	1.1	87.2	0.3	43.5	0.5	*-3.6	1.3	*-1.1	0.5	-0.5	0.7
Oklahoma	64.6	1.8	85.7	0.7	44.5	1.0	62.7	1.6	85.5	0.7	43.3	0.9	-1.9	2.4	-0.2	1.0	-1.1	1.3
Oregon	61.5	1.9	88.8	0.6	43.1	0.9	61.3	1.8	88.0	0.7	42.5	1.0	-0.2	2.6	-0.8	0.9	-0.6	1.4
Pennsylvania	58.7	1.0	88.1	0.3	44.0	0.5	57.7	1.0	87.4	0.3	45.0	0.4	-1.0	1.4	*-0.6	0.4	*1.0	0.7

Table 2. (Continued)

Area	2008						2009						Change from 2008 to 2009					
	16 to 24		25 to 54		55 and older		16 to 24		25 to 54		55 and older		16 to 24		25 to 54		55 and older	
	Rate	M.O.E.	Rate	M.O.E.	Rate	M.O.E.	Rate	M.O.E.	Rate	M.O.E.	Rate	M.O.E.	Rate	M.O.E.	Rate	M.O.E.	Rate	M.O.E.
Rhode Island	62.7	3.2	87.1	1.2	48.5	1.7	61.4	3.0	88.4	1.3	48.6	1.9	-1.4	4.4	1.3	1.8	0.1	2.5
South Carolina	58.0	1.5	86.0	0.6	42.7	0.9	56.8	1.9	85.3	0.5	42.1	0.9	-1.2	2.5	-0.7	0.8	-0.5	1.2
South Dakota	71.4	3.4	90.0	1.1	50.9	1.5	68.6	4.2	91.0	1.1	48.3	2.0	-2.8	5.4	1.0	1.6	*-2.5	2.5
Tennessee	62.3	1.3	87.2	0.4	44.2	0.7	60.4	1.2	86.2	0.5	42.3	0.9	*-1.8	1.8	*-1.0	0.7	*-1.9	1.1
Texas	62.2	0.7	89.1	0.2	48.3	0.5	59.6	0.7	88.2	0.3	48.6	0.4	*-2.6	1.0	*-0.9	0.3	0.3	0.6
Utah	70.7	2.1	92.4	0.5	48.4	1.3	70.6	1.9	92.1	0.6	49.1	1.4	-0.2	2.8	-0.3	0.8	0.6	1.9
Vermont	60.2	3.1	92.0	1.1	52.3	1.6	66.1	2.8	89.9	1.1	50.7	1.6	*5.9	4.2	*-2.1	1.5	-1.6	2.2
Virginia	61.5	1.2	89.2	0.4	49.3	0.7	59.1	1.4	88.7	0.4	49.0	0.7	*-2.4	1.8	-0.5	0.6	-0.3	1.0
Washington	62.5	1.3	89.2	0.4	45.7	0.7	59.2	1.4	88.4	0.4	45.5	0.7	*-3.2	1.9	*-0.9	0.6	-0.1	1.0
West Virginia	56.8	2.3	82.0	1.0	34.0	1.3	57.2	2.6	81.7	0.9	35.4	1.3	0.5	3.4	-0.3	1.4	1.4	1.8
Wisconsin	69.4	1.1	91.0	0.4	45.6	0.7	67.5	1.3	90.0	0.4	46.4	0.6	*-1.9	1.7	*-0.9	0.5	0.9	0.9
Wyoming	69.8	4.0	93.2	1.1	52.3	2.3	70.7	4.1	92.1	1.2	51.1	2.5	0.9	5.7	-1.1	1.6	-1.2	3.4
Puerto Rico	41.4	1.3	74.3	0.8	26.4	0.8	40.5	1.3	75.2	1.0	25.4	0.9	-0.9	1.8	0.9	1.3	-1.0	1.2

* Statistically different at the 90 percent confidence level.

– Represents or rounds to zero.

[1] Data are based on a sample and are subject to sampling variability. A margin of error is a measure of an estimate's variability. The larger the margin of error in relation to the size of the estimate, the less reliable the estimate. When added to and subtracted from the estimate, the margin of error forms the 90 percent confidence interval.

Sources: U.S. Census Bureau, American Community Surveys, 2008 and 2009, Puerto Rico Community Surveys, 2008 and 2009.

Table 3. Labor Force Participation Rate by State and Age: 2008 and 2009; Women Only (In percent)

Area	2008						2009						Change from 2008 to 2009					
	16 to 24		25 to 54		55 and older		16 to 24		25 to 54		55 and older		16 to 24		25 to 54		55 and older	
	Rate	M.O.E.	Rate	M.O.E.	Rate	M.O.E.	Rate	M.O.E.	Rate	M.O.E.	Rate	M.O.E.	Rate	M.O.E.	Rate	M.O.E.	Rate	M.O.E.
United States	60.4	0.2	77.0	0.1	32.8	0.1	58.7	0.2	77.1	0.1	33.2	0.1	*-1.7	0.3	*0.1	0.1	*0.4	0.1
Alabama.	55.5	1.5	73.9	0.7	27.2	0.7	54.9	2.0	73.3	0.8	28.2	0.7	-0.6	2.5	-0.7	1.1	*-1.0	1.0
Alaska	65.6	4.3	78.2	1.8	46.0	2.3	60.4	4.4	77.6	1.6	46.0	2.8	-5.2	6.1	-0.7	2.4	–	3.6
Arizona	58.7	1.5	73.8	0.8	30.0	0.7	57.4	1.6	73.5	0.8	29.3	0.8	-1.4	2.2	-0.3	1.1	-0.8	1.1
rkansas	58.1	2.2	74.6	0.8	28.9	0.9	57.0	2.3	74.1	1.0	28.8	0.9	-1.1	3.2	-0.5	1.3	-0.1	1.3
California	55.4	0.6	73.6	0.3	32.2	0.3	53.3	0.5	74.6	0.2	33.6	0.3	*-2.1	0.8	*1.0	0.4	*1.4	0.4
Colorado.	63.5	1.6	78.7	0.7	37.3	0.7	62.6	1.5	78.3	0.6	38.1	0.8	-0.9	2.2	-0.4	1.0	0.8	1.1
Connecticut	65.8	1.9	79.6	0.7	37.1	0.7	62.9	1.6	80.9	0.7	38.4	0.8	*-2.9	2.5	*1.3	1.0	*1.3	1.1
Delaware	61.1	4.1	80.4	1.4	32.7	1.7	61.5	3.8	80.0	1.5	34.3	1.7	0.4	5.6	-0.4	2.1	1.6	2.4
District of Columbia	52.1	4.3	84.2	1.7	39.1	2.7	46.9	4.2	82.0	1.8	39.9	1.9	-5.3	6.0	-2.3	2.5	0.8	3.3
Florida	59.1	0.9	77.6	0.4	29.1	0.4	57.1	1.0	77.9	0.4	28.9	0.4	*-2.1	1.4	0.3	0.5	-0.2	0.5
Georgia	54.6	1.1	76.6	0.6	33.9	0.6	53.0	1.4	76.8	0.5	32.8	0.7	-1.6	1.8	0.2	0.8	*-1.0	1.0
Hawaii	57.9	3.2	80.1	1.4	35.5	1.3	56.4	3.6	79.7	1.5	36.2	1.3	-1.5	4.8	-0.4	2.0	0.7	1.8
Idaho	64.7	2.9	73.5	1.5	33.2	1.3	61.4	2.6	74.1	1.3	33.5	1.2	-3.3	3.8	0.7	2.0	0.3	1.8
Illinois	61.5	1.0	78.2	0.3	34.7	0.4	60.0	1.0	78.7	0.4	34.2	0.5	*-1.4	1.4	*0.5	0.5	-0.5	0.6
Indiana	63.4	1.3	78.4	0.6	33.4	0.6	60.7	1.4	77.8	0.6	33.8	0.6	*-2.8	1.9	-0.6	0.8	0.4	0.9
Iowa	73.5	1.3	83.9	0.7	35.8	0.7	71.3	1.4	84.1	0.9	36.4	0.7	*-2.1	1.9	0.3	1.1	0.6	1.0
Kansas	70.6	1.6	80.7	0.8	36.6	0.8	65.8	2.3	80.6	0.8	36.1	0.8	*-4.7	2.8	-0.1	1.1	-0.5	1.1
Kentucky	60.2	1.8	72.7	0.8	27.5	0.7	57.5	1.8	72.3	0.8	29.0	0.6	*-2.7	2.5	-0.4	1.1	*1.4	0.9
Louisiana	56.3	2.0	73.1	0.9	29.4	0.8	57.9	2.0	74.3	0.7	29.5	0.9	1.6	2.8	*1.2	1.2	0.1	1.2
Maine	65.4	3.2	80.5	1.2	34.7	1.2	66.9	2.4	79.9	1.1	33.7	1.1	1.5	4.0	-0.6	1.6	-1.0	1.6

Table 3. (Continued)

Area	2008						2009						Change from 2008 to 2009					
	16 to 24		25 to 54		55 and older		16 to 24		25 to 54		55 and older		16 to 24		25 to 54		55 and older	
	Rate	M.O.E.	Rate	M.O.E.	Rate	M.O.E.	Rate	M.O.E.	Rate	M.O.E.	Rate	M.O.E.	Rate	M.O.E.	Rate	M.O.E.	Rate	M.O.E.
Maryland.	63.7	1.4	82.8	0.6	38.1	0.5	62.1	1.4	82.4	0.6	39.0	0.7	-1.7	2.0	-0.4	0.9	*-0.9	0.9
Massachusetts	64.8	1.2	81.0	0.6	37.4	0.6	62.3	1.5	81.5	0.5	37.6	0.6	*-2.5	1.9	0.5	0.8	0.2	0.8
Michigan	62.7	0.9	77.1	0.4	30.0	0.4	62.7	1.1	77.3	0.5	30.1	0.4	–	1.5	0.2	0.6	–	0.6
Minnesota.	72.3	1.3	84.8	0.4	37.2	0.6	69.8	1.0	84.3	0.5	37.3	0.5	*-2.5	1.6	-0.5	0.6	0.1	0.8
Mississippi	53.1	2.3	74.1	1.0	28.3	1.0	53.7	1.9	73.6	1.1	27.9	1.1	0.7	3.0	-0.5	1.5	-0.4	1.5
Missouri	66.1	1.3	79.1	0.6	32.8	0.6	65.7	1.1	78.1	0.7	33.2	0.7	-0.4	1.7	*-1.0	0.9	0.4	0.9
Montana	65.6	3.5	79.1	1.6	35.1	1.4	64.4	3.4	80.2	1.5	34.9	1.4	-1.1	4.9	1.1	2.2	-0.2	2.0
Nebraska	73.7	1.9	83.8	0.9	37.8	0.8	73.7	2.3	83.0	0.9	38.6	0.9	-0.1	3.0	-0.8	1.3	0.8	1.3
Nevada	61.4	2.4	77.3	0.8	37.7	1.3	59.0	2.4	77.1	1.0	37.1	1.1	-2.4	3.4	-0.2	1.3	-0.6	1.7
New Hampshire	68.8	2.3	82.2	1.1	38.3	1.2	68.1	2.1	82.8	1.2	39.7	1.5	-0.7	3.2	0.6	1.7	1.4	1.9
New Jersey	59.9	1.2	78.6	0.5	36.1	0.5	57.8	1.1	78.3	0.5	36.5	0.6	*-2.1	1.6	-0.2	0.7	0.4	0.8
New Mexico	60.5	2.8	74.8	1.3	31.9	1.3	56.8	2.7	74.4	1.3	32.5	1.4	-3.6	3.9	-0.3	1.8	0.6	1.9
New York	56.4	0.8	77.5	0.3	32.6	0.4	53.5	0.9	77.3	0.4	34.0	0.4	*-2.8	1.2	-0.3	0.5	*-1.4	0.5
North Carolina	59.4	1.2	77.6	0.4	32.8	0.6	55.5	1.1	77.1	0.5	32.2	0.5	*-3.9	1.6	-0.5	0.7	-0.6	0.7
North Dakota	72.3	2.8	84.7	1.3	36.3	1.4	70.8	3.0	86.0	1.2	35.5	1.6	-1.5	4.1	1.3	1.8	-0.8	2.1
Ohio	65.2	0.9	78.9	0.5	32.1	0.5	64.3	0.9	78.3	0.4	32.8	0.5	-0.9	1.3	-0.5	0.6	*-0.7	0.7
Oklahoma	60.7	1.8	74.6	0.8	31.8	0.9	57.7	1.8	73.6	0.9	31.4	0.8	*-3.0	2.6	-1.0	1.2	-0.5	1.2
Oregon.	63.6	1.7	77.1	0.8	32.3	0.7	62.1	1.7	78.4	1.0	33.0	0.9	-1.6	2.4	*-1.3	1.2	0.7	1.1
Pennsylvania	60.8	1.1	78.1	0.4	31.3	0.4	59.5	0.9	78.3	0.5	31.7	0.5	-1.3	1.4	0.2	0.6	0.5	0.5
Rhode Island	61.2	3.8	80.8	1.4	34.2	1.2	61.6	3.2	81.6	1.4	36.0	1.7	0.5	5.0	0.8	2.0	1.8	2.0
South Carolina	57.9	1.7	75.7	0.8	30.0	0.8	57.3	1.8	77.3	0.7	31.1	0.8	-0.6	2.5	*1.6	1.1	1.0	1.1
South Dakota.	72.1	3.2	85.0	1.6	37.7	1.7	68.1	3.0	84.2	1.5	39.0	1.6	-4.0	4.4	-0.8	2.2	1.3	2.4

Table 3. (Continued)

Area	2008						2009						Change from 2008 to 2009					
	16 to 24		25 to 54		55 and older		16 to 24		25 to 54		55 and older		16 to 24		25 to 54		55 and older	
	Rate	M.O.E.	Rate	M.O.E.	Rate	M.O.E.	Rate	M.O.E.	Rate	M.O.E.	Rate	M.O.E.	Rate	M.O.E.	Rate	M.O.E.	Rate	M.O.E.
Tennessee	60.9	1.4	74.7	0.6	31.2	0.7	56.9	1.2	75.1	0.8	30.7	0.6	*–4.0	1.9	0.4	1.0	–0.4	0.9
Texas	55.5	0.7	72.9	0.4	32.7	0.4	55.6	0.7	73.8	0.3	32.9	0.4	0.1	1.0	*0.9	0.5	0.2	0.5
Utah	72.0	1.7	70.5	1.0	33.7	1.1	69.7	1.8	70.9	1.1	34.7	1.0	–2.3	2.5	0.4	1.4	1.1	1.5
Vermont	66.3	3.1	84.0	1.7	41.2	1.7	65.1	3.2	83.2	1.3	39.8	1.8	–1.2	4.5	–0.8	2.1	–1.4	2.5
Virginia	61.6	1.2	79.0	0.4	35.3	0.6	58.0	1.5	78.5	0.5	35.6	0.6	*–3.6	1.9	–0.4	0.7	0.3	0.8
Washington	62.2	1.1	76.1	0.6	34.0	0.6	61.1	1.2	76.0	0.5	35.6	0.7	–1.1	1.6	–	0.8	*1.5	0.9
West Virginia	52.4	2.6	69.8	1.1	25.9	1.0	52.2	3.2	68.0	1.1	26.6	1.0	–0.2	4.1	*–1.8	1.5	0.6	1.4
Wisconsin	73.0	1.1	83.7	0.5	34.8	0.5	70.7	1.1	83.5	0.5	36.0	0.5	*–2.4	1.6	–0.2	0.7	*1.2	0.7
Wyoming	64.1	3.8	78.8	2.0	41.1	2.4	64.2	3.9	79.3	1.8	39.5	2.3	0.2	5.4	0.5	2.7	–1.5	3.3
Puerto Rico	33.3	1.5	62.0	0.8	13.8	0.6	34.1	1.5	63.6	0.9	13.6	0.6	0.8	2.1	*1.6	1.2	–0.2	0.8

* Statistically different at the 90 percent confidence level.

– Represents or rounds to zero.

[1] Data are based on a sample and are subject to sampling variability. A margin of error is a measure of an estimate's variability. The larger the margin of error in relation to the size of the estimate, the less reliable the estimate. When added to and subtracted from the estimate, the margin of error forms the 90 percent confidence interval.

Sources: U.S. Census Bureau, American Community Surveys, 2008 and 2009, Puerto Rico Community Surveys, 2008 and 2009.

End Notes

[1] Hipple, Steven F., "The Labor Market in 2009: Recession Drags On," *Monthly Labor Review*, March 2010, Vol. 133, No. 3, pp. 3–22.

[2] Hipple, 2010.

[3] See Bureau of Labor Statistics, *Issues in Labor Statistics*, March 2010, at <www.bls.gov /opub/ils/pdf/opbils81 .pdf>.

[4] Hipple, 2010.

[5] Hipple, 2010.

[6] See Greenhouse, Steven, "Recession Drives Women Back to the Work Force," New York Times, September 1 9, 2009, at <www.nytimes.com /2009/09/19/business/1 9women.html>.

7 See Bureau of Labor Statistics, Issues in Labor Statistics, April 2009, at *<www.bls .gov/ opub/ ils/pdf/opbils74.pdf>*.

[8] U.S. Census Bureau, American Community Surveys, 2008 and 2009. College enrollment rates for 18 to 24 year olds increased from 38.6 percent in 2008 to 39.5 percent in 2009 (author's tabulations).

[9] See Woodring (2010), "Employment Status of Married-Couple Families by Presence of Own Children Under 18 Years: 2008 and 2009" at <www.census.gov/prod/2010pubs /acsbr09- 1 0.pdf>, and Greenhouse, Steven, "Recession Drives Women Back to the Work Force," New York Times, September 19, 2009, at <www.nytimes.com/2009/09/19 /business/1 9women. html>.

[10] See Bureau of Labor Statistics, Occupational Outlook Handbook, 2010–11 Edition at <www.bls.gov/oco/oco2003.htm>, and McQueen, M. P., "Better Education Shields Women from Worst of Job Cuts," *Wall Street Journal*, February 12, 2010, at <online.wsj .com/article/NA_WSJ_PUB:SB1 000142405274 87033890045750337624821141 90.html>.

In: The American Community Survey ...   ISBN: 978-1-61324-362-6
Editors: B. M. Russo and A. D. Haffner   ©2011 Nova Science Publishers, Inc.

Chapter 11

EMPLOYMENT STATUS OF MARRIED-COUPLE FAMILIES BY PRESENCE OF OWN CHILDREN UNDER 18 YEARS: 2008 AND 2009

United States Census Bureau

INTRODUCTION

Although the current recession has impacted the country in a variety of ways, a common scenario emerging from this economic climate is an increase in the number of women who are the sole worker within a married-couple family.[1] In some cases, husbands have lost their jobs while their wives have not. In others, wives have reentered the labor force to help off set lost family income after their husbands' job loss. Between 2008 and 2009, the largest job losses were reported in male-dominated industries such as construction and manufacturing, whereas female-dominated industries such as healthcare have fared relatively better over the course of the recession.[2]

According to data from the Bureau of Labor Statistics (BLS), the unemployment rate for women was 2.2 percentage points lower than the rate for men in 2009, one of the largest unemployment rate gender gaps reported by BLS.[3] Reinforcing this diff erence in unemployment rates is the increasing likelihood that women possess education levels, such as advanced degrees, required to attain and hold on to jobs in today's evolving economy.[4] The unemployment rate gender gap may have consequences for family spending power since, on average, women earn less than men do.[5] Given the rising costs of education, childcare, and healthcare, married-couple families with children will face an even greater strain on their family budgets.

Unemployed: All civilians 16 years old and over are classifi ed as unemployed if they (1) were neither "at work" nor "with a job but not at work" during the reference week, and (2) were actively looking for work during the last 4 weeks, and (3) were available to accept a job. Also included as unemployed are civilians who did not work at all during the reference week, were waiting to be called back to a job from which they had been laid off , and were available for work except for temporary illness.

Own children: A child under 18 years old who is a son or daughter by birth, marriage (stepchild), or adoption.

Family: A group of two or more people who reside together and who are related by birth, marriage, or adoption.

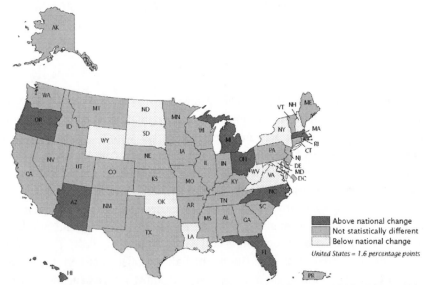

Sources: U.S. Census Bureau, American Community Survey, 2009, Puerto Rico Community Survey, 2009.

Figure 1. Employment Status of Married-Couple Families With Own Children by State and Puerto Rico: 2008 Versus 2009.

Employment Status of Married-Couple Families with Own Children Under 18 Years and Percent Change in Total Employment in Select Industries (In percent)

Area	Married-couple families with own children						Employment change in select industries			
	2009		2008		Percentage point change 2008–2009		Percent change 2008–2009		Percent change 2008–2009	
	Husband unemployed/wife employed	Margin of error[1]	Husband unemployed/wife employed	Margin of error[1]	Husband unemployed/wife employed	Margin of error[1]	Construction and manufacturing employment	Margin of error[1]	Educational services and health care and social assistance	Margin of error[1]
United States	**3.4**	**0.1**	**1.8**	**0.1**	***1.6**	**0.1**	***-10.8**	**0.4**	***0.9**	**0.4**
Alabama	2.4	0.4	0.9	0.2	*1.5	0.5	*-11.0	3.4	-1.0	3.1
Alaska	2.3	1.1	1.4	0.6	1.0	1.3	*-13.4	11.8	6.9	8.1
Arizona	4.0	0.4	1.4	0.3	*2.7	0.5	*-14.9	3.4	*4.3	3.0
Arkansas	2.9	0.6	1.5	0.4	*1.3	0.7	*-5.0	4.2	4.0	4.3
California	3.7	0.2	2.2	0.1	*1.5	0.2	*-8.9	1.3	-0.8	1.3
Colorado	2.8	0.4	1.2	0.3	*1.6	0.5	*-12.5	3.2	2.6	3.1
Connecticut	3.5	0.6	1.5	0.4	*2.0	0.7	*-5.8	3.9	*5.1	3.6
Delaware	3.1	1.3	2.1	1.1	1.1	1.7	*-9.4	7.8	*11.1	7.3
District of Columbia	4.3	2.5	2.1	2.2	2.3	3.3	*-19.3	18.6	-4.6	9.0
Florida	4.9	0.3	2.5	0.2	*2.3	0.4	*-14.6	2.4	1.6	1.7
Georgia	3.3	0.4	1.7	0.3	*1.6	0.5	*-13.3	2.3	1.7	2.6
Hawaii	3.9	1.1	1.0	0.5	*2.9	1.2	*-18.2	8.5	5.8	6.6
Idaho	3.5	0.8	2.4	0.7	*1.1	1.1	*-14.8	4.9	2.8	5.3
Illinois	4.1	0.3	2.2	0.2	*1.9	0.4	*-11.6	1.9	1.2	1.9
Indiana	4.2	0.5	2.5	0.3	*1.6	0.6	*-10.4	2.3	1.9	2.4

(Continued)

Area	Married-couple families with own children						Employment change in select industries			
	2009		2008		Percentage point change 2008–2009		Percent change 2008–2009		Percent change 2008–2009	
	Husband unemployed/wife employed	Margin of error[1]	Husband unemployed/wife employed	Margin of error[1]	Husband unemployed/wife employed	Margin of error[1]	Construction and manufacturing employment	Margin of error[1]	Educational services and health care and social assistance	Margin of error[1]
Iowa	2.7	0.4	1.2	0.4	*1.5	0.6	*-8.6	3.1	-1.5	3.2
Kansas	2.7	0.6	1.1	0.3	*1.7	0.7	*-7.5	3.9	*-6.2	3.2
Kentucky	3.0	0.5	1.7	0.4	*1.2	0.6	*-11.5	3.1	*5.2	3.1
Louisiana	1.8	0.5	1.0	0.2	*0.8	0.6	-1.8	3.6	*7.2	3.4
Maine	3.3	0.8	2.0	0.6	*1.3	1.1	*-8.0	5.1	1.9	5.1
Maryland	2.7	0.4	1.7	0.3	*1.0	0.5	*-9.7	3.5	-0.5	2.6
Massachusetts	4.1	0.5	1.9	0.3	*2.3	0.6	*-8.6	3.1	1.7	2.5
Michigan	5.9	0.4	3.0	0.3	*2.9	0.5	*-16.6	2.0	*-2.3	1.9
Minnesota	3.7	0.4	1.9	0.3	*1.8	0.5	*-9.1	2.2	*3.4	2.4
Mississippi	2.4	0.6	1.4	0.5	*1.1	0.8	*-11.3	4.3	-3.2	4.4
Missouri	3.3	0.4	2.0	0.3	*1.4	0.5	*-10.1	2.6	1.5	2.6
Montana	2.3	0.7	1.5	0.6	0.8	0.9	*-20.6	7.8	-4.8	5.4
Nebraska	1.9	0.5	0.8	0.3	*1.1	0.6	*-8.3	4.6	0.8	4.4
Nevada	4.6	0.9	2.2	0.6	*2.4	1.1	*-21.2	5.5	*9.0	5.8
New Hampshire	2.5	0.6	1.8	0.6	0.7	0.8	*-9.4	5.1	-0.8	5.0
New Jersey	3.6	0.3	1.7	0.2	*1.9	0.4	*-12.4	2.7	*-4.7	2.1

(Continued)

Area	Married-couple families with own children						Employment change in select industries			
	2009		2008		Percentage point change 2008–2009		Percent change 2008–2009		Percent change 2008–2009	
	Husband unemployed/ wife employed	Margin of error¹ (∓)	Husband unemployed/ wife employed	Margin of error¹ (∓)	Husband unemployed/ wife employed	Margin of error¹ (∓)	Construction and manufacturing employment	Margin of error¹ (∓)	Educational services and health care and social assistance	Margin of error¹ (∓)
New Mexico	3.1	0.8	1.6	0.6	*1.5	1.0	*–15.9	6.1	–2.9	4.6
New York	2.5	0.2	1.8	0.2	*0.7	0.2	*–9.4	2.0	0.3	1.5
North Carolina	3.9	0.4	1.7	0.2	*2.1	0.4	*–13.2	2.2	–0.7	2.2
North Dakota	1.2	0.6	0.5	0.4	0.6	0.7	–1.0	8.3	3.5	5.5
Ohio	4.4	0.3	2.0	0.3	*2.3	0.4	*–13.4	1.6	1.0	1.8
Oklahoma	2.1	0.4	1.3	0.4	*0.8	0.6	*–9.9	3.4	2.2	3.9
Oregon	4.7	0.5	2.3	0.4	*2.4	0.7	*–17.3	3.5	0.6	3.9
Pennsylvania	3.3	0.2	1.8	0.2	*1.5	0.3	*–8.1	1.8	1.1	1.6
Rhode Island	3.7	1.2	3.0	1.0	0.7	1.6	*–10.5	6.9	3.8	6.3
South Carolina	3.7	0.6	1.7	0.4	*2.0	0.7	*–13.4	3.3	1.4	3.5
South Dakota	1.7	0.7	1.1	0.5	0.6	0.9	*–11.7	7.9	–5.6	6.2
Tennessee	3.2	0.4	1.8	0.3	*1.4	0.5	*–14.7	2.8	–0.4	2.8
Texas	2.7	0.2	1.3	0.1	*1.4	0.2	*–7.0	1.6	*3.3	1.5
Utah	2.1	0.5	0.9	0.3	*1.2	0.6	*–6.1	4.1	–0.5	4.0
Vermont	3.1	1.0	2.2	0.9	1.0	1.4	*–9.6	6.7	–4.6	4.9
Virginia	2.1	0.3	1.3	0.3	*0.9	0.4	*–9.4	3.0	0.7	2.8
Washington	3.5	0.4	1.5	0.2	*2.0	0.5	*–11.2	2.7	2.0	3.0

(Continued)

Area	Married-couple families with own children						Employment change in select industries			
	2009		2008		Percentage point change 2008–2009		Percent change 2008–2009		Percent change 2008–2009	
	Husband unemployed/ wife employed	Margin of error[1] (∓)	Husband unemployed/ wife employed	Margin of error[1] (∓)	Husband unemployed/ wife employed	Margin of error[1] (∓)	Construction and manufacturing employment	Margin of error[1] (∓)	Educational services and health care and social assistance	Margin of error[1] (∓)
West Virginia	2.3	0.7	1.6	0.6	0.7	0.9	*–9.7	5.9	1.0	4.8
Wisconsin	3.6	0.4	1.7	0.3	*1.9	0.5	*–12.4	2.1	2.0	2.3
Wyoming	1.2	0.7	0.4	0.3	*0.8	0.8	–4.7	11.2	8.3	9.0
Puerto Rico	3.3	0.6	2.5	0.5	*0.8	0.8	*–11.3	4.7	*–4.3	4.1

* Statistically different at the 90 percent confi dence level.

[1] Data are based on a sample and are subject to sampling variability. A margin of error is a measure of an estimate's variability. The larger the margin of error in relation to the size of the estimate, the less reliable the estimate. This number when added to and subtracted from the estimate forms the 90 percent confi dence interval.

Sources: U.S. Census Bureau, American Community Surveys, 2008 and 2009, Puerto Rico Community Surveys, 2008 and 2009.

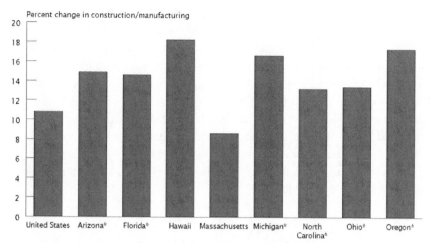

*Statistically different from the change for the United States at the 90 percent confidence level.

Sources: U.S. Census Bureau, American Community Surveys, 2008 and 2009.

Figure 2. Percent Change in Total Construction and Manufacturing Employment for Select States and the Nation, 2008–09.

CHANGE IN EMPLOYMENT STATUS FOR MARRIED-COUPLE FAMILIES WITH OWN CHILDREN

Nationally, 3.4 percent of married- couple families with own children under 18 years old had an unemployed husband and employed wife in 2009—up from 1.8 percent in 2008.[6] Between 2008 and 2009, 41 states saw an increase in the percentage of married-couple families in this situation.

Compared with the national increase of 1.6 percentage points, Arizona, Florida, Hawaii, Michigan, Massachusetts, North Carolina, Ohio, and Oregon all reported a larger increase in the percentage of married-couple families with own children with an unemployed husband and employed wife. Six of these states (Arizona, Florida, Michigan, North Carolina, Ohio, and Oregon) experienced larger percentage decreases in total construction and manufacturing employment than the nation (see Figure 2).[7] Employment losses in construction and manufacturing industries, which are consistently male-dominated industries, may have contributed to larger increases in the percentage of marriedcouple families with own children with an unemployed husband and employed wife for these states.[8]

While male-dominated industries experienced considerable employment losses over the past year, female-dominated industries fared relatively better between 2008 and 2009. For example, national employment in the educational services and health care and social assistance industry group increased nearly 1 .0 percent between 2008 and 2009, compared with a 3.7 percent decline in total national employment during the same time period.[9] Given diff erences in gender composition between industries, in addition to differences in educational attainment between men and women, women have been more likely to maintain current employment or reenter the labor force, likely contributing to the increase in married-couple families with own children with an unemployed husband and employed wife.[10]

SOURCE AND ACCURACY

Data presented in this report are based on people and households that responded to the ACS in 2008 and 2009. The resulting estimates are representative of the entire population. All comparisons presented in this report have taken sampling error into account and are signifi cant at the 90 percent confidence level unless otherwise noted.

Due to rounding, some details may not sum to totals. For information on sampling and estimation methods, confidentiality protection, and sampling and nonsampling errors, please see the "2009 ACS Accuracy of the Data" document located at <www.census.gov/acs /www/Down loads/data _docu mentation/Accuracy/ACS _Accuracy_of_Data_2009.pdf>.

End Notes

[1] Bureau of Labor Statistics, Employment Characteristics of Families, Economic News Release, Table 4. Families with own children: Employment status of parents by age of youngest child and family type, 2008-09 annual averages.

[2] Hipple, Steven F., "The Labor Market in 2009: Recession Drags On," *Monthly Labor Review*, March 2010, Vol. 133, No.3, pp. 3–22 and U.S. Census Bureau, American Community Surveys, 2008 and 2009, table S2403.

[3] Bureau of Labor Statistics CPS Annual Averages: <bls.gov/cps/cpsaat2.pdf>.

[4] For example, between 2008 and 2009, the num-ber of females over the age of 25 with a graduate or professional degree increased 3.7 percent while the number of male graduate and professional degree holders over the age of 25 remained unchanged (U.S. Census Bureau, American Community Surveys, 2008 and 2009, author's tabulations). Also see McQueen, M. P., "Better Education Shields Women from Worst of Job Cuts," *The Wall Street Journal*, Feb. 12, 2010, at<online.wsj.com/article/NA_WSJ_PUB :SB10001 42405

27487033890045750337624821141 90.html> and Bureau of Labor Statistics, *Occupational Outlook Handbook,* 2010–11 Edition, <www.bls.gov /oco/oco2003.htm>.

[5] "Men's and Women's Earnings for States and Metropolitan Statistical Areas: 2009," American Community Survey Briefs, <www .census.gov/prod/2010pubs/acsbr09-3.pdf>.

[6] Nationally, there were 23,411,061 married-couple families with own children under 18 years old in 2009. centage of married-couple families in this situation.

[7] Although Hawaii did not experience a signifi cantly larger decrease in total construction and manufacturing employment compared to the nation, the state did experience a signifi cantly larger decrease in construction employment separately. Between 2008 and 2009, Hawaii reported a 27 percent decrease in construction employment. Information on industry classifi cations can be found at <www.census.gov/acs/www/UseData/Def.htm>. The decrease in construction and manufacturing employment for Massachusetts was not signifi cantly diff erent than the decrease for the United States.

[8] According to American Community Survey data, males made up 78.6 percent of construction and manufacturing employment in 2009. Please see table C24030 for additional information at <http://factfinder .census.gov/servlet/DTTable?_bm=y& -geo_id=01 000US&- ds_name=ACS_2009_1 YR _G00_&- ang=en&-mt_name=ACS_2009_1 YR _G2000_ C24030&format=&-CONTEXT=dt>.

[9] According to American Community Survey data, females made up 74.8 percent of employment in the educational services and health care and social assistance industry group in 2009.

[10] Women in the prime working age group of 25 to 54 experienced increases in labor force participation between 2008 and 2009 while men of the same age experienced decreases. For more information, see "Labor Force Participation Rate for Selected Age Groups: 2008 and 2009," *American Community Survey Briefs,* <www.census.gov /prod/201 0pubs/acsbr09-9.pdf>. Also see Greenhouse, Steven, "Recession Drives Women Back to the Work Force," *The New York Times,* September 18, 2009, at <www .nytimes.com/2009/09/19 /business/1 9women.html>.

In: The American Community Survey ...   ISBN: 978-1-61324-362-6
Editors: B. M. Russo and A. D. Haffner   ©2011 Nova Science Publishers, Inc.

Chapter 12

HEALTH INSURANCE COVERAGE OF CHILDREN UNDER AGE 19: 2008 AND 2009

United States Census Bureau

INTRODUCTION

Health insurance coverage, whether private or public, improves children's access to health care services and the regularity with which children receive medical care. This improved access to care leads to better health for insured children compared to uninsured children.[1]

Insured children are either covered by private health insurance as dependents on a parent's or guardian's plan or through public coverage available to eligible low- income children. Children's health insurance coverage is susceptible to changes in adults' insurance coverage status as well as changes in a child's eligibility for public programs.

Between 2008 and 2009, changes in children's health insurance coverage type concurred with reduced access to private insurance and increased eligibility for public coverage. There were 9.4 million families with at least one unemployed member in 2009, up from 6.1 million in 2008.[2] This increase suggests decreased access to private insurance for parents and children.[3] The increase in the poverty rate for children under age 18, from 18.3 percent in

2008 to 20.0 percent in 2009, indicates that more children were eligible for public coverage.

Two federal laws increased access to public coverage in 2009. First, the federal government reauthorized the Children's Health Insurance Program— a program designed to provide health insurance coverage to uninsured children in families with income-levels above standards to qualify for Medicaid. The reauthorization took effect in April of 2009 and included funds for outreach and enrollment grants as well as provisions to remove barriers to enrollment. Second, the federal government passed the American Recovery and Reinvestment Act of 2009, which included funds to help states maintain Medicaid services for current enrollees and to defray costs associated with new enrollment from October 2008 through December 2010.[4] It is likely that these two Acts boosted enrollment in public programs shortly after the provisions in the Acts took effect.[5,6]

This report presents data on health insurance coverage of children under age 19 in the 2008 and 2009 American Community Surveys (ACS).[7] The data presented in this report are for the civilian noninstitutionalized population, which excludes active-duty military and persons in prisons and nursing homes.

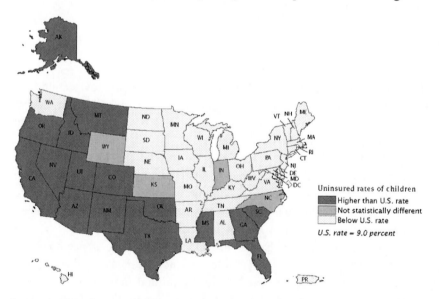

Sources: U.S. Census Bureau, American Community Survey, 2009, Puerto Rico Community Survey, 2009.

Figure 1. Uninsured Rates of Children by State and Puerto Rico: 2009.

HIGHLIGHTS

- Between 2008 and 2009, the percentage of insured children in the United States increased from 90.3 percent to 91.0 percent.
- In 2009, the uninsured rate of children in the United States was 9.0 percent, and among the states the uninsured rate ranged from 1 8.4 percent in Nevada to 1 .5 percent in Massachusetts.
- Between 2008 and 2009, the uninsured rate for children decreased in the United States as well as in 1 7 states. The uninsured rate increased in two states (Alaska and Minnesota), and it was not statistically different in 32 states and Puerto Rico.
- The percentage of insured children with private insurance decreased from 71.3 percent in 2008 to 68.0 percent in 2009. The percentage of insured children with public coverage increased from 32.7 percent in 2008 to 35.7 percent in 2009.

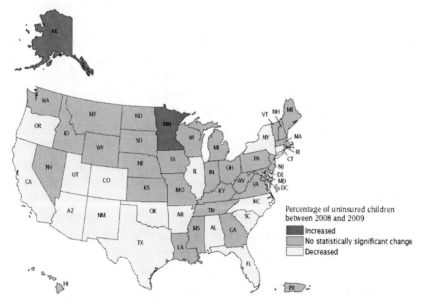

Sources: U.S. Census Bureau, American Community Surveys, 2008 and 2009, Puerto Rico Community Surveys, 2008 and 2009.

Figure 2. Change in Uninsured Rates of Children by State and Puerto Rico: 2008 and 2009.

HEALTH INSURANCE COVERAGE

The percentage of insured children in the United States increased from 90.3 percent in 2008 to 91.0 percent in 2009, with 1.1 million more insured children in 2009 compared to 2008 (see table). Conversely, the percentage of uninsured children in the United States decreased from 9.7 percent in 2008 to 9.0 percent in 2009, with 517,669 fewer uninsured children in 2009 compared to 2008.

In 2009, Nevada had the highest percentage of uninsured children, 18.4 percent, and Massachusetts had the lowest percentage of uninsured children, 1 .5 percent. Compared to the percentage of uninsured children nationally, the percentage of uninsured children was higher in 1 6 states, lower in 31 states and Puerto Rico, and not statistically different in 4 states (Figure 1). Between 2008 and 2009, the percentage of uninsured children increased in 2 states (Alaska and Minnesota), decreased in 1 7 states, and did not change significantly in 32 states and Puerto Rico (Figure 2).

The increases in the number and percent of insured children in the United States between 2008 and 2009 were accompanied by shifts in the coverage types held by insured children. The number of insured children with private coverage decreased from 50.5 million in 2008 to 48.9 million in 2009, while the percentage decreased from 71 .3 percent to 68.0 percent. The number of insured children with public coverage increased from 23.1 million in 2008 to 25.7 million in 2009, while the percentage increased from 32.7 percent to 35.7 percent. The net effect of the change in overall coverage was 517,669 fewer uninsured children in 2009 than in 2008—even though about 400,000 more parents were uninsured and the U.S. economy was in recession. Specifically, the percentage of insured children with employer-based insurance, the percentage with direct purchase, and the percentage with Medicare decreased, while the percentage of insured children with Medicaid or other means-tested public coverage increased between 2008 and 2009 (Figure 3).

Measuring Health Insurance Coverage

The ACS asks respondents about current health insurance coverage at the time of the interview.

Respondents select one or more types of health insurance from a list or explain their coverage in a written response. Respondents who do not indicate a form of coverage or only select Indian Health Service (IHS) are considered uninsured.

Health insurance coverage in the ACS is broadly classified as private or public coverage. The follow-ing are definitions for the types of coverage captured by the ACS and discussed in this report.

Private Health Insurance

Employer-based: Insurance through a current or former employer or union.

Direct-purchase: Insurance purchased directly from an insurance company.

TRICARE or other military health coverage: Coverage for active duty service members, National Guard and Reserve members, retirees, their families, survivors, and certain former spouses.

Public Coverage

Medicare: Coverage for people 65 and older or people with certain disabilities.

Medicaid or other means-tested public coverage: Medicaid, medical assistance, or any kind of government-assistance plan for those with low incomes or a disability (for example, Children's Health Insurance Program— CHIP).

VA Health Care: Provided through the Department of Veterans Affairs (includes those who have ever used or enrolled in VA Health Care).

FOR MORE INFORMATION

For more information about health insurance estimates, go to the U.S. Census Bureau health insurance Web site at < *www.census.gov/hhes /www/ hlthins/hlthins.html*> or contact the Health and Disability Statistics Branch of the U.S. Census Bureau at 301-763-9112.

SOURCE AND ACCURACY

Data presented in this report are based on people and households that responded to the ACS in 2008 and 2009. The resulting estimates are representative of the entire population. All comparisons presented in this report have taken sampling error into account and are significant at the 90 percent confidence level unless otherwise noted. Due to rounding, some details may not sum to totals. For information on sampling and estimation methods, confidentiality protection, and sampling and nonsampling errors, please see the "2009 ACS Accuracy of the Data" document located at <*www.census gov/acs/www /Downloads/data_documentation /Accu* racy/ACS_Accu racy_of _Data_2009.pdf>.

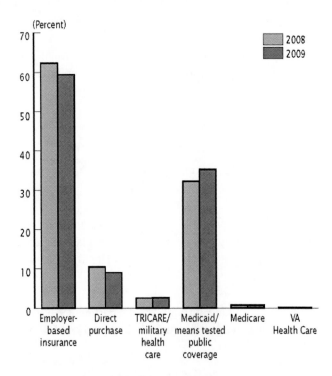

Sources: U.S. Census Bureau, American Community Surveys, 2008 and 2009.

Figure 3. Health Insurance Coverage of Insured Children by Type: 2008 and 2009 (Percent).

Health Insurance coverage of children by state and Puerto Rico: 2008 and 2009 (Numbers in thousands)

Area	2008 health insurance coverage				2009 health insurance coverage				Change in health insurance coverage (2009 less 2008)			
	Number	Margin of error[1] (±)	Percent	Margin of error[1] (±)	Number	Margin of error[1] (±)	Percent	Margin of error[1] (±)	Number	Margin of error[1] (±)	Percent	Margin of error[1] (±)
United States[2]	70,827	78	90.3	0.10	71,895	70	91.0	0.09	*1,068	105	*0.72	0.14
Alabama	1,094	7	92.1	0.58	1,120	8	93.8	0.53	*26	11	*1.76	0.79
Alaska	169	3	87.5	1.31	169	3	85.4	1.62	–	5	*-2.11	2.09
Arizona	1,514	13	84.4	0.73	1,590	11	87.3	0.56	*75	17	*2.86	0.91
Arkansas	682	6	91.2	0.80	697	6	93.0	0.67	*15	8	*1.78	1.04
California	8,898	27	89.5	0.26	8,988	23	90.0	0.23	*90	35	*0.55	0.35
Colorado	1,095	10	85.9	0.79	1,161	11	89.4	0.75	*65	15	*3.42	1.09
Connecticut	822	5	95.1	0.55	826	5	96.0	0.53	3	7	*0.90	0.76
Delaware	201	3	92.4	1.40	210	3	94.4	1.21	*9	5	*2.05	1.85
District of Columbia	119	3	96.3	1.37	122	2	96.6	1.30	3	3	0.28	1.89
Florida	3,513	21	82.7	0.48	3,635	21	84.7	0.46	*123	30	*1.94	0.66
Georgia	2,381	14	88.6	0.49	2,419	14	88.4	0.46	*38	20	-0.20	0.68
Hawaii	290	3	96.4	0.85	297	3	97.1	0.67	*7	4	0.63	1.08
Idaho	382	6	87.2	1.19	392	5	88.2	1.04	*10	7	1.02	1.58
Illinois	3,194	13	94.4	0.33	3,197	12	95.1	0.30	3	18	*0.70	0.44
Indiana	1,513	13	90.1	0.66	1,524	11	90.9	0.62	11	17	0.82	0.91
Iowa	715	5	94.7	0.57	717	6	95.1	0.53	2	8	0.37	0.77
Kansas	685	7	92.2	0.66	679	6	91.3	0.71	-6	9	-0.96	0.97

(Continued)

Area	2008 health insurance coverage				2009 health insurance coverage				Change in health insurance coverage (2009 less 2008)			
	Number	Margin of error[1] (±)	Percent	Margin of error[1] (±)	Number	Margin of error[1] (±)	Percent	Margin of error[1] (±)	Number	Margin of error[1] (±)	Percent	Margin of error[1] (±)
Kentucky	992	8	93.1	0.63	1,001	7	93.1	0.59	9	11	-0.02	0.86
Louisiana	1,084	9	92.2	0.59	1,106	8	92.8	0.57	*22	12	0.67	0.82
Maine	274	3	93.1	1.20	273	3	94.2	0.82	-1	5	1.14	1.46
Maryland	1,350	8	94.6	0.47	1,360	7	94.9	0.39	10	11	0.31	0.61
Massachusetts	1,498	7	98.2	0.24	1,517	6	98.5	0.20	*18	9	0.26	0.31
Michigan	2,420	9	94.7	0.30	2,372	9	94.9	0.27	*-48	13	0.14	0.40
Minnesota	1,248	5	94.0	0.36	1,246	7	93.3	0.43	-2	9	*-0.69	0.56
Mississippi	716	8	87.8	1.05	728	9	89.1	0.96	*12	12	1.29	1.42
Missouri	1,392	7	92.8	0.40	1,404	9	92.7	0.51	*12	12	-0.14	0.65
Montana	205	4	86.2	1.42	206	4	86.9	1.31	1	6	0.72	1.93
Nebraska	440	4	92.8	0.78	442	4	93.4	0.82	2	6	0.59	1.13
Nevada	561	9	80.0	1.28	585	10	81.6	1.38	*24	14	1.64	1.88
New Hampshire	295	3	94.8	0.84	295	3	95.1	0.82	–	4	0.26	1.17
New Jersey	2,010	10	92.9	0.40	2,019	8	93.3	0.32	9	12	0.36	0.51
New Mexico	461	6	86.2	1.00	482	8	87.7	1.08	*21	10	*1.59	1.47
New York	4,449	14	94.4	0.24	4,473	13	95.1	0.24	*24	19	*0.65	0.34
North Carolina	2,144	13	90.1	0.49	2,205	13	91.3	0.39	*61	18	*1.21	0.63
North Dakota	141	3	92.8	1.41	144	2	94.3	0.96	3	4	1.54	1.71
Ohio	2,690	12	92.9	0.39	2,696	13	93.3	0.38	5	17	0.36	0.55

(Continued)

Area	2008 health insurance coverage				2009 health insurance coverage				Change in health insurance coverage (2009 less 2008)			
	Number	Margin of error[1] (±)	Percent	Margin of error[1] (±)	Number	Margin of error[1] (±)	Percent	Margin of error[1] (±)	Number	Margin of error[1] (±)	Percent	Margin of error[1] (±)
Oklahoma	837	7	87.0	0.68	860	7	88.3	0.68	*23	10	*1.30	0.96
Oregon	803	9	87.7	0.87	827	9	89.1	0.73	*24	12	*1.45	1.14
Pennsylvania	2,783	12	94.0	0.39	2,796	10	94.4	0.32	13	16	0.42	0.51
Rhode Island	232	3	94.8	0.87	230	3	94.3	1.04	–2	4	–0.53	1.35
S. Carolina	998	8	87.9	0.68	1,030	8	89.5	0.68	*32	11	*1.58	0.96
South Dakota	192	3	91.2	1.28	193	3	92.2	1.14	–	5	0.91	1.71
Tennessee	1,456	9	93.2	0.51	1,479	10	93.6	0.49	*24	13	0.35	0.71
Texas	5,846	23	82.4	0.31	6,022	27	83.1	0.38	*177	35	*0.63	0.49
Utah	783	9	87.1	0.93	822	8	89.4	0.88	*39	12	*2.32	1.28
Vermont	134	2	95.9	1.00	133	2	96.5	0.80	–1	3	0.56	1.28
Virginia	1,789	11	92.5	0.47	1,841	10	93.1	0.43	*52	15	0.62	0.64
Washington	1,506	9	92.0	0.51	1,544	9	92.6	0.50	*38	12	0.68	0.71
West Virginia	384	4	93.4	0.83	385	4	94.0	0.85	1	6	0.55	1.19
Wisconsin	1,322	6	94.9	0.40	1,313	7	94.7	0.45	–9	10	–0.15	0.60
Wyoming.	125	3	91.1	1.71	124	3	90.7	2.03	–1	4	–0.35	2.65
Puerto Rico	994	6	95.1	0.47	976	5	95.3	0.47	*–18	8	0.19	0.66

* Statistically different at the 90 percent confidence level. – Represents or rounds to zero.

[1] Data are based on a sample and are subject to sampling variability. A margin of error is a measure of an estimate's variability. The larger the margin of error in relation to the size of the estimate, the less reliable the estimate. This number when added to and subtracted from the estimate forms the 90 percent confidence interval.

[2] The U.S. estimates do not include Puerto Rico.

Sources: U.S. Census Bureau, American Community Surveys, 2008 and 2009, Puerto Rico Community Surveys, 2008 and 2009.

End Notes

[1] Institute of Medicine, *Health Insurance Is a Family Matter*, The National Academies Press, Washington DC, 2002.

[2] Bureau of Labor Statistics, U.S. Department of Labor, "Employment Characteristics of Families— 2009," June 10, 2010, <www.bls.gov/news.release /famee.nr0.htm> (August 10, 2010).

[3] Gerry L. Fairbrother et al., "The Impact of Parental Job Loss on Children's Health Insurance Coverage," *Health Affairs*, vol. 29, no. 7, 2010.

[4] Kaiser Commission on Medicaid and the Uninsured, "American Recovery and Reinvestment Act (ARRA): Medicaid and Health Care Provisions," March 4, 2009, <www.kff.org/medicaid/7872.cfm> (August 10, 2010).

[5] Vernon K. Smith, et al., "The Crunch Continues: Medicaid Spending, Coverage and Policy in the Midst of a Recession," September 2009, <www.kff.org /medicaid/7985.cfm> (August 30, 2010).

[6] Vernon K. Smith, et al., "CHIP Enrollment June 2009: An Update on Current Enrollment and Policy Directions," April 2010, <www.kff.org/ medicaid/7642 .cfm> (August 30, 2010).

[7] Data for children under 19 are presented because both Medicaid and the Children's Health Insurance Program are available to eligible children under 19.

In: The American Community Survey ...   ISBN: 978-1-61324-362-6
Editors: B. M. Russo and A. D. Haffner   ©2011 Nova Science Publishers, Inc.

Chapter 13

DISABILITY AMONG THE WORKING AGE POPULATION: 2008 AND 2009

United States Census Bureau

INTRODUCTION

Many policies directed toward the population of people with disabilities have focused on expanding employment opportunities. Federal laws, like the Rehabilitation Act of 1 972 and the Americans with Disabilities Act of 1 990 (ADA), have attempted to improve workplace conditions by encouraging reasonable accommodation and reducing job discrimination. Over the two decades since the ADA was signed, countless numbers of people with disabilities have credited the legislation with improving their lives.[1] Despite the progress made, barriers still remain that limit full participation in the labor force.[2]

This report presents data on disability and employment among the population 16 to 64 years old to help assess the economic differences between people with and without disabilities in the 2008 and 2009 American Community Surveys (ACS). The data presented in this report are for the civilian noninstitutionalized population, which exclude people in prisons, nursing homes, and active duty military.

Disability: Difficulty with any of the six types of disability collected in the American Community Survey: vision, hearing, ambulatory, cognitive, self-care, and independent living. It covers functional limitations in the three domains of disability (communication, mental, and physical[3]), activities of daily living (ADLs), and instrumental activities of daily living (IADLs).

Vision difficulty: Blindness or serious difficulty seeing, even when wearing glasses or contacts.

Hearing difficulty: Deafness or serious difficulty hearing.

Cognitive difficulty: Serious difficulty remembering, concentrating, or making decisions.

Ambulatory difficulty: Serious difficulty walking or climbing stairs.

Self-care difficulty: Difficulty dressing or bathing. This type relates to ADLs.

Independent living difficulty: Difficulty doing errands alone such as visiting a doctor's office or shopping. This type relates to IADLs.

Employment-to-population ratio: The ratio of people who are currently employed to the total population, in terms of percentage.

HIGHLIGHTS

- In 2009, 19.5 million people, or 9.9 percent of the civilian noninstitutionalized population aged 16 to 64, had a disability. Between 2008 and 2009, both the number and percent of people with disabilities did not change.
- In 2009, West Virginia had the highest disability rate for people aged 16 to 64 years at 1 6.8 percent. Hawaii had the lowest rate, not statistically different from California, Colorado, Illinois, Minnesota, New Jersey, and Utah.
- About 34.7 percent of people with disabilities were employed compared with 71.9 percent of people without a disability. North

Dakota[4] had the highest employment-to-population ratio for people with disabilities, whereas the District of Columbia[5] had the lowest employment-to-population ratio for people with disabilities.

DISABILITY IN THE WORKING-AGE POPULATION

Of the 197.6 million people aged 16 to 64 in the civilian noninstitutionalized population in 2009, about 9.9 percent, or 1 9.5 million people, had a disability (see table). Neither the number nor percent of people with a disability were statistically different from the 2008 estimates.

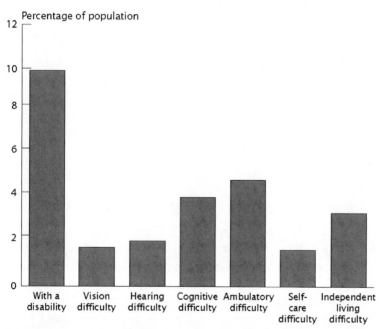

Note: Data are for the civilian noninstitutionalized population aged 16 to 64 years. This excludes people in correctional facilities, nursing homes, other institutions, and the armed forces.

Source: U.S. Census Bureau, American Community Survey, 2009.

Figure 1. Disability Status and Type: 2009.

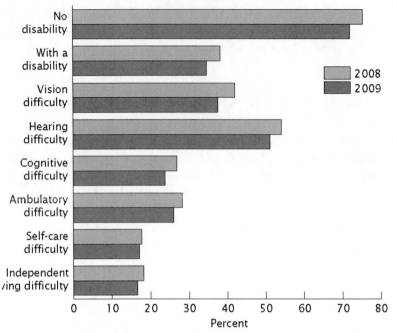

Note: Data are for the civilian noninstitutionalized population aged 1 6 to 64 years.
   This excludes people in correctional facilities, nursing homes, other institutions,
   and the armed forces.
Sources: U.S. Census Bureau, American Community Surveys, 2008 and 2009.

Figure 2. Employment-to-Population Ratio by Disability Status and Type: 2008 and
2009.

Ambulatory difficulty was the most prevalent disability type at 5.0 percent
of the population, as shown in Figure 1. About 1 .7 percent of the population
had a vision difficulty, 2.0 percent had a hearing difficulty, and 4.1 percent
had a cognitive difficulty. Self-care and independent living difficulties were
present in1.7 percent and 3.4 percent of the population, respectively.[6]

As shown in the table, West Virginia had the highest prevalence of disability of any state at 1 6.8 percent. Hawaii had the lowest prevalence of
disability at 7.5 percent, not statistically different from California, Colorado,
Illinois, Minnesota, New Jersey, and Utah. Between 2008 and 2009, seven
states experienced changes in the rates of disability. The disability prevalence
rates for Arizona, Illinois, Mississippi, and Texas decreased while the
prevalence rates for Michigan, Minnesota, and Ohio increased.

Number and Percent of People 16 to 64 Years With a Disability by State and Puerto Rico: 2008 and 2009

Area	With a disability in 2008				With a disability in 2009				Change in disability (2009 less 2008)	
	Number[1]	Margin of error[2] (±)	Percent	Margin of error[2] (±)	Number[1]	Margin of error[2] (±)	Percent	Margin of error[2] (±)	Number[1]	Percent
United States	19,470,362	70,857	9.9	0.1	19,511,992	83,745	9.9	0.1	41,630	-0.1
Alabama	424,476	11,477	14.3	0.4	433,364	10,030	14.5	0.3	8,888	0.2
Alaska	52,574	4,093	11.7	0.9	49,765	5,116	10.7	1.1	-2,809	-0.9
Arizona	410,819	11,598	10.2	0.3	390,228	11,418	9.5	0.3	*-20,591	*-0.7
Arkansas	278,740	8,005	15.5	0.4	284,750	8,978	15.7	0.5	6,010	0.2
California	1,920,577	26,636	8.0	0.1	1,898,118	22,046	7.9	0.1	-22,459	-0.1
Colorado	262,288	7,436	8.0	0.2	263,655	8,832	7.9	0.3	1,367	–
Connecticut	183,631	7,420	8.1	0.3	189,190	7,138	8.3	0.3	5,559	0.2
Delaware	60,439	3,988	10.8	0.7	60,525	4,248	10.7	0.7	86	-0.1
District of Columbia	36,831	3,690	8.9	0.9	42,254	4,185	10.0	1.0	5,423	1.1
Florida	1,083,669	20,469	9.5	0.2	1,095,352	19,800	9.5	0.2	11,683	–
Georgia	631,345	13,542	10.1	0.2	632,084	15,463	10.0	0.2	739	-0.1
Hawaii	58,251	3,523	7.3	0.4	59,788	4,052	7.5	0.5	1,537	0.2
Idaho	95,287	4,986	9.9	0.5	101,522	5,148	10.5	0.5	6,235	0.5
Illinois	678,493	15,627	8.1	0.2	654,101	13,743	7.8	0.2	*-24,392	*-0.3
Indiana	444,183	10,531	10.8	0.3	437,399	10,592	10.6	0.3	-6,784	-0.2
Iowa	174,908	5,993	9.1	0.3	171,419	6,344	8.9	0.3	-3,489	-0.2
Kansas	178,979	6,948	10.1	0.4	182,259	6,642	10.2	0.4	3,280	0.1
Kentucky	425,754	9,088	15.4	0.3	425,914	11,424	15.3	0.4	160	-0.1

(Continued)

Area	With a disability in 2008				With a disability in 2009				Change in disability (2009 less 2008)	
	Number[1]	Margin of error[2] (±)	Percent	Margin of error[2] (±)	Number[1]	Margin of error[2] (±)	Percent	Margin of error[2] (±)	Number[1]	Percent
Louisiana	365,227	9,585	12.9	0.3	359,341	10,354	12.5	0.4	−5,886	−0.4
Maine	115,125	5,102	13.3	0.6	118,589	4,737	13.6	0.5	3,464	0.4
Maryland	302,269	10,986	8.2	0.3	302,745	9,787	8.1	0.3	476	−0.1
Massachusetts	394,320	11,727	9.1	0.3	387,683	11,558	8.8	0.3	−6,637	−0.3
Michigan	730,896	13,322	11.2	0.2	749,726	16,508	11.6	0.3	18,830	*0.3
Minnesota	261,782	7,304	7.6	0.2	277,105	7,888	8.0	0.2	*15,323	*0.4
Mississippi	285,712	10,009	15.5	0.5	261,201	10,373	14.2	0.6	*−24,511	*−1.3
Missouri	455,257	10,978	12.0	0.3	463,093	10,727	12.1	0.3	7,836	0.1
Montana	68,861	4,010	11.0	0.6	68,373	3,612	10.9	0.6	−488	−0.1
Nebraska	95,848	4,837	8.5	0.4	98,624	4,711	8.7	0.4	2,776	0.2
Nevada	138,799	7,042	8.3	0.4	142,605	6,157	8.4	0.4	3,806	0.1
New Hampshire	78,265	4,819	8.8	0.5	77,659	4,398	8.7	0.5	−606	−0.1
New Jersey	413,816	11,299	7.3	0.2	426,109	11,444	7.5	0.2	12,293	0.2
New Mexico	148,053	6,326	11.8	0.5	147,955	6,252	11.7	0.5	−98	−0.1
New York	1,115,645	18,070	8.7	0.1	1,109,513	16,133	8.6	0.1	−6,132	—
North Carolina	661,171	14,039	11.2	0.2	661,450	12,346	11.1	0.2	279	−0.1
North Dakota	34,108	2,493	8.3	0.6	36,675	2,959	8.8	0.7	2,567	0.5
Ohio	819,340	13,974	11.1	0.2	850,393	15,028	11.4	0.2	*31,053	*0.4
Oklahoma	334,713	9,331	14.6	0.4	329,344	8,731	14.3	0.4	−5,369	−0.3
Oregon	271,816	9,585	10.9	0.4	265,448	8,388	10.6	0.3	−6,368	−0.3
Pennsylvania	848,251	15,020	10.6	0.2	853,417	16,252	10.5	0.2	5,166	−0.1

(Continued)

Area	With a disability in 2008				With a disability in 2009				Change in disability (2009 less 2008)	
	Number[1]	Margin of error[2] (±)	Percent	Margin of error[2] (±)	Number[1]	Margin of error[2] (±)	Percent	Margin of error[2] (±)	Number[1]	Percent
South Carolina	341,719	9,717	11.9	0.3	335,492	9,622	11.6	0.3	-6,227	-0.4
Rhode Island	70,313	4,393	10.2	0.6	68,807	4,602	9.9	0.7	-1,506	-0.2
South Dakota	43,281	2,764	8.6	0.6	45,753	3,665	9.0	0.7	2,472	0.3
Tennessee	515,808	11,118	12.8	0.3	533,193	11,713	13.1	0.3	*17,385	0.3
Texas	1,549,366	23,094	10.0	0.1	1,532,691	22,256	9.8	0.1	-16,675	*-0.2
Utah	131,896	7,058	7.8	0.4	134,701	6,568	7.8	0.4	2,805	0.1
Vermont	46,336	3,282	11.0	0.8	47,698	3,064	11.4	0.7	1,362	0.4
Virginia	437,151	11,992	8.7	0.2	449,973	11,462	8.8	0.2	12,822	0.1
Washington	438,653	11,194	10.2	0.3	448,492	12,597	10.2	0.3	9,839	0.1
West Virginia	203,209	6,838	17.2	0.6	197,633	6,479	16.8	0.6	-5,576	-0.5
Wisconsin	316,718	7,848	8.6	0.2	320,825	7,356	8.7	0.2	4,107	0.1
Wyoming	35,394	2,831	10.2	0.8	37,999	3,582	10.7	1.0	2,605	0.5
Puerto Rico	480,184	10,833	19.0	0.4	448,039	10,191	17.6	0.4	*-32,145	*-1.4

– Represents or rounds to zero.

* Statistically different at the 90 percent confidence level.

[1] The numbers and percents shown in this table are for the civilian noninstitutionalized population . This excludes people in correctional facilities, nursing homes, other institutions and the armed forces.

[2] Data are based on a sample and are subject to sampling variability. A margin of error is a measure of an estimate's variability. The larger the margin of error in relation to the size of the estimate, the less reliable the estimate. This number when added to and subtracted from the estimate forms the 90 percent confidence interval.

Sources: U .S . Census Bureau, American Community Surveys, 2008 and 2009, Puerto Rico Community Surveys, 2008 and 2009.

EMPLOYMENT OF PEOPLE WITH DISABILITIES

Because a large proportion of people with disabilities are not in the labor force, an employment-topopulation ratio is a more descriptive measure of this population's economic situation. Nationally, 34.7 percent of people aged 1 6 to 64 years with a disability were employed in 2009, down from 38.2 percent in 2008. For people without a disability, the employment-to-population ratio decreased from 75.2 percent in 2008 to 71 .9 percent in 2009. While the declines between the two groups were not statistically different from each other, people with disabilities were differentially affected by the economic downturn due to their lower overall employment.[7]

Of the six disability types, people with hearing difficulties had the highest employment-to-population ratio at 51.1 percent in 2009 (Figure 2). People with independent living difficulties had the lowest employment-to-population ratio at 1 6.6 percent. For each disability type, the ratio decreased from 2008 to 2009. People with vision difficulty experienced the greatest decline in the employment-to- population ratio, falling 4.3 percentage points from 42.0 percent in 2008 to 37.7 percent in 2009. People with self-care difficulty experienced the smallest decline from 17.7 percent in 2008 to 17.2 percent in 2009.[8]

In 2009, 26 states had employment- to-population ratios greater than the national estimate while 14 states and the District of Columbia had ratios that were lower than the national estimate. As shown in Figure 3, areas with low employment-to-population ratios appear concentrated in the southeastern area of the United States.

North Dakota had the highest employment-to-population ratio for people with disabilities at 56.0 percent, not statistically different from Wyoming. The District of Columbia had the lowest employment-to-population ratio at 26.8 percent, not statistically different from Alabama, Kentucky, Michigan, Mississippi, South Carolina, Tennessee, and West Virginia.

NOTE

In 2008, the Census Bureau changed the way it asks about disability status in the ACS. Because of this change, 2008 and 2009 estimates about the population of people with disabilities should not be compared to ACS disability estimates from prior years. For more information see Review of Changes to the Meas*urement* of Disability in the 2008 American Community Survey, available at <www.census .gov/hhes/www/disability /2008ACS_ disability.pdf>.

FOR MORE INFORMATION

For more information about the population of people with disabilities, go to the U.S. Census

Bureau Web site on disability at <www.census.gov/hhes/www /d isabi l ity/d isabi l ity. html>, contact the Health and Disability Statistics Branch of the U.S. Census Bureau at 301-763-9112, or e-mail <*matthew.w.brault@ census.gov*>. For monthly employment statistics about people with disabilities, go to the Bureau of Labor Statistics Web site for disability data in the Current Population Survey at <www.bls.gov/cps/cpsdisability .htm>.

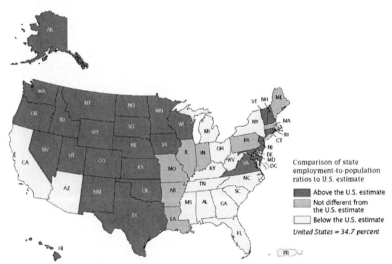

Comparison of state employment-to-population ratios to U.S. estimate

- Above the U.S. estimate
- Not different from the U.S. estimate
- Below the U.S. estimate

United States = 34.7 percent

Note: Data are for the civilian noninstitutionalized population aged 16 to 64 years. This excludes people in correctional facilities, nursing homes, other institutions, and the armed forces.

Sources: U.S. Census Bureau, American Community Survey, 2009, Puerto Rico Community Survey, 2009.

Figure 3. Employment-to-Population Ratio for the Population With a Disability by State: 2009.

SOURCE AND ACCURACY

Data presented in this report are based on people and households that responded to the ACS in 2008 and 2009. The resulting estimates are representative of the civilian noninstitutionalized population. All comparisons presented in this report have taken sampling error into account and are significant at the 90 percent confidence level unless otherwise noted. Due to rounding, some details may not sum to totals. For information on sampling and estimation methods, confidentiality protection, and sampling and nonsampling errors, please see the "2009 ACS Accuracy of the Data" document located at < *www.census.gov/acs/www/Downloads/data_documentation/Accu* racy/ACS_ Accu racy_of_Data_2009.pdf>.

End Notes

[1] National Council on Disability, "The Impact of the Americans with Disabilities Act: Assessing the Progress Toward Achieving the Goals of the ADA," Washington, DC. July 26, 2007.

[2] National Council on Disability, "National Disability Policy: A Progress Report," Washington, DC. March 31, 2009.

[3] The three domains of disability are used to broadly categorize types of disability. See *Americans With Disabilities: 2005* (P70-1 1 7) available at <*www.census.gov/p rod/ 2008 pubs /p70-1 1 7.pdf*>.

[4] Not statistically different from Wyoming.

[5] Not statistically different from Alabama, Kentucky, Michigan, Mississippi, South Carolina, Tennessee, and West Virginia.

[6] The percentage with a vision difficulty and percentage with a self-care difficulty round to the same number but are statistically different.

[7] The percent decline in the employmentto-population ratio for people with disabilities was 9.1 percent, compared with the percent decline in the ratio for people without disabilities at 4.4 percent.

[8] The employment-to-population ratio for people with self-care difficulty in 2008 was not statistically different from the ratio for people with independent living difficulty in the same year.

In: The American Community Survey ...   ISBN: 978-1-61324-362-6
Editors: B. M. Russo and A. D. Haffner   ©2011 Nova Science Publishers, Inc.

Chapter 14

PUBLIC ASSISTANCE RECEIPT
IN THE PAST 12 MONTHS
FOR HOUSEHOLDS: 2008 AND 2009

United States Census Bureau

INTRODUCTION

This report presents data on public assistance receipt at the national and state levels based on the 2008 and 2009 American Community Surveys (ACS). Public assistance income, or welfare, provides cash payments to poor families and includes general assistance and Temporary Assistance to Needy Families (TANF), which replaced Aid to Families with Dependent Children (AFDC) in 1997. Public assistance income does not include Supplemental Security Income (SSI), noncash benefits such as food stamps, or separate payments received for hospital or other medical care (vendor payments). To qualify for public assistance benefits, the income and/or assets of an individual or family must fall below specified thresholds. However, unlike AFDC benefits, TANF benefits are time-limited, require most adult recipients to work, and give states increased flexibility in program design.

The ACS questions on participation in public assistance were designed to identify households in which one or more current members received public assistance during the past 12 months. These data are for households, not individuals. If any person living at the sample address at the time of the interview received public assistance, the household is included in the count.

PUBLIC ASSISTANCE RECEIPT

In 2009, 3.0 million households had received public assistance during the past 12 months, an increase of about 0.4 million from the 2008 estimate. Among the states with the highest public assistance participation in 2009 were Alaska (6.3 percent), Maine (4.9 percent), Washington (4.1 percent), and Michigan (3.9 percent), as well as the District of Columbia (5.3 percent).[1] Although not statistically different when compared with some other states, states with the lowest public assistance participation rates included Louisiana (1.3 percent), Wyoming (1.5 percent), and Alabama (1.6 percent).

The public assistance participation rate for U.S. households was 2.6 percent in 2009 —0.3 percentage points higher than in 2008. Fourteen states, the District of Columbia, and Puerto Rico had a statistically higher participation rate when compared to the national average in 2009. These states were concentrated in the Northeast (Maine, Vermont, Pennsylvania, New York, and Connecticut) and West (Alaska, Washington, Hawaii, California, and Oregon). The remaining states included Michigan, Oklahoma, Ohio, and Minnesota.

Twenty-one states had statistically lower participation rates when compared to the national average in 2009. Ten of them were located in the South (Louisiana, Alabama, Florida, Georgia, South Carolina, North Carolina, Texas, Maryland, Virginia, and Arkansas). The remaining states were Wyoming, Wisconsin, Colorado, Nebraska, North Dakota, Utah, Rhode Island, Illinois, Missouri, Iowa, and New Jersey.

Twenty states (Alabama, Arizona, California, Florida, Georgia, Illinois, Maryland, Michigan, Mississippi, Nevada, New Jersey, North Carolina, Ohio, Oregon, Tennessee, Texas, Utah, Virginia, Washington, and Wisconsin), the District of Columbia, and Puerto Rico had increases in the number and percentages of households receiving public assistance between 2008 and 2009. In Hawaii, the number of households receiving public assistance grew, but the rate was statistically unchanged. In all the remaining states, the rates and the number of households receiving public assistance were not statistically different from the 2008 estimates.

Public Assistance Receipt in the Past 12 Months for Households by state and Puerto Rico: 2008 and 2009

Area	Public assistance receipt in 2008				Public assistance receipt in 2009				Change in public assistance receipt (2009 less 2008)			
	Estimate	Margin of error[1] (±)	Percent	Margin of error[1] (±)	Estimate	Margin of error[1] (±)	Percent	Margin of error[1] (±)	Estimate	Margin of error[1] (±)	Percent	Margin of error[1] (±)
United States	**2,649,499**	**26,671**	**2.3**	**0.1**	**3,009,319**	**28,071**	**2.6**	**0.1**	***359,820**	**38,721**	***0.3**	**–**
Alabama	22,608	2,338	1.2	0.1	29,804	2,639	1.6	0.1	*7,196	3,526	*0.4	0.2
Alaska	14,902	1,682	6.3	0.7	14,993	2,262	6.3	0.9	91	2,819	0.1	1.2
Arizona	47,519	3,588	2.1	0.2	57,416	4,182	2.5	0.2	*9,897	5,510	*0.4	0.2
Arkansas	22,098	2,160	2.0	0.2	23,257	2,627	2.1	0.2	1,159	3,401	0.1	0.3
California	395,008	10,756	3.2	0.1	449,059	10,015	3.7	0.1	*54,051	14,697	*0.4	0.1
Colorado	33,597	2,947	1.8	0.2	37,466	3,057	2.0	0.2	3,869	4,246	0.2	0.2
Connecticut	36,922	2,742	2.8	0.2	38,919	3,025	2.9	0.2	1,997	4,083	0.2	0.3
Delaware	7,349	1,160	2.2	0.4	8,567	1,542	2.6	0.5	1,218	1,930	0.4	0.6
District of Columbia	10,686	1,636	4.3	0.6	13,308	1,984	5.3	0.8	*2,622	2,571	*1.1	1.0
Florida	96,884	5,482	1.4	0.1	115,630	5,168	1.7	0.1	*18,746	7,534	*0.3	0.1
Georgia	45,775	3,547	1.3	0.1	57,584	3,608	1.7	0.1	*11,809	5,060	*0.3	0.1
Hawaii	13,466	1,778	3.1	0.4	16,443	2,130	3.7	0.5	*2,977	2,775	0.6	0.6
Idaho	13,758	1,732	2.4	0.3	15,193	1,672	2.7	0.3	1,435	2,407	0.3	0.4
Illinois	87,947	5,057	1.8	0.1	111,669	5,728	2.3	0.1	*23,722	7,641	*0.5	0.2
Indiana	65,145	3,995	2.6	0.2	68,643	4,151	2.8	0.2	3,498	5,761	0.1	0.2
Iowa	27,096	2,426	2.2	0.2	29,483	2,907	2.4	0.2	2,387	3,786	0.2	0.3
Kansas	25,769	2,842	2.3	0.3	28,182	2,637	2.6	0.2	2,413	3,877	0.2	0.3
Kentucky	40,520	3,201	2.4	0.2	42,486	3,497	2.5	0.2	1,966	4,741	0.1	0.3

(Continued)

Area	Public assistance receipt in 2008				Public assistance receipt in 2009				Change in public assistance receipt (2009 less 2008)			
	Estimate	Margin of error[1] (±)	Percent	Margin of error[1] (±)	Estimate	Margin of error[1] (±)	Percent	Margin of error[1] (±)	Estimate	Margin of error[1] (±)	Percent	Margin of error[1] (±)
Louisiana	21,748	2,130	1.3	0.1	22,468	2,138	1.3	0.1	720	3,018	–	0.2
Maine	25,405	2,604	4.7	0.5	26,669	2,406	4.9	0.4	1,264	3,545	0.2	0.7
Maryland	33,169	3,280	1.6	0.2	41,470	3,352	2.0	0.2	*8,301	4,690	*0.4	0.2
Massachusetts	66,470	4,514	2.7	0.2	70,320	4,365	2.8	0.2	3,850	6,279	0.1	0.3
Michigan	131,772	4,692	3.5	0.1	147,919	6,773	3.9	0.2	*16,147	8,240	*0.4	0.2
Minnesota	63,058	3,347	3.0	0.2	66,091	4,162	3.2	0.2	3,033	5,340	0.2	0.3
Mississippi	19,925	2,129	1.8	0.2	27,666	2,392	2.5	0.2	*7,741	3,202	*0.7	0.3
Missouri	53,787	3,929	2.3	0.2	55,963	3,627	2.4	0.2	2,176	5,347	0.1	0.2
Montana	7,905	1,335	2.1	0.4	8,728	1,203	2.3	0.3	823	1,797	0.2	0.5
Nebraska	16,055	2,232	2.3	0.3	15,482	1,818	2.2	0.3	–573	2,879	–0.1	0.4
Nevada	20,192	1,919	2.1	0.2	26,176	2,707	2.7	0.3	*5,984	3,318	*0.6	0.3
New Hampshire	12,053	1,680	2.4	0.3	14,663	2,163	2.9	0.4	2,610	2,739	0.5	0.5
New Jersey	64,838	3,553	2.1	0.1	76,828	4,092	2.4	0.1	*11,990	5,419	*0.4	0.2
New Mexico	18,473	2,300	2.5	0.3	18,027	2,108	2.4	0.3	–446	3,120	–0.1	0.4
New York	214,142	8,210	3.0	0.1	224,674	7,769	3.1	0.1	10,532	11,304	0.1	0.2
North Carolina	56,035	3,667	1.6	0.1	64,936	4,165	1.8	0.1	*8,901	5,549	*0.2	0.2
North Dakota	5,197	1,125	1.9	0.4	6,155	1,211	2.2	0.4	958	1,653	0.3	0.6
Ohio	118,763	4,887	2.6	0.1	150,463	5,757	3.3	0.1	*31,700	7,552	*0.7	0.2
Oklahoma	46,465	3,271	3.3	0.2	47,863	2,797	3.3	0.2	1,398	4,304	–	0.3

(Continued)

Area	Public assistance receipt in 2008				Public assistance receipt in 2009				Change in public assistance receipt (2009 less 2008)			
	Estimate	Margin of error[1] (±)	Percent	Margin of error[1] (±)	Estimate	Margin of error[1] (±)	Percent	Margin of error[1] (±)	Estimate	Margin of error[1] (±)	Percent	Margin of error[1] (±)
Oregon	36,149	2,827	2.5	0.2	51,179	4,011	3.4	0.3	*15,030	4,908	*1.0	0.3
Pennsylvania	158,603	6,549	3.2	0.1	161,311	5,903	3.3	0.1	2,708	8,816	–	0.2
Rhode Island	10,940	1,505	2.7	0.4	9,218	1,396	2.3	0.3	–1,722	2,053	–0.5	0.5
South Carolina	29,542	2,646	1.7	0.2	29,891	2,906	1.7	0.2	349	3,930	–	0.2
South Dakota	7,005	1,070	2.2	0.3	7,520	1,091	2.4	0.3	515	1,528	0.2	0.5
Tennessee	58,193	3,356	2.4	0.1	65,543	3,673	2.7	0.2	*7,350	4,976	*0.3	0.2
Texas	132,310	5,150	1.6	0.1	155,207	6,067	1.8	0.1	*22,897	7,958	*0.2	0.1
Utah	12,695	1,669	1.5	0.2	19,194	1,908	2.2	0.2	*6,499	2,535	*0.7	0.3
Vermont	7,349	1,160	2.9	0.5	9,121	1,475	3.6	0.6	1,772	1,876	0.7	0.7
Virginia	49,535	3,969	1.7	0.1	60,292	3,952	2.0	0.1	*10,757	5,601	*0.4	0.2
Washington	87,372	4,576	3.4	0.2	103,993	5,106	4.1	0.2	*16,621	6,857	*0.6	0.3
West Virginia	17,147	1,940	2.3	0.3	19,865	2,044	2.7	0.3	2,718	2,818	0.4	0.4
Wisconsin	37,559	2,912	1.7	0.1	43,101	3,002	1.9	0.1	*5,542	4,182	*0.2	0.2
Wyoming	2,599	801	1.2	0.4	3,221	837	1.5	0.4	622	1,159	0.3	0.6
Puerto	64,826	3,266	5.5	0.3	70,263	3,446	5.9	0.3	*5,437	4,748	*0.5	0.4

* Statistically different at the 90 percent confidence level .

– Represents or rounds to zero .

[1] Data are based on a sample and are subject to sampling variability . A margin of error is a measure of an estimate's variability . The larger the margin of error in relation to the size of the estimate, the less reliable the estimate . When added to and subtracted from the estimate, the margin of error forms the 90 percent confidence interval .

Sources: United States Census Bureau, American Community Surveys, 2008 and 2009, Puerto Rico Community Surveys, 2008 and 2009..

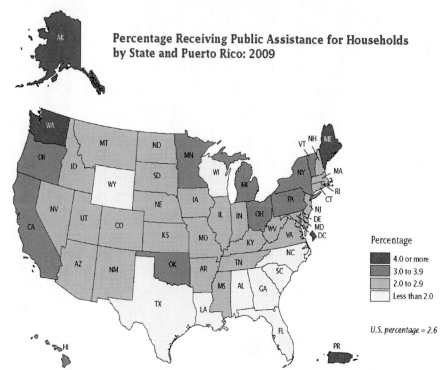

Percentage Receiving Public Assistance for Households
by State and Puerto Rico: 2009

Percentage

	4.0 or more
	3.0 to 3.9
	2.0 to 2.9
	Less than 2.0

U.S. percentage = 2.6

Sources: U.S. Census Bureau, American Community Survey, 2009, Puerto Rico
Community Survey, 2009.

SOURCE AND ACCURACY

Data presented in this report are based on people and households that
responded to the ACS in 2008 and 2009. The resulting estimates are
representative of the entire population. All comparisons presented in this
report have taken sampling error into account and are significant at the 90
percent confidence level unless otherwise noted. Due to rounding, some details
may not sum to totals. For information on sampling and estimation methods,
confidentiality protection, and sampling and nonsampling errors, please see
the "2009 ACS Accuracy of the Data" document located at *<www.census.
gov/acs/www/*Down loads/data_docu mentation /Accuracy/accuracy2009.pdf>.

End Notes

[1] Alaska's and Maine's 2009 ACS public assistance participation rates were not statistically different from the rate for the District of Columbia (5.3 percent). Washington's 2009 ACS public assistance participation rate was not statistically different from the rates for Michigan (3.9 percent), Hawaii (3.7 percent), and Vermont (3.6 percent). Michigan's 2009 ACS public assistance participation rate was not statistically different from the rates for Washington (4.1 percent), Hawaii (3.7 percent), California (3.7 percent), and Vermont (3.6 percent). The District of Columbia's 2009 ACS public assistance participation rate was not statistically different from the rates for Alaska (6.3 percent) and Maine (4.9 percent).

In: The American Community Survey ...   ISBN: 978-1-61324-362-6
Editors: B. M. Russo and A. D. Haffner   ©2011 Nova Science Publishers, Inc.

Chapter 15

SCIENCE AND ENGINEERING DEGREES: 2009

United States Census Bureau

INTRODUCTION

This brief presents data on reported field of bachelor's degrees for the nation, the 50 states, the District of Columbia, and Puerto Rico based on the 2009 American Community Survey (ACS). It focuses on the distribution of degrees in science and engineering fields (S&E) compared to all other degree fields. The science and engineering category includes fields such as animal sciences, biology, psychology, engineering, and anthropology. Examples of nonscience and nonengineering fields include agriculture, business, communications, education, and social work.

Information on field of bachelor's degree was first collected by the ACS in 2009. Respondents who reported their highest degree completed was a bachelor's degree, master's degree, professional degree, or doctoral degree were also asked to list the specific major(s) of the bachelor's degree. Respondents with more than one bachelor's degree, or with more than one major field, were allowed to report multiple fields of degree. Field(s) of degree for levels of education other than the bachelor's (such as vocational, master's, or doctorate) were not collected.

SCIENCE AND ENGINEERING DEGREES IN THE UNITED STATES

The map displays the variation in S&E degrees by state for 2009. The table contains the estimated number of people with any bachelor's degree, the number of people with at least one S&E bachelor's degree, and the percentage of people with at least one bachelor's degree in an S&E field. The estimated number of people in the United States age 25 and over with a bachelor's degree or higher was 56.3 million. Of this group, 20.5 million, or 36.4 percent, held at least one S&E degree.

The percentages of all bachelor's degrees in the S&E fields were 28 or less in Mississippi, North Dakota, and Puerto Rico, and as high as 51 in the District of Columbia.

The District of Columbia and the five states of California, Maryland, Massachusetts, Virginia, and Washington had a percentage of S&E degrees above 40 percent. Nine additional states were also above the national average of 36.4 percent: Alaska, Colorado, Connecticut, New Hampshire, New Jersey, New Mexico, New York, Oregon, and Vermont.

SOURCE AND ACCURACY

Data presented in this report are based on people and households that responded to the ACS in 2009. The resulting estimates are representative of the entire population. All comparisons presented in this report have taken sampling error into account and are significant at the 90 percent confidence level unless otherwise noted. Due to rounding, some details may not sum to totals. For information on sampling and estimation methods, confidentiality protection, and sampling and nonsampling errors, please see the "2009 ACS Accuracy of the Data" document located at <www .census.gov/acs/www/ Downloads /data_documentation/Accuracy/ACS _Accu racy_of_Data_2 009. pdf>.

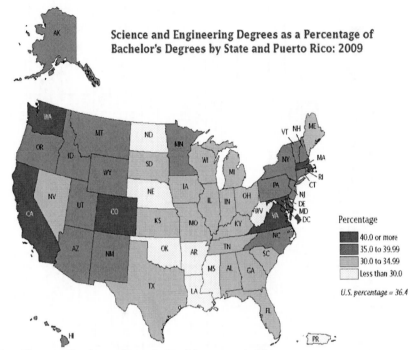

Science and Engineering Degrees as a Percentage of
Bachelor's Degrees by State and Puerto Rico: 2009

Percentage

40.0 or more
35.0 to 39.99
30.0 to 34.99
Less than 30.0

U.S. percentage = 36.4

Note: Data are for the total population 25 years and older.
Sources: U.S. Census Bureau, American Community Survey, 2009, Puerto Rico
    Community Survey, 2009.

Total Population with Bachelor's Degrees and with Science and Engineering Degrees by State and Puerto Rico: 2009

Area	Total population with bachelor's degrees		Total population with science and engineering degrees			
	Estimate[1]	Margin of error[2] (±)	Estimate[1]	Margin of error[2] (±)	Percent	Margin of error[2] (±)
United States	56,335,654	171,795	20,498,538	89,611	36.4	0.1
Alabama	686,543	12,245	216,050	7,084	31.5	0.8
Alaska	114,535	5,559	44,526	3,503	38.9	2.4
Arizona	1,085,753	14,044	380,717	9,279	35.1	0.8
Arkansas	358,933	9,504	102,173	4,972	28.5	1.2
California	7,110,449	41,480	2,990,726	27,567	42.1	0.3
Colorado	1,181,594	15,302	479,385	8,638	40.6	0.6
Connecticut	843,502	11,640	332,553	9,396	39.4	0.9
Delaware	171,091	6,009	62,715	3,870	36.7	1.8
District of Columbia	200,382	5,000	102,203	4,239	51.0	1.8
Florida	3,233,714	25,701	1,072,760	15,536	33.2	0.4
Georgia	1,716,045	21,504	570,366	12,109	33.2	0.5
Hawaii	261,095	6,888	92,436	5,791	35.4	1.8
Idaho	230,252	6,022	83,210	3,928	36.1	1.3
Illinois	2,581,463	17,778	894,174	13,837	34.6	0.5
Indiana	944,320	14,704	289,498	8,057	30.7	0.7
Iowa	496,918	9,576	152,511	6,123	30.7	1.0
Kansas	533,004	9,566	160,737	5,749	30.2	0.9
Kentucky	603,567	12,395	183,213	6,610	30.4	0.9

(Continued)

Area	Total population with bachelor's degrees		Total population with science and engineering degrees			
	Estimate[1]	Margin of error[2] (±)	Estimate[1]	Margin of error[2] (±)	Percent	Margin of error[2] (±)
Louisiana	620,131	11,881	173,913	5,803	28 0	0 8
Maine	249,275	7,829	86,810	4,509	34 8	1 4
Maryland	1,355,268	16,700	591,897	11,532	43 7	0 7
Massachusetts	1,716,578	18,229	720,463	12,902	42 0	0 6
Michigan	1,628,826	21,418	561,935	10,722	34 5	0 5
Minnesota	1,098,041	13,828	386,044	8,771	35 2	0 6
Mississippi	365,660	9,502	97,918	4,861	26 8	1 2
Missouri	999,095	14,352	302,013	8,819	30 2	0 7
Montana	177,632	6,493	62,283	4,350	35 1	2 1
Nebraska	315,465	7,589	89,526	4,176	28 4	1 0
Nevada	376,423	8,862	123,040	5,200	32 7	1 3
New Hampshire	288,873	6,998	111,128	4,562	38 5	1 3
New Jersey	2,037,481	21,317	799,085	13,454	39 2	0 6
New Mexico	327,130	6,924	126,062	4,798	38 5	1 4
New York	4,275,463	30,486	1,575,997	18,928	36 9	0 4
North Carolina	1,632,573	19,109	591,311	12,068	36 2	0 6
North Dakota	108,035	3,947	29,134	2,072	27 0	1 4
Ohio	1,866,776	19,330	600,768	11,293	32 2	0 5
Oklahoma	540,276	9,481	153,529	5,470	28 4	0 9
Oregon	754,459	12,227	299,923	8,343	39 8	0 9
Pennsylvania	2,271,270	19,144	807,225	11,500	35 5	0 4

(Continued)

Area	Total population with bachelor's degrees		Total population with science and engineering degrees			
	Estimate[1]	Margin of error[2] (±)	Estimate[1]	Margin of error[2] (±)	Percent	Margin of error[2] (±)
Rhode Island	217,976	7,157	82,276	4,326	37 7	1 5
South Carolina	734,662	12,752	251,180	7,175	34 2	0 8
South Dakota	131,554	5,248	39,560	3,091	30 1	1 9
Tennessee	969,266	13,985	301,117	7,492	31 1	0 6
Texas	3,917,304	30,669	1,369,822	19,252	35 0	0 4
Utah	448,121	9,764	160,223	6,016	35 8	1 0
Vermont	140,634	4,400	54,377	2,726	38 7	1 8
Virginia	1,770,257	19,314	742,583	14,150	41 9	0 6
Washington	1,379,728	15,657	586,533	11,716	42 5	0 6
West Virginia	218,270	6,542	63,536	3,555	29 1	1 5
Wisconsin	965,428	11,464	316,503	7,601	32 8	0 6
Wyoming	84,564	3,800	30,871	2,269	36 5	2 5
Puerto Rico	556,734	9,136	149,685	5,811	26 9	1 0

[1] The estimates in this table are for the total population 25 years and older.

[2] Data are based on a sample and are subject to sampling variability . A margin of error is a measure of an estimate's variability. The larger the margin of error in relation to the size of the estimate, the less reliable the estimate . When added to and subtracted from the estimate, the margin of error forms the 90 percent confidence interval.

Sources: U .S . Census Bureau, American Community Survey, 2009, Puerto Rico Community Survey, 2009.

In: The American Community Survey …   ISBN: 978-1-61324-362-6
Editors: B. M. Russo and A. D. Haffner   ©2011 Nova Science Publishers, Inc.

Chapter 16

PLACE OF BIRTH
OF THE FOREIGN-BORN
POPULATION: 2009

United States Census Bureau

INTRODUCTION

This report presents data on the foreign- born population at the national and state levels based on the 2009 American Community Survey (ACS). During the last four decades, the foreign-born population of the United States has continued to increase in size and as a percent of the total population: from 9.6 million or 4.7 percent in 1970, to 14.1 million or 6.2 percent in 1980, 19.8 million or 7.9 percent in 1990, and 31.1 million or 11.1 percent in 2000.[1] According to the 2009 ACS, there were 38.5 million foreign-born residents, representing 12.5 percent of the total population.[2] While the number of foreign born repre-sents a historical high, the proportion of the total population is lower than during the great migration of the late 1800s and early 1900s, when it fluctuated between 13 percent and 15 percent.[3] But more notable than the growth of the foreign- born population is the change in the distribution of origin countries over time.

Defining Nativity Status: Who Is Foreign Born?

Nativity status refers to whether a person is native or foreign born. The native-born population includes anyone who was a U.S. citizen at birth. Respondents who were born in the United States, Puerto Rico, a U.S. Island Area (U.S. Virgin Islands, Guam, American Samoa, or the Commonwealth of the Northern Mariana Islands), or abroad of a U.S. citizen parent or parents, are defined as native. The foreign-born population includes anyone who was not a U.S. citizen at birth, including those who have become U.S. citizens through naturalization.

In 1960, 75 percent of the foreign born were from countries in Europe. By 2009, over 80 percent of the foreign born were from countries in Latin America and Asia. Also since 1960, the foreign born increasingly have settled in states beyond the traditional gateway states of New York, California, Texas, Florida, and Illinois. This report will discuss the size, country of origin, and distribution of the foreign- born population in 2009.

Size, Country of Birth, and Distribution
of the Foreign-Born Population

In 2009, there were 307 million people living in the United States, including 38.5 million foreign born representing 1 in 8 residents. Between 2000 and 2009, the foreign-born population increased by 7.4 million persons, or by about 24 percent.

Over half (53 percent) of all foreign born were from Latin America (see Figure 1). Another 28 percent were from Asia. The next largest region-of-origin group —the foreign born from Europe—represented 13 percent of all foreign born, less than half the size of the foreign born from Asia. About 4 percent of the foreign born were from Africa, followed by about 3 percent from other regions, including Oceania and Northern America.

Mexico was the largest of all country-of-birth groups (see Figure 2). There were 11.5 million foreign born from Mexico in the United States, representing 30 percent of the total foreign-born population. Mexico was also the predominant country in the Latin America region-of-origin group. Of the 20.5 million foreign born from Latin America, 56 percent were born in Mexico. The next largest country-of-birth group, the foreign born from China, was considerably smaller than the foreign-born population from Mexico. There were 2 million foreign born from China, comprising over 5 percent of the total foreign-born population. The remaining largest country-ofbirth groups, with about 1 million foreign born each, included the Philippines, India, Vietnam, El Salvador, Korea, and Cuba.[4]

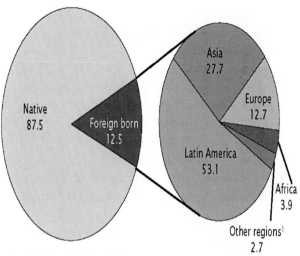

[1] Other regions include Oceania and Northern America.
Source: U.S. Census Bureau, American Community Survey, 2009.

Figure 1. Total Population by Nativity and Foreign-Born Population by Region of Birth: 2009.
(Percent distribution. Data based on sample. For information on confidentiality protection, sampling error, nonsampling error, and definitions, see www.census.gov/acs/www).

California had the largest number of foreign-born residents (9.9 million), followed by New York (4.2 million), Texas (4.0 million), and Florida (3.5 million) (see Figure 3). When combined, 21 .6 million foreign born —or more than half (56 percent) of the total foreign-born population —lived in just these four states. California's foreign born alone represented over one-fourth of all foreign born.

California also had the largest proportion of foreign born in its total population (see Figure 4). Over one-fourth (27 percent) of all residents of California were foreign born. Approximately 1 in 5 residents were foreign born in two other states —New York (21 percent) and New Jersey (20 percent). An additional nine states had proportions of foreign born that were higher than the national average (1 2.5 percent): Nevada, Florida, Hawaii, Texas, Massachusetts, Arizona, Illinois, Connecticut, and Maryland.[5]

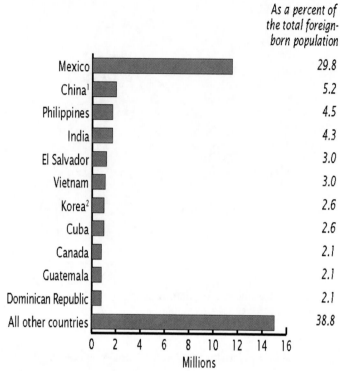

As a percent of the total foreign-born population

Country	As a percent of the total foreign-born population
Mexico	29.8
China[1]	5.2
Philippines	4.5
India	4.3
El Salvador	3.0
Vietnam	3.0
Korea[2]	2.6
Cuba	2.6
Canada	2.1
Guatemala	2.1
Dominican Republic	2.1
All other countries	38.8

[1] Includes respondents who reported their country of birth as China, Hong Kong, Macau, Paracel Islands, or Taiwan.

[2] Includes respondents who reported their country of birth as Korea, North Korea, or South Korea.

Source: U.S. Census Bureau, American Community Survey, 2009.

Figure 2. Foreign-Born Population by Country of Birth for Countries With 750,000 or More Foreign Born: 2009.
(Data based on sample. For information on confidentiality protection, sampling error, nonsampling error, and definitions, see www.census.gov/acs/www).

The composition of the foreign- born population by region of birth varied among states. The foreign born from Latin America represented over 65 percent of the state foreign-born population in New Mexico (78 percent), Florida (75 percent), Texas (73 percent), and Arizona (69 percent) (see Table

1). In addition to these 4 states, there were 1 3 other states where over 50 percent of the foreign-born population was from Latin America. The foreign born from Asia comprised more than 50 percent of the total foreign-born population in one state: Hawaii (78 percent). An additional 10 states had more than one-third of their foreign-born populations from Asia. In three states, the foreign born from Africa represented more than 15 percent of the foreign-born population: North Dakota (22 percent), Minnesota (18 percent), and Maryland (1 6 percent).[6] One of the states with the highest proportion of foreign born from Europe in its total foreign-born population was Vermont (39 percent).[7]

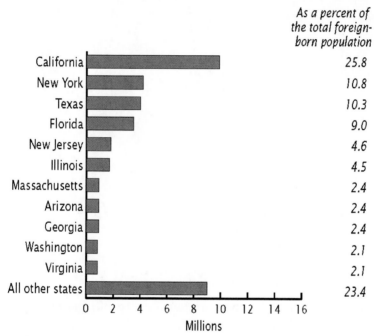

	As a percent of the total foreign-born population
California	25.8
New York	10.8
Texas	10.3
Florida	9.0
New Jersey	4.6
Illinois	4.5
Massachusetts	2.4
Arizona	2.4
Georgia	2.4
Washington	2.1
Virginia	2.1
All other states	23.4

Millions

Source: U.S. Census Bureau, American Community Survey, 2009.

Figure 3. Foreign-Born Population by State for States With 750,000 or More Foreign Born: 2009.
(Data based on sample. For information on confidentiality protection, sampling error, nonsampling error, and definitions, see *www.census.gov/acs/www*).

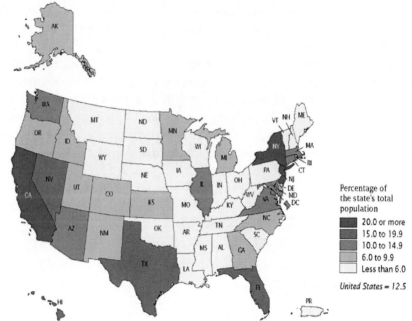

Sources: U.S. Census Bureau, American Community Survey, 2009, Puerto Rico
Community Survey, 2009.

Figure 4. Foreign-Born Population by State and Puerto Rico: 2009.
(Data based on sample. For information on confidentiality protection, sampling error,
nonsampling error, and definitions, see www.census.gov/acs/www).

SOURCE AND ACCURACY

Data presented in this report are based on people and households that
responded to the ACS in 2009. The resulting estimates are representative of
the entire population. All comparisons presented in this report have taken
sampling error into account and are significant at the 90-percent confidence
level unless otherwise noted. Due to rounding, some details may not sum to
totals. For information on sampling and estimation methods, confidentiality
protection, and sampling and nonsampling errors, please see the "ACS
Accuracy of the Data (2009)" document located at <*www.census.gov /acs/
www/Downloads/data_documentation/Accu*racy/ACS_Accuracy_of_Data_
2009.pdf>.

Additional information about the foreign-born population is available on
the Census Bureau's Web site at <www.census.gov/population. html>.

Table 1. The Foreign-Born Population, Showing Percentage of the Population by Region of Birth and by State and Puerto Rico: 2009

(Numbers in thousands. Data based on sample. For information on confidentiality protection, sampling error, nonsampling error, and definitions, see www.census.gov/acs/www).

Area	Foreign born		Africa		Asia		Europe		Latin America		Other regions[1]	
	Total	Margin of error[2] (±)	Percent of total	Margin of error[2] (±)	Percent of total	Margin of error[2] (±)	Percent of total	Margin of error[2] (±)	Percent of total	Margin of error[2] (±)	Percent of total	Margin of error[2] (±)
United States	**38,517**	**116**	**3.9**	**0.1**	**27.7**	**0.1**	**12.7**	**0.1**	**53.1**	**0.1**	**2.7**	**–**
Alabama	147	4	5.2	1.5	28.3	1.6	12.5	1.4	51.0	2.1	3.1	0.8
Alaska	49	3	3.4	2.0	51.6	3.7	13.3	2.3	23.7	3.9	8.0	1.9
Arizona	925	20	2.2	0.4	15.0	0.7	8.9	0.6	69.4	0.9	4.5	0.4
Arkansas	120	5	1.7	0.8	20.2	2.2	9.6	1.7	65.5	2.3	3.0	0.8
California	9,947	47	1.4	0.1	35.1	0.2	6.7	0.2	54.8	0.3	2.1	0.1
Colorado	487	15	3.8	0.7	21.5	1.1	13.5	0.9	58.0	1.4	3.2	0.5
Connecticut	460	12	3.8	0.7	21.5	0.7	28.1	1.2	42.7	1.3	3.9	0.4
Delaware	74	5	9.6	2.7	31.0	3.5	14.6	2.8	41.9	4.2	2.9	1.5
District of Columbia	72	5	13.1	3.2	17.3	2.0	16.9	2.6	49.0	3.1	3.7	1.2
Florida	3,484	37	1.4	0.1	10.0	0.2	10.5	0.3	74.8	0.4	3.3	0.2
Georgia	920	17	8.2	0.8	25.0	0.8	10.0	0.7	54.6	0.8	2.2	0.3
Hawaii	224	9	0.8	0.4	78.2	2.2	5.5	0.9	4.8	0.9	10.8	1.7
Idaho	98	6	3.0	1.3	15.3	2.2	17.1	2.5	59.1	3.0	5.5	1.3
Illinois	1,741	24	2.6	0.3	25.8	0.5	22.7	0.7	47.6	0.7	1.3	0.1
Indiana	281	9	4.7	1.1	27.6	1.4	16.4	1.7	47.8	1.6	3.5	0.5
Iowa	116	4	6.5	1.6	33.8	2.0	15.2	2.1	42.0	2.2	2.5	0.6

Table 1. (Continued)

Area	Foreign born		Africa		Asia		Europe		Latin America		Other regions[1]	
	Total	Margin of error[2] (±)	Percent of total	Margin of error[2] (±)	Percent of total	Margin of error[2] (±)	Percent of total	Margin of error[2] (±)	Percent of total	Margin of error[2] (±)	Percent of total	Margin of error[2] (±)
Kansas	171	6	4.3	0.9	26.8	1.3	8.8	1.3	57.8	1.8	2.4	1.0
Kentucky	128	6	7.3	1.8	30.7	2.5	18.0	2.5	40.4	2.6	3.5	0.9
Louisiana	152	7	4.5	1.8	32.4	1.9	10.7	1.4	49.5	2.2	2.9	0.8
Maine	44	4	15.3	5.0	22.6	2.6	24.9	3.4	8.1	2.2	29.0	4.0
Maryland	730	14	16.1	1.1	32.8	0.9	12.2	0.7	37.6	1.0	1.3	0.2
Massachusetts	943	19	8.1	0.9	27.6	0.8	25.9	0.9	34.8	1.1	3.5	0.3
Michigan	614	15	3.6	0.6	45.5	1.3	25.0	1.2	19.3	1.0	6.6	0.5
Minnesota	358	10	17.9	1.5	36.3	1.2	12.9	1.2	29.2	1.3	3.8	0.6
Mississippi	60	5	3.2	1.4	31.1	3.6	12.5	2.7	49.5	4.0	3.6	1.7
Missouri	213	8	7.4	1.3	35.7	1.8	23.6	1.8	30.1	1.7	3.1	0.6
Montana	19	2	2.0	2.0	28.1	5.6	33.1	6.5	16.2	4.1	20.6	4.6
Nebraska	106	4	7.8	1.7	26.2	2.1	5.9	1.1	57.4	2.6	2.7	1.0
Nevada	507	11	2.9	0.6	26.8	0.9	8.7	0.9	58.7	1.0	2.9	0.5
New Hampshire	68	5	8.1	1.9	29.8	2.7	25.7	2.8	22.9	3.3	13.6	2.5
New Jersey	1,759	24	4.5	0.4	31.1	0.6	18.1	0.5	45.2	0.7	1.0	0.1
New Mexico	196	10	1.7	0.6	9.5	0.8	7.9	1.0	78.3	1.4	2.6	0.6
New York	4,178	36	4.0	0.3	26.4	0.3	19.2	0.4	48.8	0.5	1.6	0.1
North Carolina	665	14	5.7	0.8	22.2	0.8	11.7	0.7	57.3	1.0	3.2	0.4
North Dakota	15	2	21.6	4.1	25.7	4.9	16.1	4.2	11.5	4.6	25.1	5.1
Ohio	433	11	11.3	1.3	36.6	1.3	27.7	1.3	20.5	1.0	4.0	0.5

Table 1. (Continued)

Area	Foreign born Total	Foreign born Margin of error[2] (±)	Africa Percent of total	Africa Margin of error[2] (±)	Asia Percent of total	Asia Margin of error[2] (±)	Europe Percent of total	Europe Margin of error[2] (±)	Latin America Percent of total	Latin America Margin of error[2] (±)	Other regions[1] Percent of total	Other regions[1] Margin of error[2] (±)
Oklahoma	190	7	4.3	1.1	23.4	1.4	7.9	0.9	60.4	1.9	4.0	1.2
Oregon	367	12	2.3	0.5	27.7	1.2	16.4	1.3	48.0	1.3	5.6	0.7
Pennsylvania	691	16	7.7	0.9	36.4	1.0	26.4	1.1	26.9	1.2	2.6	0.3
Rhode Island	133	7	12.5	2.0	16.6	1.5	23.6	2.3	43.4	2.5	3.9	1.1
South Carolina	205	8	3.0	1.1	24.1	1.6	16.6	1.6	52.3	1.8	4.1	0.9
South Dakota	22	3	17.4	4.4	31.4	5.3	23.2	8.7	22.4	5.0	5.6	1.9
Tennessee	266	10	7.7	1.6	29.6	1.9	12.0	1.3	46.9	1.5	3.8	0.7
Texas	3,985	37	3.1	0.2	17.6	0.3	4.6	0.2	73.4	0.4	1.3	0.1
Utah	218	7	2.3	0.9	18.5	1.6	11.1	1.3	59.6	1.8	8.6	1.1
Vermont	21	2	4.5	2.5	24.3	4.5	38.7	5.6	6.1	2.1	26.4	4.2
Virginia	806	15	8.7	0.8	41.4	0.9	11.7	0.7	35.7	0.8	2.5	0.3
Washington	811	15	5.2	0.6	39.0	0.8	18.4	1.0	30.2	0.9	7.1	0.5
West Virginia	23	2	8.4	4.1	51.6	6.3	16.5	4.2	19.8	5.0	3.6	1.9
Wisconsin	256	9	3.8	0.9	31.2	1.4	20.3	1.7	41.2	1.8	3.4	0.7
Wyoming	17	2	3.2	3.1	16.4	6.2	13.2	4.4	59.0	6.8	8.2	3.1
Puerto Rico	108	7	0.1	0.2	2.7	1.3	3.8	1.0	92.9	1.7	0.4	0.3

– Represents or rounds to zero.

[1] Other regions include Oceania and Northern America.

[2] Data are based on a sample and are subject to sampling variability. A margin of error is a measure of an estimate's variability. The larger the margin of error in relation to the size of the estimates, the less reliable the estimate. When added to and subtracted from the estimate, the margin of error forms the 90 percent confidence interval.

Source: U.S. Census Bureau, American Community Survey, 2009.

End Notes

[1] Gibson, Campbell and Kay Jung. 2006.
"Historical Census Statistics on the Foreign-Born Population in the United States: 1850 to 2000." U.S. Census Bureau: Population Division Working Paper, Number 81 available on the U.S. Census Bureau's Web site at <www.census.gov/population .html>.

[2] In addition, since 1970, as the foreign-born population increased in size, it also became, on average, a younger population. In 1970, the median age of the foreign-born population was 52 years; by 2009, it was 41 years (Campbell and Jung, 2006; 2009 American Community Survey).

[3] The foreign-born population represented 13.3 percent of the total population in 1880, 14.8 percent in 1890, 13.6 percent in 1900, 14.7 percent in 1910, and 13.2 percent in 1920. See Campbell and Jung, 2006.

[4] The estimates for Vietnam and El Salvador are not statistically different. The estimates for Korea and Cuba are not statistically different.

[5] The estimates for Nevada and Florida are not statistically different. The estimates for Massachusetts and Arizona are not statistically different. The estimates for Connecticut and Maryland are not statistically different.

[6] The estimates for North Dakota and Minnesota are not statistically different. The estimates for Minnesota and Maryland are not statistically different.

[7] The estimates for Vermont and Montana are not statistically different.

In: The American Community Survey ...   ISBN: 978-1-61324-362-6
Editors: B. M. Russo and A. D. Haffner   ©2011 Nova Science Publishers, Inc.

Chapter 17

NATIVITY STATUS AND CITIZENSHIP IN THE UNITED STATES: 2009

United States Census Bureau

INTRODUCTION

This report presents data on nativity status and citizenship at the national and state levels based on the 2009 American Community Survey (ACS). During the last four decades, both the native and foreign- born populations have increased in size.[1] While the native-born population has remained the majority during this period, the foreign-born population has come to represent a greater share of the total population, increasing from 9.6 million or 4.7 percent in 1970, to 31.1 million or 11.1 percent in 2000.[2] According to the 2009 ACS, 38.5 million of the 307 million residents in the United States were foreign- born, representing 12.5 percent of the total population (see Table 1).

NATIVITY STATUS AND CITIZENSHIP

Historically, the majority of the population of the United States have been citizens— either native-born or naturalized—and this has remained unchanged in recent decades. Since 1920, over 92 percent of the total population have been citizens.[3] However, as the size of the foreign-born population has increased, the citizenship composition of this population has changed. In 1970,

64 percent of the foreign-born population were naturalized citizens; by 2000, the percent naturalized had declined to 40 percent. In 2009, 44 percent of the foreign born were naturalized (see Figure 1). Of the 16.8 million naturalized U.S. citizens, 41 percent reported being naturalized in 2000 or later, while 59 percent reported naturalizing before 2000.

DEFINING NATIVITY STATUS: WHO IS FOREIGN BORN?

Nativity status refers to whether a person is native or foreign born. The native-born population includes anyone who was a U.S. citizen or U.S. national at birth. Respondents who were born in the United States, Puerto Rico, a U.S. Island Area (U.S. Virgin Islands, Guam, American Samoa, or the Commonwealth of the Northern Mariana Islands), or abroad of a U.S. citizen parent or parents, are defined as native. The foreign-born population includes anyone who was not a U.S. citizen at birth, including those who have become U.S. citizens through naturalization.

Considerable variation in citizenship status is evident by region and country of birth (see Figure 2), as more recent migrants are less likely to be naturalized. For example, over 55 percent of the foreign born from Europe and Asia were naturalized citizens, while only 32 percent of the foreign born from Latin America (including Mexico and other Central American countries) were naturalized citizens. Similarly, less than one-fourth of the foreign born from Mexico were naturalized.

The states also exhibited notable differences in the percent of their foreign-born populations who have naturalized. States with the highest percent naturalized included Hawaii (58 percent), Vermont (57 percent), and Maine (55 percent), while states having among the lowest percent naturalized included Nebraska (30 percent), Mississippi (31 percent), North Carolina (31 percent), and Alabama (30 percent) (see Figure 3).[4,5] In general, states in the Northeast and Midwest regions tend to have higher proportions of naturalized citizens in their foreign-born populations than states in the South.[6] Texas had the lowest proportion naturalized (32 percent) among the four states with the largest foreign- born populations: California (9.9 million), New York (4.2 million), Texas (4.0 million), and Florida (3.5 million).

Table 1. population by Nativity Status and citizenship: 2009
(Numbers in thousands. Data based on sample. For information
on confi-dentiality protection, sampling error, nonsampling error,
and definitions, see www.census.gov/acs/www)

Characteristic	Number	Margin of error[1] (±)	Percent	Margin of error[1] (±)
Total	**307,007**	**(X)**	**100 .0**	**(X)**
Native	**268,489**	**116**	**87 .5**	–
U.S. citizen, born in the United States	264,367	119	86.1	–
U.S. citizen, born in Puerto Rico or U.S. Island Areas	1,704	30	0.6	–
U.S. citizen, born abroad of American parent(s)	2,418	28	0.8	–
Foreign born	**38,517**	**116**	**12 .5**	–
U.S. citizen by naturalization	16,846	68	5.5	–
Not a U.S. citizen	21,671	120	7.1	–

(X) Not applicable.

– Represents or rounds to zero.

[1] Data are based on a sample and are subject to sampling variability. A margin of error is a measure of an estimate's variability. The larger the margin of error in relation to the size of the estimates, the less reliable the estimate. When added to and subtracted from the estimate, the margin of error forms the 90 percent confidence interval.

Source: U.S. Census Bureau, American Community Survey, 2009.

California was the state with the largest foreign-born population, at almost 10 million, and also had the largest percent of any state's total population who were foreign born, at 27 percent (see Table 2). Because of its large foreign-born population, California had the largest percentage of naturalized citizens in its total population (12 percent) of all states, as well as the highest pro-portion of noncitizens (1 5 percent). Other states with high proportions of naturalized citizens were New York (11 percent) and New Jersey (10 percent).

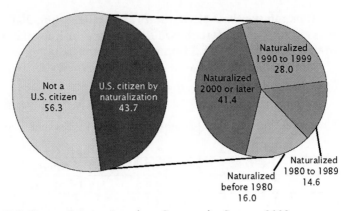

Source: U.S. Census Bureau, American Community Survey, 2009.

Figure 1. The Foreign-Born Population by Citizenship Status, Showing Year of Naturalization for Naturalized Citizens: 2009.
(Percent distribution. Data based on sample. For information on confidentiality protection, sampling error, nonsampling error, and definitions, see www.census.gov/acs/www).

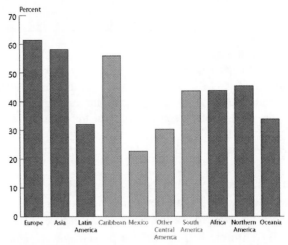

Note: Latin America consists of the subcategories Caribbean, Mexico, Other Central America, and South America.
Source: U.S. Census Bureau, American Community Survey, 2009.

Figure 2. Percentage of the Foreign-Born Population Who Are Naturalized by Place of Birth: 2009.
(Percent distribution. Data based on sample. For information on confidentiality protection, sampling error, nonsampling error, and definitions, see www.census.gov/acs/www).

SOURCE AND ACCURACY

Data presented in this report are based on people and households that responded to the ACS in 2009. The resulting estimates are representative of the entire population. All comparisons presented in this report have taken sampling error into account and are significant at the 90 percent confidence level unless otherwise noted. Due to rounding, some details may not sum to totals. For information on sampling and estimation methods, confidentiality protection, and sampling and nonsampling errors, see the "ACS Accuracy of the Data (2009)" document located at <*www.census.gov/acs/www /Downloads/data_documentation/Accu*racy/ACS_Accuracy_of _Data_2009.pdf>.

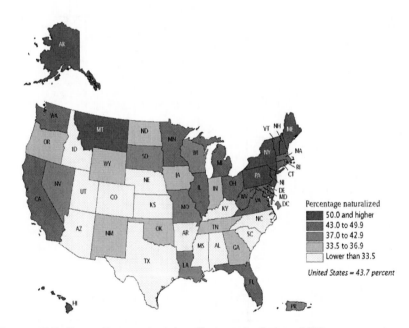

Source: U.S. Census Bureau, American Community Survey, 2009.

Figure 3. Percentage of the Foreign-Born Population Who Are Naturalized, by State: 2009.
(Data based on sample. For information on confidentiality protection, sampling error, nonsampli ng error, and definitions, see www.census.gov/acs/www)

Table 2. Population by Nativity and citizenship Status for States and puerto Rico: 2009

(Numbers in thousands. Data based on sample. For information on confidentiality protection, sampling error, nonsampling error, and definitions, see www.census.gov/acs/www)

Area	Total population	Native		Foreign born					
				Total		Naturalized U.S. citizen		Not a U.S. citizen	
		Percent	Margin of error[1] (±)	Percent	Margin of error[1] (±)	Percent	Margin of error[1] (±)	Percent	Margin of error[1] (±)
United States	307,007	87.5	–	12.5	–	5.5	–	7.1	–
Alabama	4,709	96.9	0.1	3.1	0.1	0.9	0.1	2.2	0.1
Alaska	698	93.0	0.5	7.0	0.5	3.7	0.4	3.3	0.5
Arizona	6,596	86.0	0.3	14.0	0.3	4.5	0.2	9.5	0.3
Arkansas	2,889	95.8	0.2	4.2	0.2	1.3	0.1	2.9	0.2
California	36,962	73.1	0.1	26.9	0.1	12.3	0.1	14.6	0.1
Colorado	5,025	90.3	0.3	9.7	0.3	3.2	0.1	6.5	0.3
Connecticut	3,518	86.9	0.3	13.1	0.3	6.0	0.2	7.1	0.3
Delaware	885	91.6	0.6	8.4	0.6	3.5	0.4	4.8	0.5
District of Columbia	600	88.0	0.8	12.0	0.8	4.6	0.4	7.4	0.7
Florida	18,538	81.2	0.2	18.8	0.2	9.1	0.1	9.7	0.2
Georgia	9,829	90.6	0.2	9.4	0.2	3.2	0.1	6.1	0.2
Hawaii	1,295	82.7	0.7	17.3	0.7	10.0	0.5	7.3	0.5
Idaho	1,546	93.7	0.4	6.3	0.4	2.1	0.2	4.2	0.3
Illinois	12,910	86.5	0.2	13.5	0.2	6.1	0.1	7.4	0.2
Indiana	6,423	95.6	0.1	4.4	0.1	1.5	0.1	2.8	0.1
Iowa	3,008	96.1	0.1	3.9	0.1	1.4	0.1	2.5	0.2
Kansas	2,819	93.9	0.2	6.1	0.2	1.9	0.1	4.2	0.2
Kentucky	4,314	97.0	0.1	3.0	0.1	0.9	0.1	2.0	0.2

Table 2. (Continued)

Area	Total population	Native		Foreign born					
				Total		Naturalized U.S. citizen		Not a U.S. citizen	
		Percent	Margin of error[1] (±)	Percent	Margin of error[1] (±)	Percent	Margin of error[1] (±)	Percent	Margin of error[1] (±)
Louisiana	4,492	96.6	0.2	3.4	0.2	1.5	0.1	1.9	0.2
Maine	1,318	96.7	0.3	3.3	0.3	1.8	0.2	1.5	0.2
Maryland	5,699	87.2	0.2	12.8	0.2	5.8	0.2	7.0	0.2
Massachusetts	6,594	85.7	0.3	14.3	0.3	7.0	0.2	7.3	0.2
Michigan	9,970	93.8	0.1	6.2	0.1	3.0	0.1	3.2	0.1
Minnesota	5,266	93.2	0.2	6.8	0.2	3.0	0.1	3.8	0.2
Mississippi	2,952	98.0	0.2	2.0	0.2	0.6	0.1	1.4	0.2
Missouri	5,988	96.4	0.1	3.6	0.1	1.5	0.1	2.0	0.1
Montana	975	98.0	0.3	2.0	0.3	1.0	0.1	0.9	0.2
Nebraska	1,797	94.1	0.2	5.9	0.2	1.8	0.2	4.1	0.2
Nevada	2,643	80.8	0.4	19.2	0.4	7.6	0.3	11.6	0.5
New Hampshire	1,325	94.8	0.4	5.2	0.4	2.7	0.3	2.5	0.2
New Jersey	8,708	79.8	0.3	20.2	0.3	10.1	0.2	10.1	0.2
New Mexico	2,010	90.2	0.5	9.8	0.5	3.3	0.2	6.4	0.4
New York	19,541	78.6	0.2	21.4	0.2	11.2	0.1	10.2	0.2
North Carolina	9,381	92.9	0.1	7.1	0.1	2.2	0.1	4.9	0.1
North Dakota	647	97.6	0.3	2.4	0.3	0.9	0.2	1.5	0.3
Ohio	11,543	96.2	0.1	3.8	0.1	1.9	0.1	1.9	0.1
Oklahoma	3,687	94.9	0.2	5.1	0.2	1.8	0.1	3.4	0.2
Oregon	3,826	90.4	0.3	9.6	0.3	3.5	0.2	6.1	0.3
Pennsylvania	12,605	94.5	0.1	5.5	0.1	2.8	0.1	2.7	0.1

Table 2. (Continued)

Area	Total population	Native		Foreign born					
				Total		Naturalized U.S. citizen		Not a U.S. citizen	
		Percent	Margin of error[1] (±)	Percent	Margin of error[1] (±)	Percent	Margin of error[1] (±)	Percent	Margin of error[1] (±)
Rhode Island	1,053	87.3	0.7	12.7	0.7	6.0	0.4	6.6	0.6
South Carolina	4,561	95.5	0.2	4.5	0.2	1.5	0.1	3.0	0.2
South Dakota	812	97.3	0.4	2.7	0.4	1.0	0.2	1.6	0.3
Tennessee	6,296	95.8	0.2	4.2	0.2	1.5	0.1	2.7	0.1
Texas	24,782	83.9	0.1	16.1	0.1	5.1	0.1	10.9	0.1
Utah	2,785	92.2	0.3	7.8	0.3	2.6	0.2	5.2	0.2
Vermont	622	96.7	0.4	3.3	0.4	1.9	0.2	1.4	0.3
Virginia	7,883	89.8	0.2	10.2	0.2	4.6	0.1	5.6	0.2
Washington	6,664	87.8	0.2	12.2	0.2	5.4	0.2	6.7	0.2
West Virginia	1,820	98.7	0.1	1.3	0.1	0.6	0.1	0.7	0.1
Wisconsin	5,655	95.5	0.2	4.5	0.2	1.9	0.1	2.6	0.1
Wyoming	544	96.9	0.4	3.1	0.4	1.1	0.2	2.0	0.4
Puerto Rico	3,967	97.3	0.2	2.7	0.2	1.0	0.1	1.7	0.1

– Represents or rounds to zero.

[1] Data are based on a sample and are subject to sampling variability. A margin of error is a measure of an estimate's variability. The larger the margin of error in relation to the size of the estimates, the less reliable the estimate. When added to and subtracted from the estimate, the margin of error forms the 90 percent confidence interval.

Source: U.S. Census Bureau, American Community Survey, 2009.

End Notes

[1] The terms native and native born are used interchangeably in this report.

[2] Gibson, Campbell and Kay Jung. 2006. "Historical Census Statistics on the Foreign-Born Population in the United States: 1850 to 2000." U.S. Census Bureau: Population Division Working Paper, Number 81. Available on the U.S. Census Bureau's Web site at <www.census.gov/population>.

[3] Note that information on citizenship was not collected in the 1960 census.

[4] The percents for Hawaii, Vermont, and Maine are not statistically different.

[5] The percents for Nebraska, Mississippi, North Carolina, and Alabama are not statistically different.

[6] The Northeast region includes Connecticut, Maine, Massachusetts, New Hampshire, New Jersey, New York, Pennsylvania, Rhode Island, and Vermont. The South region includes Alabama, Arkansas, Delaware, the District of Columbia, Florida, Georgia, Kentucky, Louisiana, Maryland, Mississippi, North Carolina, Oklahoma, South Carolina, Tennessee, Texas, Virginia, and West Virginia. The West region includes Alaska, Arizona, California, Colorado, Hawaii, Idaho, Montana, Nevada, New Mexico, Oregon, Utah, Washington, and Wyoming. The Midwest region includes Illinois, Indiana, Iowa, Kansas, Michigan, Minnesota, Missouri, Nebraska, North Dakota, Ohio, South Dakota, and Wisconsin.

In: The American Community Survey ...   ISBN: 978-1-61324-362-6
Editors: B. M. Russo and A. D. Haffner   ©2011 Nova Science Publishers, Inc.

Chapter 18

YEAR OF ENTRY OF THE FOREIGN-BORN POPULATION: 2009

United States Census Bureau

INTRODUCTION

This report presents data on the year of entry of the foreign-born population at the national and state levels based on the 2009 American Community Survey (ACS).[1] In 2009, an estimated 38.5 million foreign-born people lived in the United States, representing roughly 12.5 percent of the total population. The foreign-born population includes anyone who was not a U.S. citizen at birth.

Data on year of entry is important because it can be used as an indicator of time spent in the United States by the foreign born. For example, in 2009, 14 percent of the foreign-born popula-tion reported having lived in the country less than 5 years. Additional information about the foreign born can be gained when year of entry is analyzed with other variables. For example, combining year of entry with data on place of birth shows that 83 percent of the foreign-born population who reported entering the United States in 2000 or later were from Asian or Latin American countries compared with 68 percent of those who reported entering prior to 1980. Also, data showing year of entry by state of residence can provide information on the proportion of recent entrants in each state. For example, the foreign-born population in North Dakota represents less than 1 percent of the total foreign born; however, one-third of this state's foreign-born population entered the country within the past 5 years. By comparison, over one-fourth of all foreign born lived in California, but only 10 percent had entered in the past 5 years. This report examines differences in the size, place of birth, and geographic distribution of foreign-born year of entry cohorts.[2]

SIZE, PLACE OF BIRTH, AND GEOGRAPHIC DISTRIBUTION OF FOREIGN-BORN YEAR OF ENTRY COHORTS

Among the 38.5 million foreign-born U.S. residents in 2009, 21 percent reported a year of entry prior to 1980, compared with 32 percent who reported entering in 2000 or later (Table 1). Over half (59 percent) of the foreign-born population entered the United States during the last two decades.

Table 1. Foreign-Born Population by Period of Entry: 2009
(Numbers in thousands. Data based on sample. For information on confidentiality protection, sampling error, nonsampling error, and definitions, see www.census.gov/acs/www)

Period of entry	Number	Margin of error[1] (±)	Percent	Margin of error[1] (±)
Total	38,517	116	100 .0	(X)
Prior to 1980	8,041	54	20 .9	0 .2
1980 to 1989	7,577	60	19 .7	0 .1
1990 to 1999	10,736	74	27 .9	0 .2
2000 or later	12,163	97	31 .6	0 .2

(X) Not applicable .

[1] Data are based on a sample and are subject to sampling variability. A margin of error is a measure of an estimate's variability. The larger the margin of error in relation to the size of the estimates, the less reliable the estimate. When added to and subtracted from the estimate, the margin of error forms the 90 percent confidence interval.

Source: U .S . Census Bureau, American Community Survey, 2009.

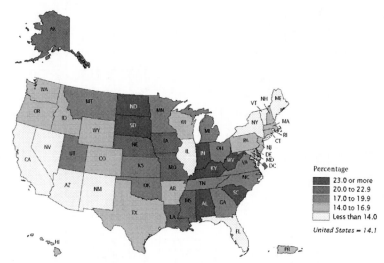

Sources: U.S. Census Bureau, American Community Survey, 2009, Puerto Rico Community Survey, 2009.

Figure 1. Percentage of State Foreign-Born Population That Entered the United States: 2005 to 2009.
(Data based on sample. For information on confidentiality protection, sampling error, nonsampling error, and definitions, see www.census.gov/acs/www).

The distribution of the foreign-born population by world region of birth varies considerably across entry cohorts. For example, 13 percent of the total foreign- born population was born in Europe (Table 2). However, 1 in 4 who entered prior to 1980 was born in Europe compared with less than 1 in 10 (8.9 percent) who entered in 2000 or later. When compared to Europe, the foreign born from Latin America show a different pattern. Over half (53 percent) of all foreign born were from Latin America. Of the foreign born who entered prior to 1980, 45 percent were born in Latin America, compared with 54 percent of those who entered in 2000 or later. This trend has been driven especially by those born in Central American countries, representing 37 percent of the total foreign-born population, 28 percent of those who entered before 1 980, and 39 percent of those who entered in 2000 or later. The foreign born from Asia, when examined by entry cohort, also show a noteworthy pattern. Over one-fourth (28 percent) of the total foreign- born population was from Asia, and the Asian foreign born represented approximately one-fourth or more of each entry cohort, peaking at 31 percent of all foreign born who entered between 1980 and 1989.

Table 2. Foreign-Born Population by Period of Entry and Place of Birth: 2009
(Percent distribution. Data based on sample. For information on confidentiality protection, sampling error, nonsampling error, and definitions, see www.census.gov/acs/www).

Place of birth	Total Percent	Total Margin of error[1] (±)	Prior to 1980 Percent	Prior to 1980 Margin of error[1] (±)	1980 to 1989 Percent	1980 to 1989 Margin of error[1] (±)	1990 to 1999 Percent	1990 to 1999 Margin of error[1] (±)	2000 or later Percent	2000 or later Margin of error[1] (±)
Total	**100.0**	(X)	**100.0**	(X)	**100.0**	(X)	**100.0**	(X)	**100.0**	(X)
Africa	3.9	0.1	1.8	0.1	2.8	0.1	3.9	0.1	5.9	0.2
Americas	55.2	0.1	49.1	0.3	57.6	0.4	57.8	0.3	55.6	0.4
Latin America	53.1	0.1	44.6	0.3	56.3	0.3	56.2	0.4	54.0	0.4
Caribbean	9.0	0.1	11.6	0.2	10.1	0.3	8.3	0.2	7.2	0.2
Central America	37.4	0.2	27.7	0.2	39.7	0.4	41.4	0.3	38.8	0.4
South America	6.7	0.1	5.3	0.2	6.5	0.2	6.5	0.2	8.1	0.2
Northern America	2.1	–	4.5	0.1	1.2	0.1	1.6	0.1	1.6	0.1
Asia	27.7	0.1	23.7	0.3	31.5	0.3	26.6	0.3	28.8	0.4
Europe	12.7	0.1	24.9	0.3	7.7	0.2	11.3	0.2	8.9	0.2
Oceania	0.5	–	0.5	–	0.4	–	0.5	–	0.7	0.1
Total	**100.0**	(X)	**100.0**	(X)	**100.0**	(X)	**100.0**	(X)	**100 0**	(X)
Eight largest countries of birth[2]	54.9	0.2	46.4	0.3	58.3	0.4	58.3	0.4	55.5	0.4
China[3]	5.2	0.1	4.1	0.1	5.7	0.2	5.4	0.1	5.3	0.1

Table 2. (Continued)

Place of birth	Total		Prior to 1980		1980 to 1989		1990 to 1999		2000 or later	
	Percent	Margin of error[1] (±)	Percent	Margin of error[1] (±)	Percent	Margin of error[1] (±)	Percent	Margin of error[1] (±)	Percent	Margin of error[1] (±)
Cuba	2.6	0.1	4.8	0.1	1.9	0.1	1.8	0.1	2.2	0.1
El Salvador	3.0	0.1	1.5	0.1	4.4	0.2	3.1	0.1	3.0	0.1
India	4.3	0.1	2.3	0.1	3.2	0.1	4.4	0.1	6.3	0.2
Korea[4]	2.6	0.1	2.9	0.1	3.4	0.1	2.1	0.1	2.4	0.1
Mexico	29.8	0.2	23.5	0.2	30.0	0.3	33.7	0.3	30.3	0.4
Philippines	4.5	0.1	4.8	0.1	5.6	0.2	4.0	0.1	4.0	0.1
Vietnam	3.0	0.1	2.5	0.1	4.1	0.2	3.8	0.1	1.9	0.1
All other countries	45.1	0.2	53.6	0.3	41.7	0.4	41.7	0.4	44.5	0.4

(X) Not applicable .

– Represents or rounds to zero .

[1] Data are based on a sample and are subject to sampling variability . A margin of error is a measure of an estimate's variability . The larger the margin of error in relation to the size of the estimate, the less reliable the estimate . When added to and subtracted from the estimate, the margin of error forms the 90 percent confidence interval .

[2] Eight largest countries of birth determined for total foreign-born population . Countries listed alphabetically .

[3] Includes respondents who reported their country of birth as China, Hong Kong, Macau, Paracel Islands, or Taiwan .

[4] Includes respondents who reported their country of birth as Korea, North Korea, or South Korea .

Note: Data exclude population born at sea .

Source: U .S . Census Bureau, American Community Survey, 2009 .

Table 3. Foreign-Born Population by Period of Entry by State and Puerto Rico: 2009

(Numbers in thousands. Data based on sample. For information on confidentiality protection, sampling error, nonsampling error, and definitions, see www.census.gov/acs/www)

Area	Total		Prior to 1980		1980 to 1989		1990 to 1999		2000 or later	
	Number	Margin of error[1] (±)	Percent of total	Margin of error[1] (±)	Percent of total	Margin of error[1] (±)	Percent of total	Margin of error[1] (±)	Percent of total	Margin of error[1] (±)
United States	**38,517**	**116**	**20.9**	**0.2**	**19.7**	**0.1**	**27.9**	**0.2**	**31.6**	**0.2**
Alabama.	147	4	14.7	1.6	11.4	1.3	26.3	2.4	47.6	2.6
Alaska.	49	3	18.3	3.5	21.0	3.1	24.9	3.3	35.7	5.5
Arizona	925	20	19.2	0.8	18.9	1.1	29.2	1.2	32.7	1.3
Arkansas	120	5	13.8	1.8	16.6	2.2	31.7	3.2	37.8	3.8
California	9,947	47	23.4	0.3	25.2	0.3	26.5	0.3	24.9	0.4
Colorado	487	15	16.3	0.9	13.9	1.1	33.8	1.7	36.0	2.1
Connecticut	460	12	24.3	1.2	15.8	1.1	25.4	1.1	34.5	1.6
Delaware	74	5	16.0	2.3	12.0	1.8	27.7	3.7	44.3	4.1
District of Columbia	72	5	19.1	2.9	17.8	2.7	23.5	2.5	39.6	3.8
Florida	3,484	37	24.0	0.5	18.7	0.5	25.5	0.5	31.8	0.6
Georgia	920	17	12.0	0.6	14.9	0.8	31.7	1.2	41.4	1.4
Hawaii	224	9	30.2	1.9	19.1	1.5	24.3	1.6	26.4	2.4
Idaho	98	6	20.9	2.2	16.9	2.6	28.0	3.1	34.1	4.0
Illinois	1,741	24	22.6	0.7	17.7	0.6	31.4	0.9	28.4	0.9
Indiana	281	9	16.2	1.2	11.7	1.1	27.2	1.9	44.8	2.3
Iowa	116	4	12.5	1.4	14.0	2.0	33.6	2.8	39.8	3.0

Table 3. (Continued)

Area	Total		Prior to 1980		1980 to 1989		1990 to 1999		2000 or later	
	Number	Margin of error[1] (±)	Percent of total	Margin of error[1] (±)	Percent of total	Margin of error[1] (±)	Percent of total	Margin of error[1] (±)	Percent of total	Margin of error[1] (±)
Kansas	171	6	13.6	1.4	15.3	1.7	31.1	2.0	39.9	2.3
Kentucky	128	6	11.5	1.4	7.7	1.5	26.8	2.6	54.0	3.1
Louisiana	152	7	24.0	2.2	15.3	1.9	21.1	1.9	39.5	2.9
Maine	44	4	37.4	4.5	11.1	2.3	17.6	4.3	33.9	5.2
Maryland	730	14	16.6	0.7	18.7	1.0	28.4	1.2	36.4	1.5
Massachusetts	943	19	21.6	0.7	18.0	0.9	26.2	1.1	34.2	1.2
Michigan	614	15	22.3	1.0	13.3	0.8	27.8	1.2	36.5	1.4
Minnesota	358	10	12.4	1.0	15.8	1.1	30.0	1.7	41.8	2.0
Mississippi	60	5	16.0	2.9	12.4	2.6	23.5	3.7	48.1	4.9
Missouri	213	8	16.8	1.2	12.8	1.2	28.3	1.7	42.2	2.3
Montana	19	2	35.1	5.1	15.2	4.1	19.4	4.2	30.3	6.1
Nebraska	106	4	11.2	1.5	12.7	2.1	31.7	2.7	44.4	3.5
Nevada	507	11	19.2	1.1	20.2	1.4	28.6	1.6	32.1	1.6
New Hampshire	68	5	31.5	2.8	14.6	2.8	23.1	3.2	30.8	3.9
New Jersey	1,759	24	21.1	0.6	19.1	0.6	27.7	0.7	32.1	0.8
New Mexico	196	10	24.1	2.1	20.7	1.9	25.3	2.5	29.9	2.6
New York	4,178	36	22.9	0.4	20.9	0.4	28.1	0.4	28.2	0.6
North Carolina	665	14	11.4	0.6	13.0	0.9	31.3	1.1	44.2	1.6
North Dakota	15	2	19.5	4.6	9.2	4.1	18.2	5.3	53.1	7.5
Ohio	433	11	24.5	1.0	12.6	1.1	25.5	1.3	37.4	1.4

Table 3. (Continued)

Area	Total		Prior to 1980		1980 to 1989		1990 to 1999		2000 or later	
	Number	Margin of error[1] (±)	Percent of total	Margin of error[1] (±)	Percent of total	Margin of error[1] (±)	Percent of total	Margin of error[1] (±)	Percent of total	Margin of error[1] (±)
Oklahoma	190	7	16.7	1.3	15.6	1.7	27.7	2.2	40.0	2.3
Oregon	367	12	16.9	1.0	17.8	1.1	29.8	1.6	35.5	1.7
Pennsylvania	691	16	21.7	0.8	16.1	0.9	26.7	1.1	35.5	1.4
Rhode Island	133	7	26.8	2.0	20.8	2.1	25.4	2.6	27.0	3.1
South Carolina	205	8	18.0	1.5	12.3	1.4	24.0	2.0	45.7	2.3
South Dakota	22	3	16.0	3.9	14.3	4.5	27.6	8.1	42.2	7.3
Tennessee	266	10	12.8	1.3	12.1	1.4	32.5	2.5	42.6	2.6
Texas	3,985	37	17.5	0.4	19.1	0.4	29.8	0.6	33.5	0.7
Utah	218	7	14.2	1.1	16.6	1.5	31.1	2.0	38.1	2.3
Vermont	21	2	38.5	5.3	11.1	2.8	30.2	6.2	20.2	4.3
Virginia	806	15	16.1	0.7	16.7	0.8	29.4	1.1	37.8	1.5
Washington	811	15	19.5	0.9	18.3	0.9	29.0	1.1	33.2	1.3
West Virginia	23	2	26.6	4.5	14.6	4.1	21.5	4.5	37.2	6.1
Wisconsin	256	9	21.8	1.4	14.3	1.3	27.3	2.0	36.6	2.1
Wyoming	17	2	26.7	7.3	12.4	4.4	19.8	6.0	41.1	8.9
Puerto Rico	108	7	25.3	2.3	15.8	1.9	29.8	2.8	29.2	2.0

[1] Data are based on a sample and are subject to sampling variability . A margin of error is a measure of an estimate's variability . The larger the margin of error in relation to the size of the estimates, the less reliable the estimate . When added to and subtracted from the estimate, the margin of error forms the 90 percent confidence interval .

Source: U .S . Census Bureau, American Community Survey, 2009 .

Immigration from Africa shows a pattern similar to the foreign born from Latin America, albeit on a smaller scale. The proportion born in Africa increased in each subsequent entry cohort from a low of 1 .8 percent of those who entered prior to 1980 to 5.9 percent of those who entered in 2000 or later.

There are some interesting differences by country across each entry cohort. For example, Mexico accounted for the largest share of foreign-born residents (30 percent). Less than one-fourth of all foreign born who entered prior to 1 980 were from Mexico; however, there were 30 percent or more in each subsequent period. The foreign born from China represented 4.1 percent of those who entered the United States prior to 1 980 and 5.7 percent of those entering between 1980 and 1989. The foreign born from India represented a comparatively small percentage—2.3 percent—of the cohort entering before 1 980. However, this proportion almost tripled for those who entered after 2000, increasing to 6.3 percent.

Individual states differed considerably in terms of the year of entry to the United States of their foreign- born populations. California and New York, with large foreign-born populations, exhibited relatively consistent proportions of foreign- born individuals throughout their entry cohorts (Table 3). More interesting is the higher proportion of recent entrants in the foreign- born populations of several less populous states. For example, in five such states (Alabama, Indiana, Kentucky, Mississippi, and South Carolina) less than 20 percent of the foreign-born population in those states entered prior to 1 980, compared with 45 percent or more who entered in 2000 or later.

When focusing on the most recent immigrants, 14 percent of the foreign-born population entered the United States between 2005 and 2009. More than half of these new immigrants lived in just six states: California, Florida, Illinois, New Jersey, New York, and Texas. However, a slightly different picture emerges when considering the proportion of the foreign-born population within each state that entered the United States within the past 5 years. Of those states with more than 1.0 million foreign born, four states (California, Florida, Illinois, and New York) had a lower proportion of recent entrants than the national average (Figure 1). Several states beyond these traditional immigrant destinations had considerably higher proportions of recent entrants. North Dakota (34 percent), Kentucky (28 percent), and South Dakota (26 percent) had among the largest proportions of foreign-born population entering between 2005 and 2009. An additional three states, including Alabama, Indiana, and South Carolina, had over 20 percent of their foreign born entering between 2005 and 2009.[3] Although these states account for a small percentage of the total foreign-born population, they illustrate widening geographic distribution of the foreign born, particularly among more recent entrants.

SOURCE AND ACCURACY

Data presented in this report are based on people and households that responded to the ACS in 2009. The resulting estimates are representative of the entire population. All comparisons presented in this report have taken sampling error into account and are significant at the 90 percent confidence level unless otherwise noted. Due to rounding, some details may not sum to totals. For information on sampling and estimation methods, confidentiality protection, and sampling and nonsampling errors, please see the "ACS Accuracy of the Data (2009)" document located at < *www.census.gov/ acs/www/Down*load/data_documentation/Accuracy/ACS_Accuracy_of_Data _ 2 009. pdf>.

End Notes

[1] Data on the year of entry of the foreign-born population are derived from the question: "When did this person come to live in the United States?" The year respondents report that they "came to live" is considered their "year of entry." Respondents who "came to live" in the United States more than once were asked to report their most recent year of entry.

[2] In this report the term "year of entry cohorts" refers to individuals who reported coming to live in the United States during specific periods of time: prior to 1980, 1980 to 1989, 1990 to 1999, and 2000 or later.

[3] The percentages for North Dakota, Kentucky, and South Dakota were not statistically different from each other. South Dakota's percentage was also not statistically different from 20 percent.

In: The American Community Survey ...   ISBN: 978-1-61324-362-6
Editors: B. M. Russo and A. D. Haffner   ©2011 Nova Science Publishers, Inc.

Chapter 19

THE POPULATION WITH HAITIAN ANCESTRY IN THE UNITED STATES: 2009

United States Census Bureau

INTRODUCTION

This report describes the population with Haitian ancestry living in the United States based on the 2009 American Community Survey (ACS). It also presents the distribution of people with Haitian ancestry across the United States.

Haitian is a relatively small, yet growing, ancestry group in the United States, increasing from 290,000 people with Haitian ancestry (0.1 percent of the total population) in 1990 to 548,000 (0.2 percent) in 2000.[1] By 2009, an estimated 830,000 people with Haitian ancestry were living in the United States, or 0.3 percent of the total population.[2]

GEOGRAPHIC DISTRIBUTION OF THE POPULATION WITH HAITIAN ANCESTRY

Of the estimated 830,000 people in the United States in 2009 with Haitian ancestry, about two-thirds lived in two states: Florida, with around 376,000, and New York, with 191,000. Five states had a higher percentage of Haitians than the national percentage of 0.3 percent (Florida, with 2.0 percent; New

York, with 1.0 percent; Massachusetts, with 0.9 percent; New Jersey, with 0.7 percent; and Connecticut, with 0.5 percent).[3, 4, 5]

HOW IS HAITIAN ANCESTRY DETERMINED?

The ACS asks each person to write in his or her "ancestry or ethnic origin." From the responses collected, the U.S. Census Bureau considers anyone who wrote in "Haitian" or "Haiti" to be of Haitian ancestry.

Ancestry is a broad concept. The Census Bureau defines ancestry as the ethnic origin, descent, roots, heritage, or place of birth of the person or of the person's ancestors. The question was not intended to measure the degree of attachment to a group, but simply to establish the ethnic group(s) with which the respondent self-identifies.

CHARACTERISTICS OF HAITIANS IN THE UNITED STATES

In 2009, people with Haitian ancestry were, on average, younger than the total U.S. population. Specifically, the median age of the Haitian population was 30, compared with 37 for the total population.

Haitian households were more likely to be family households and to be larger, on average, than households in the total popula-tion.[6] Around 79 percent of Haitian households were family households, compared with 67 percent of households in the total population. The average household size where there was a Haitian householder was 3.7 people, compared with 2.6 people for the total population.

Approximately 59 percent of the population with Haitian ancestry was foreign born, compared with 13 percent of the total U.S. population. This is reflected in the high proportion of Haitians aged 5 and over who speak a language other than English at home (81 percent, compared with 20 percent in the total population).

Also, among Haitians 25 years and over, 18 percent of both males and females had a bachelor's degree or more, compared with 28 percent of males and 27 percent of females in the total population.

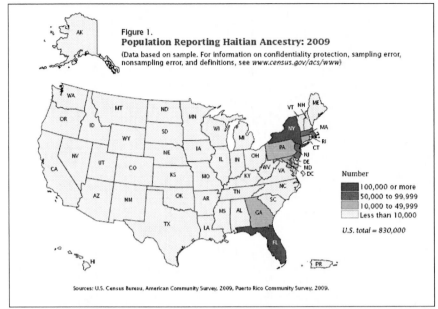

Figure 1.
Population Reporting Haitian Ancestry: 2009
(Data based on sample. For information on confidentiality protection, sampling error, nonsampling error, and definitions, see www.census.gov/acs/www)

Number
■ 100,000 or more
■ 50,000 to 99,999
□ 10,000 to 49,999
□ Less than 10,000

U.S. total = 830,000

Sources: U.S. Census Bureau, American Community Survey, 2009, Puerto Rico Community Survey, 2009.

Sources: U.S. Census Bureau, American Community Survey, 2009, Puerto Rico Community Survey, 2009.

Figure 1. Population Reporting Haitian Ancestry: 2009
(Data based on sample. For information on confidentiality protection, sampling error, nonsampling error, and definitions, see www.census.gov/acs/www)

In 2009, Haitians were involved in the U.S. labor market at a higher rate than the total population. Seventy-one percent of those aged 16 and over were in the civilian labor force, compared with 65 percent of the total population. However, the median earnings of full-time, year-round workers were lower for both Haitian males and females—$33,000 for men and $29,000 for women, compared with $45,000 for men and $36,000 for women in the total population. Median Haitian family income was also lower than for the total population, at $46,000 compared with $61,000. Around 14 percent of Haitians were unemployed, compared with 1 0 percent in the total population.

One in 5 Haitians in the United States was living in poverty (20 percent) compared with 1 in 7 in the total population (14 percent).[7] Homeownership was lower for Haitian households; less than half (47 percent) were owner-occupied, compared with 66 percent of total U.S. households.

Table 1. Demographic, social, Economic, and Housing characteristics for the population Who Reported Haitian Ancestry: 2009

(In percent. Data based on sample. For information on confidentiality protection, sampling error, nonsampling error, and definitions, see www.census.gov/acs/www).

Characteristic	Total population	Margin of error[1] (±)	Haitian population	Margin of error[1] (±)
Total Population (in thousands)	**307,007**	(X)	**830**	30
Median age	36.8	0.1	29.7	0.5
Sex				
Male	49.3	0.1	48.9	0.9
Female	50.7	0.1	51.1	0.9
Households by Type[2]				
Family households	66.5	0.1	78.8	1.7
Nonfamily households	33.5	0.1	21.2	1.7
Average household size	2.63	0.01	3.69	0.07
Educational Attainment (25 years and over)				
Males with a bachelor's degree or higher	28.4	0.1	18.3	1.6
Females with a bachelor's degree or higher	27.4	0.1	18.2	1.5
Nativity and Language Spoken at Home				
Foreign born	12.5	0.1	59.0	0.5
Population 5 years and over who spoke a language other than English at home	20.0	0.1	81.2	1.1

Table 1. (Continued)

Characteristic	Total population	Margin of error[1] (±)	Haitian population	Margin of error[1] (±)
Civilian Labor Force Participation and Unemployment				
Population 16 years and over in civilian labor force	64.7	0.1	70.9	1.1
Civilian labor force unemployed	9.9	0.1	14.2	1.1
Earnings and Income (dollars)				
Median earnings for males[3]	45,485	128	32,650	1,250
Median earnings for females[3]	35,549	79	28,937	974
Median family income[2]	61,082	109	45,626	2,040
Poverty				
Individuals below poverty for whom poverty was determined	14.3	0.1	19.6	1.5
Housing Tenure[2]				
Owner-occupied housing units	65.9	0.1	46.5	2.0
Renter-occupied housing units	34.1	0.1	53.5	2.0

(X) Not applicable .

[1] Data are based on a sample and are subject to sampling variability . A margin of error is a measure of an estimate's variability . The larger the margin of error in relation to the size of the estimate, the less reliable the estimate . When added to and subtracted from the estimate, the margin of error forms the 90 percent confidence interval .

[2] Based on the ancestry of the householder .

[3] Based on full-time, year-round workers .

Source: U .S . Census Bureau, American Community Survey, 2009, Selected Population Profile, S0201 .

SOURCE AND ACCURACY

Data presented in this report are based on people and households that responded to the ACS in 2009. The resulting estimates are representative of the entire population. All comparisons presented in this report have taken sampling error into account and are significant at the 90 percent confidence level unless otherwise noted. Due to rounding, some details may not sum to totals. For information on sampling and estimation methods, confidentiality protection, and sampling and nonsampling errors, please see the "ACS Accuracy of the Data (2009)" document located at <www.census.gov/acs/www/Downloads/data_documentation/Accuracy/ACS_Accuracy_of_Data_2009.pdf>.

End Notes

[1] Brittingham, Angela, and G. Patricia de la Cruz. *Ancestry: 2000*. U.S. Census Bureau. Census 2000 Brief, C2KBR-35, issued June 2004.

[2] Data are based on a sample and are subject to sampling variability; see Table 1 for margins of error.

[3] The terms "Haitians" and "Haitian population" are used in this report to refer to people who reported Haitian ancestry.

[4] Although the estimates of the percentage of the population who were Haitian in Delaware and Georgia appear higher than the U.S. percentage, they were not statistically different from the national percentage.

[5] The percentage of the population in Massachusetts with Haitian ancestry was not statistically different from the percentage in New York.

[6] Based on the ancestry of the householder.

[7] For more information, see "How Poverty Is Calculated in the American Community Survey" at <www.census.gov/hhes/www /poverty>.

In: The American Community Survey …   ISBN: 978-1-61324-362-6
Editors: B. M. Russo and A. D. Haffner   ©2011 Nova Science Publishers, Inc.

Chapter 20

PEOPLE WHO SPOKE A LANGUAGE OTHER THAN ENGLISH AT HOME BY HISPANIC ORIGIN AND RACE: 2009

United States Census Bureau

INTRODUCTION

This report presents data on the proportion of people aged 5 and over who spoke a language other than English at home, based on the 2009 American Community Survey (ACS). Data are presented at the national and state levels. Data in the state maps are reported for Hispanic origin and racial groups with a population of at least 65,000.

These data come from a three-part question. Part one asks, "Does this person speak a language other than English at home?" Part two asks, "What is this language?" Part three asks, "How well does this person speak English (very well; well; not well; not at all)?" The information presented in this report utilizes data from part one of the language question.

Data on language ability has become increasingly important as the U.S. population has become more ethnically diverse. Government and private sector service providers use data on language ability to help meet the communication needs of different communities by tailoring services to schools, hospitals, and other providers. These data are also used to monitor and enforce the Voting Rights Act of 1965.

This report highlights information about language for selected Hispanic origin and race groups. The U.S. Census Bureau collects race and ethnicity data in accordance with guidelines provided by the U.S. Office of Management and Budget (OMB). These data are based on self- identification. The question on Hispanic origin asks respondents if they are of Hispanic, Latino, or Spanish origin. The question on race asks respondents to report the race or races they consider themselves to be. People who identify their origin as Hispanic, Latino, or Spanish may be of any race.

LANGUAGE OTHER THAN ENGLISH SPOKEN AT HOME FOR THE UNITED STATES

Table 1 shows that among the major racial categories in the United States, those only choosing the Some Other Race category had the highest proportion of individuals who spoke a language other than English at home (83 percent).[1] Asian alone (77 percent) had the next highest proportion, followed by Native Hawaiian and Other Pacific Islander alone (43 percent), American Indian and Alaska Native alone (29 percent), White alone (1 5 percent), and Black alone (8 percent).[2]

People who reported Some Other Race alone were more likely to speak a language other than English at home (83 percent) compared with people who reported Some Other Race as well as one or more additional race groups (46 percent).[3] The difference between single-race Asians and Asians who reported multiple races was even larger (77 percent versus 1 8 percent).

The patterns differed for Whites and Blacks. The White alone population and the Black alone population had a lower proportion of people who spoke a language other than English at home (1 5 percent and 8 percent, respectively) compared with the White in combination population and the Black in combination population (19 percent and 1 6 percent, respectively).

Table 2 presents data on detailed Hispanic origin and racial groups in the United States. Overall, among the major race groups and Hispanic origin, Non-Hispanic Whites had the lowest proportion (6 percent) of people who spoke a language other than English at home and Asians alone and Hispanics had the highest proportion (77 percent and 76 percent, respectively).

Table 1. Population 5 years and older Who spoke a Language other Than English at Home by Race: 2009

(In percent. For information on confidentiality protection, sampling error, nonsampling error, and definitions, see www.census.gov/acs/www).

Race	Alone	Margin of error[1] (±)	In combination	Margin of error[1] (±)	Alone or in combination	Margin of error[1] (±)
White	14.5	0.1	18.9	0.4	14.6	0.1
Black or African American	7.9	0.1	15.7	0.6	8.3	0.1
American Indian and Alaska Native	29.0	0.7	12.3	0.6	20.7	0.5
Asian	77.1	0.3	17.9	0.6	70.6	0.3
Native Hawaiian and Other Pacific Islander	42.5	1.8	11.6	1.2	28.2	1.1
Some Other Race	82.9	0.3	46.4	1.0	79.9	0.3

[1]Data are based on a sample and are subject to sampling variability . A margin of error is a measure of an estimate's variability . The larger the margin of error in relation to the size of the estimate, the less reliable the estimate . When added to and subtracted from the estimate, the margin of error forms the 90 percent confidence interval .

Source: U .S . Census Bureau, American Community Survey, 2009, Selected Population Profile, S0201 .

Hispanics were much more likely to speak a language other than English at home (76 percent) compared with non-Hispanics (10 percent). Among the selected Hispanic detailed groups, Dominicans (92 percent), Salvadorans (92 percent), and Guatemalans (91 percent) were among the top three groups with the highest percent who spoke a language other than English at home.4 This was followed by Colombians (87 percent), Cubans (82 percent), Mexicans (76 percent), and Puerto Ricans (66 percent).

Among the selected American Indian and Alaska Native tribes, Navajos had the highest proportion of people who spoke a language other than English at home (60 percent), while Cherokees had the lowest (7 percent).[5]

Vietnamese (89 percent) had the highest proportion of people who spoke a language other than English at home, among the selected Asian detailed groups; Japanese had the lowest (46 percent).

Among the selected Native Hawaiian and Other Pacific Islander detailed groups, Samoans had a higher proportion of people who spoke a language other than English at home (56 percent); Native Hawaiians had a lower proportion (12 percent).

Within the selected Two or More Races category, White *and* Some Other Race had the highest proportion of people who spoke a language other than English at home (50 percent), while White *and* American Indian and Alaska Native had the lowest proportion (11 percent).[6]

LANGUAGE OTHER THAN ENGLISH SPOKEN AT HOME BY STATE

California had the largest percent of the total population who spoke a language other than English at home (43 percent), followed by New Mexico (36 percent) and Texas (34 percent).

Rhode Island (87 percent) and Florida (86 percent) had the highest proportion of Hispanics who spoke a language other than English at home; Hawaii had the lowest (23 percent).[7] For non-Hispanics who spoke a language other than English at home, Hawaii (25 percent) and California (24 percent) were the states with the highest proportion, followed by New York (19 percent) and New Jersey (18 percent).[8]

New York had the highest proportion of non-Hispanic Whites who spoke a language other than English at home (13 percent).

Massachusetts (35 percent), Minnesota (28 percent), and Washington (21 percent) had the highest proportions of Blacks who spoke a language other than English at home.

Table 2. Population 5 years and older Who spoke a Language other Than English at Home by selected Hispanic origin and Race Group: 2009 (In percent. For information on confidentiality protection, sampling error, nonsampling error, and definitions, see www.census.gov/acs/www)

Hispanic origin and race[1]	Percent	Margin of error[2] (±)
Total population 5 years and older	**20.0**	**0 .1**
Not Hispanic or Latino	10.0	0 .1
Hispanic or Latino	76.2	0 .2
Colombian	86.9	0 .8
Cuban	82.3	0 .7
Dominican	91.9	0 .6
Guatemalan	91.0	0 .7
Mexican	76.1	0 .2
PuertoRican	66.2	0 .6
Salvadoran	91.5	0 .6
White Alone	14.5	0 .1
White alone, not Hispanic or Latino	5.8	0 .1
Black or African American Alone	7.9	0 .1
American Indian and Alaska Native Alone	29.0	0 .7
Alaska Native alone[3]	29.3	2 .3
Cherokeealone	6.5	1 .0
Chippewa alone	8.4	1 .5
Choctaw alone	13.8	1 .8
Navajoalone	60.0	2 .4
Siouxalone	12.2	1 .7
Asian Alone	77.1	0 .3
AsianIndianalone	79.6	0 .5
Chinesealone	82.9	0 .4
Filipinoalone	67.4	0 .6
Japanesealone	45 .8	1 .1

Table 2. (Continued)

Hispanic origin and race[1]	Percent	Margin of error[2] (±)
Koreanalone	79 .0	0 .7
Vietnamese alone	89 .1	0 .6
Native Hawaiian and Other Pacific Islander Alone	42 .5	1 .8
Native Hawaiian alone	12 .3	1 .9
Samoan alone	55 .6	4 .2
Two or More Races	19 .6	0 .4
White; American Indian and Alaska Native	11.1	0.6
White; Asian	15.7	0.7
White; Black or African American	14.7	0.7
White; Some Other Race	50.4	1.1

[1] The American Indian and Alaska Native groups and the Native Hawaiian and Other Pacific Islander groups included in this table have estimated populations of at least 65,000 at the national level. The Hispanic, Asian, and Two or More Races groups included in this table have estimated populations of at least 750,000 at the national level.

[2] Data are based on a sample and are subject to sampling variability. A margin of error is a measure of an estimate's variability. The larger the margin of error in relation to the size of the estimate, the less reliable the estimate . When added to and subtracted from the estimate, the margin of error forms the 90 percent confidence interval.

[3] This category represents the population who specified any Alaska Native group(s) alone .

Source: U.S. Census Bureau, American Community Survey, 2009, Selected Population Profile, S0201.

New Mexico (59 percent) and Arizona (51 percent) had the highest proportion of American Indians and Alaska Natives who spoke a language other than English at home.

In nearly all states with at least 65,000 or more Asians, at least 50 percent of Asians spoke a language other than English at home. The exception was Hawaii, where 43 percent spoke a language other than English at home.

Two states had Native Hawaiian and Other Pacific Islander populations of 65,000 or more — California and Hawaii. Among Pacific Islanders in California, about half spoke a language other than English at home (52 percent), compared with one- third of Pacific Islanders in Hawaii (33 percent).

New Jersey (41 percent) and Massachusetts (38 percent) had the highest proportion of people reporting multiple races who spoke a language other than English at home.[9]

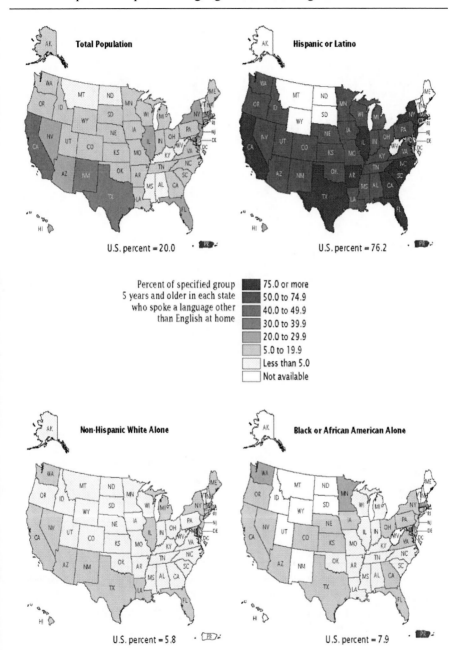

Figure 1. (Continued).

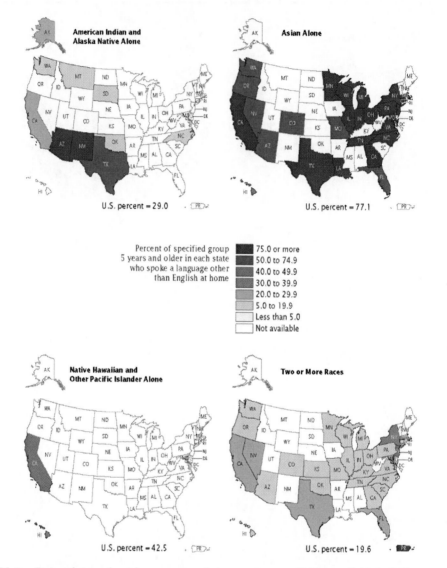

Note: Data classes based on unrounded percentages. "Not available" indicates population of specified group in state was less than 65,000.

Sources: U.S. Census Bureau, American Community Survey, 2009, Puerto Rico Community Survey, 2009.

Figure 1. Population 5 Years and Older Who Spoke a Language Other Than English at Home by Hispanic Origin and Race: 2009 (For information on confidentiality protection, sampling error, nonsampling error, and definitions, see www.census.gov/acs/www).

SOURCE AND ACCURACY

Data presented in this report are based on people and households that responded to the ACS in 2009. The resulting estimates are representative of the entire population. All comparisons presented in this report have taken sampling error into account and are significant at the 90 percent confidence level unless otherwise noted. Due to rounding, some details may not sum to totals. For information on sampling and estimation methods, confidentiality protection, and sampling and nonsampling errors, please see the "ACS Accuracy of the Data (2009)" document located at <www.census.gov/ acs/www/Downloads/data_documentation/Accuracy/ACS_Accuracy_of _Data 2009.pdf>.

End Notes

[1] The Census Bureau uses a variety of approaches for showing data for race groups. In this report, a series of maps compares data for single-race populations (e.g., Asian alone) and the Two or More Races population. However, this does not imply that it is the preferred method of presenting or analyzing data. Table 1 also presents data for the major race groups "alone," "in combination," and "alone or in combination." For example, the data for Asians summarizes characteristics for single-race Asians, for Asians who reported two or more races, and people who reported they were Asian regardless of whether they also reported another race.

[2] See the Race section of the 2009 ACS Subject Definitions Guide for detailed definitions of the racial categories used in this report <www.census.gov/acs /www/U seData/Def.htm>.

[3] Individuals who chose more than one of the six race categories are referred to as the race in combination population, or as the group who reported more than one race.

[4] The percentages speaking a language other than English at home for Dominicans, Salvadorans, and Guatemalans were not statistically different from each other.

[5] In the text and figures of this report, data for detailed race groups (e.g., Cherokee, Japanese, Samoan) are shown for people who reported only a single group. However, this does not imply that it is the preferred method of presenting or analyzing data on race; the Census Bureau uses a variety of approaches. Additional ACS data are available online in American FactFinder for a number of race groups "alone," "in combination," and "alone or in combination." For example, data are available for people who reported they were Japanese; for people who reported they were Japanese and White; and for people who reported they were Japanese, regardless of whether they also reported another race.

[6] The race-in-combination categories use the conjunction *and* in bold and italicized print to link the race groups that compose the combination.

[7] The percentages for Rhode Island and Florida were not statistically different from each other.

[8] The percentages for Hawaii and California were not statistically different from each other.

[9] The percentages for New Jersey and Massachusetts were not statistically different from each other.

INDEX

N

O

P